REFUSE TO LOSE

REFUSE TO LOSE

JOHN CALIPARI
WITH DICK WEISS

BALLANTINE BOOKS • NEW YORK

http://www.randomhouse.com

Library of Congress Catalog Card Number: 96-96955

ISBN 0-345-40801-2

Text design by Debbie Glasserman

Manufactured in the United States of America

First Edition: August 1996

10 9 8 7 6 5 4 3 2

To my wife, Ellen, and my daughters, Erin and Megan. Ellen has been through a lot as a coach's wife. She has spent hours parenting our children, often by herself. She is a fabulous mother and wife. As for my two little sweethearts, Erin and Megan, they don't care about the score. They just think their dad is the best and that means so much to me.

—J.C.

To Joan, who kept me company, put up with my changing moods, hung in there with me during the dark hours, supplied help with the copy, and offered both moral support and insight while I wrote this book. Who else would put up with a basketball junkie like me?

—D.W.

CONTENTS

FOREWORD

There are some people who think I owe my national championship to John Calipari.

As the coach of Kentucky, I felt if we had defeated UMass in the Great Eight last November, they would have been NCAA Tournament champions today. As it turned out, they gave us the motivation to succeed because they gave us something to shoot for all season.

I felt Kentucky and UMass were the two best teams in college basketball.

I never thought I'd be saying that. But I never thought UMass would be in the Final Four, either.

That achievement speaks volumes about the job John Calipari did since he arrived in Amherst eight years ago. I have not seen anything close to it in my life.

When I took my first head coaching job at Boston University, the program there was in bad shape. But UMass was much worse. Ten straight losing seasons. One secretary doing work for a couple of departments. No facilities. No weight room. No basketball camp. No support. No tradition in the Atlantic 10. No media coverage.

I was hoping John could eventually turn my alma mater into a competitive mid-major team in New England. I was hoping UMass could get to the NIT once every four years and maybe to the NCAA once every five years.

I was hoping.

But, to be honest with you, as good as John was, I didn't think even he could pull it off.

I should have known better.

I was on the selection committee to choose a new coach in 1988. When we finally went with John, it didn't take long for him to promote the program. He was on every TV station, every radio show, selling UMass basketball. He was part P. T. Barnum, part Merlin the Magician. And all John Calipari. He was doing everything humanly possible to give my school a team we could be proud of.

Most new coaches schedule weak teams to build confidence in their program. John did just the opposite. And he did it without any financial security: this was a job that had turned over every few years. If he had gotten fired, he might have been finished in this business. But he had superhuman confidence in his abilities.

Even when UMass had Julius Erving, the school never played in the NCAA tournament. Before John got there, UMass hadn't been invited since 1962, and even then, they couldn't get past the first round. In defense of our program, a school had to be No. 1 in New England to earn a bid because the NCAA field included only thirty-two teams. That usually meant getting past Providence College.

So we went to the NIT when I played.

In my mind, it was impossible to transform UMass into a national program. Best in New England? With an incredible amount of work, incredible recruiting, maybe. But we were never going national, no matter how much I prayed and believed. If I went to church every day for two years, it wasn't going to happen.

Never say never.

UMass went to its first NCAA tournament under John in 1992. They've been going back ever since. And they've been ranked No. 1 the past two years.

I watched John grow up in this business. I was a counselor at Five-Star Camp when he was a camper. He was an average player, but you could see he really knew the game.

John played for Clarion State in college. What he lacked in physical ability, he made up for in the cerebral part of the game. When he became an assistant at Kansas and then at Pitt, I could see he was a ferocious recruiter. He had a brashness even then that has made him what he is today.

I was the Knicks' coach when the UMass job opened up and I spoke to John about interviewing for the position. He was young, only twenty-eight years old at the time. The search came down to two candidates—John and Larry Shyatt, an assistant at New Mexico and later at Providence—and I bowed out of being an active committee member.

When I left for a weekend road trip, the committee had agreed it was going to be John. I was in Milwaukee for a game with the Bucks when I received a phone call. The committee had now eliminated John from consideration because two or three Big East coaches had fired in and just killed his reputation and char- acter after he had gotten into a recruiting squabble with Vil- lanova over a 6'8" prospect from Atlantic City named Bobby Martin.

I persuaded them to call an emergency meeting on Monday. The discussion was heated.

"We're not here to promote a Big East school," I said. "We're here to turn UMass around, and John Calipari's the guy to do it. These people fear Calipari. They fear him in recruiting. This is the ideal guy."

Then I asked if they had called the NCAA.

"Yes," they told me.

"That's all we need to know," I said. "All we care about is what the NCAA thinks about his character. Jealousy is the worst evil we have in sports today. And a lot of people are jealous of this young guy."

They all, I think, realized he was the right guy for the job. But the school wasn't about to hire him without hitting me up for a donation.

They had offered John a $63,000 package.

"But," they said, "we don't have $63,000. Would you be willing to kick in $5,000?"

So I did.

Before John arrived, I was really disappointed in the direction of the program. It looked like the administration had given up. They just did not care. It was almost like they said, "Well, what are you going to do? The Big East buried everybody."

Some guys might have come in with an attitude of "Let's take what's left over. Let's take our piece of the pie."

But John said, "No. Let's take their piece of the pie, too."

I feel absolutely wonderful about what he accomplished with UMass.

He's unique.

Thanks, John. And good luck with the Nets.

—Rick Pitino

ACKNOWLEDGMENTS

Let me thank the Court Club board members who helped me and my family in so many ways; the original members: executive director Ron Nathan, Jim Hunt, Bob Borawski, Dave Malek, Glenn Allen, Paul Mannheim, and Dick Covell; and the new members: Buzz Foster, John Peterson, Kathleen Teagna, Rob Burke, Wally Kelb, Rich Halpern, and Bob Kerris. Special thanks to the "Search" and later "Advisory Committee": Steve Fletcher, Frank McInerney, Ron Nathan, Dave Bischoff, Glenn Wong, and Dave Bartley. And thanks to the "Governor" John Gilmore and son Rob—two special friends.

—J.C.

I would first like to thank John Calipari; his wife, Ellen; and their two daughters, Megan and Erin, for all their kindness and cooperation during this project. I would also like to thank my wife, Joan Williamson, who helped with the manuscript; our literary agent, David Vigliano; Doug Grad, our editor at Ballantine; UMass president Bill Bulger, chancellor Dr. David Scott, athletic director Bob Marcum, executive director of athletic development John Nitardy, assistant athletic director of student-athlete services Mike Jenkins, assistant coaches and staff members John Robic, Bruiser Flint, Ed Schilling, Brian Gorman, Dave Glover, Tony Barbee, Matt "The Cheese" Komer, Jack Leaman, Mike Connors, and Bonnie Martin; the players on current and past UMass teams; Bill Strickland, Kathy Connors, Michael Reiss, Scott McConnell, Ruthie Drew, Kate Mulligan, Mike McComiskey, and Charlie Bare, all from UMass Media Relations; Dan Wetzel, a former editor with the UMass *Collegian* who now works with Larry Donald and Mike Sheridan at *Basketball Times;* Barry Werner, Dave Kaplan, John Temple, Will Pakutka, Anthony Reiber, Roger Rubin, Anthony McCarron, David Cummings, Ian O'Connor, Luke Cyphers, and Adam Berkowitz of the New York *Daily News* staff; members of the media Bob Ryan, Joe Burris, Ron Chimelis, Michael Gee, Craig Handel, Marty Dobrow, Mark Murphy, Joe Calabrese, Mark Blaudschun, Dick Vitale, Kevin Whitmer, Mike Francesa, Chris Russo, Howard Garfinkel, Dr. Carol Barr, Joe Cassidy, Larry Pearlstein, Rick Troncelliti, Frank Morgan, Marc Vandermeer, Ted Sarandis, John Feinstein, and Lesley Visser; Norb Garrett and John Roach of *College Sports* magazine; Malcom Moran; Howie Davis; Rick Bozich; Mark Coomes; Ray Didinger; Ken Denlinger; Ray Cella; and Linda Bruno; Jersey Red Ford; Rick Pitino; Mike Flynn of Blue Star Basketball Camps; Steve Wieberg; my parents, Richard and Barbara Weiss; Diane Weiss; Roger Weiss; Gene Whelan; Mary Flannery; Sam Albano; Adam Berkowitz; Jen Dorfmeister; Tom Healy; Chris Weiller; Berm; and The Guys.

—D.W.

REFUSE TO LOSE

CHAPTER 1

NETS' PROFIT

I met Pat Riley of the Miami Heat for the first time at the 1995 Basketball Hall of Fame Dinner in Springfield, Massachusetts. I was surprised he even knew who I was.

Then he asked me, "When are you coming up?"

"Coming up to what? Practice?"

"No," Riley said, "coming up to our league. With your personality and the way you are, you can coach in this league. You just have to want to do it."

I finally decided I did—late Wednesday night, June 5, 1996.

I walked away from a job I loved at UMass to accept the position of head coach, executive vice president, and head of basketball operations with the New Jersey Nets.

Coaching in the NBA had always been in the back of my mind, but I hadn't felt comfortable that I had done enough in college to merit moving on. Well, the last two years, I thought I had proved to myself I could do it.

I judge myself by looking in the mirror, not by what somebody else says. At UMass, did we go as far as we could go? I don't think so. But the opportunity that came up might never come my way again.

In a lot of ways, I felt like I was caught in a time warp.

When I became head coach at UMass in 1988, I was told the job was a coach-killer. It was a graveyard for coaches. People said the administration was soft and didn't care, and the fans were apathetic. That sounds familiar. Isn't that what I'm getting into with the Nets?

At UMass, we were in the shadow of the Big East. Now we're in the shadow of the Knicks. But that doesn't mean we won't get it done.

It took us eight years to put UMass basketball on the map, to reach the top of the AP poll, and to advance to the Final Four. The Nets have been to the NBA playoffs twice in the last twenty years.

I like the odds.

What I like about the team is they're a good group of guys. They play hard and they rebound. Think about our teams at UMass. They all played hard. They played defense. And they all rebounded.

However, the Nets don't shoot very well.

Sounds like my UMass teams, too.

I stayed eight years in Amherst. That's a long time in this business. And every year, I was offered more money to leave and go to another job.

But this was a five-year deal that was just too good to turn down. For a kid from Moon Township, Pennsylvania, it was like hitting the jackpot. I'm not going to sit here and tell you money didn't play a part in this. My family is very important to me. Security is very important to me. I was poor growing up, so the money did play a part, even though I was pretty well taken care of at UMass.

Last fall, I had signed a ten-year contract with the school. It contained a special clause that would have given me a job as a development officer in the chancellor's office until I was sixty at my last base salary if I ever decided I wanted to get out of coaching. Essentially, I had the same security as a tenured professor.

The Nets are much more of a risk. But they were willing to give me total control of an NBA franchise.

When I told that to UMass athletic director Bob Marcum, one of my closest friends, he just laughed. "Sure, John," Bob said, "but the goddamned captain of the *Titanic* thought he had total control, too."

I figured he'd say something like that. I'm sure a lot of people feel the same way. But, at age thirty-seven, this is what I want to do.

People have suggested I left because the UMass program was slipping. That's bull. UMass basketball should be a Top 20 team for the next five to ten years now that the university has promoted my former associate coach, James "Bruiser" Flint, to the position of head coach. I pushed hard for that with Bob and UMass chancellor David K. Scott because I felt it was the best way to maintain continuity.

UMass is on national television twenty-five times a year these days. It plays a national schedule. It recruits regional players who are good enough to take the program where it wants to go. UMass went to the NCAA tournament five years in a row when I was there. It won the Atlantic 10 tournament five straight times. UMass has started to put up banners—like North Carolina does. Every year that we were in the Top 20 in the AP poll we put up a banner. Hopefully, next year they'll add another one.

I've also heard speculation I left because of reports in *The Hartford Courant* on Tuesday, June 4, that Marcus Camby had accepted cash and jewelry from two prospective agents while he was still playing college basketball.

Wrong again.

My attorney, Craig Fenech, had spoken to the Nets before that situation ever came up. I'd had initial talks with Michael Rowe, the team president, the previous Friday night in Providence, Rhode Island. In fact, Marcus's situation almost got me to say "I'm not leaving" until I looked into it more. Once I decided everything was going to be okay with Marcus, I moved on.

This was the second year in a row I had been contacted by NBA teams. I spoke to three different NBA teams in 1995, including the Boston Celtics. I think they had to talk to me because everybody wanted them to. M. L. Carr, who was the acting GM then, called me. I told him at the time, "I don't think I have an interest in the job, but I will talk to you."

Afterwards he said, "I don't think you have any interest in this job."

"You're probably right," I told him.

He probably wanted the job. That's okay.

Since that experience, I've learned that you don't deal on your own behalf in the NBA. At UMass, whenever there had been a shoe deal, or a speaking engagement, I used to do it all myself. An administrator, a college AD, or an apparel guy doesn't want to deal with an agent. He'd rather look me in the eye.

In the NBA, I can't do that.

At this point, I will not deal with anybody from the NBA on a personal level. I direct them to Craig.

This spring, the phone calls started again. In May, I was contacted by the Philadelphia 76ers, and we began to speak. When the Nets job opened and Rick Pitino turned down a deal that included equity in the team, I was really surprised I hadn't heard from them. But I wasn't going to approach them. I wasn't going to call them. I was talking with Philadelphia at the time.

Then I got a call from someone close to the organization who broached the subject and asked if I would be willing to listen to the Nets.

I was scheduled to give a motivational speech with UMass professor and bestselling author of *The One Minute Manager* Ken Blanchard to a group in Providence on Friday, May 31, when I received a phone call from Michael Rowe.

He called at noon. I told him what my schedule was and he said, "I'll be right there."

He drove all the way up from New Jersey to talk with me and we met at 9:30 P.M. At that time, I didn't know how serious they were. I didn't even have enough time to tell Bob Marcum.

Anyway, we met. He gave me the outline. We didn't talk any numbers. I told him I would talk to Craig Fenech. The next morning, Michael left. Craig called the Nets on Sunday and told them we were interested. They talked and it got close. Craig threw numbers at Michael. Michael threw numbers at Craig. I wanted control of the organization. I wanted a certain number because I was making a lot of money. I was giving up a lot. People don't realize it wasn't just the salary at UMass, it was everything else.

I was giving up a job I could have had the rest of my life to come to an organization for a job people looked at as a dead end.

But I looked at it and said, "What an opportunity. I'll get some time to do it. If they give me some control and I'm making the decisions, I can put an image and a face on it that I want it to have. I can surround myself with my people, and we can go in and fight like heck and turn this thing around."

That's what I looked at.

I called Bruiser that Monday and said, "Bru, if they do the right thing in New Jersey, I'm going to take that job. You're going to be the new head coach."

At that point, I had already talked to Bob and asked him, "If I do this, what will you do?"

He said, "What do you think I should do?"

I said, "I think there's no question you should hire Bruiser."

He came back, without hesitation, and said, "You're absolutely right. That's exactly what I feel."

That way, I told him, there would be a smooth transition and there wouldn't be any major changes. I said, "I think the kids will stay. The recruits will stay, and I think you'll be okay."

Before I did anything, though, I wanted to make sure Marcus Camby was all right. *The Hartford Courant* claimed Marcus had told a *Courant* reporter he'd accepted a diamond pendant worth $2,500 and a chain worth $950 from childhood friends Tamia Murray and Boris Wray. He said they later gave him a Cuban-link chain worth $1,829. Afterwards, they told him the jewelry had been bought by Wesley Spears, a Hartford attorney who was trying to become Marcus's agent. Marcus said that Murray and Wray received cash, which they spent on clothing and rental cars as well as airline tickets and expenses so they could watch him play at the Atlantic 10 tournament in Philadelphia and the NCAA East Regional in Atlanta. After the season, Marcus said, he went to Spears's home and was given $1,000. He said it was the only time he had ever taken cash from Spears. In addition, the *Courant* reported that Marcus said he had received "a couple thousand" from Signature Sports agent John Loundsbury, also from Hartford.

The *Courant* quoted Marcus as saying that he would do it over again, too, if he had the chance. "They didn't have anything," he

"They have been my boys since I was growing up. It was an opportunity to do things for them . . . I mean, I'm going to be the No. 2 pick in the draft, they're back home chilling. They took it as free money."

Marcus has since denied ever accepting money from Loundsbury. Loundsbury has also denied the allegations. Marcus's attorney, James Bryant of ProServ, acknowledged that his client had received money from Spears—after the season—but denied Marcus had accepted jewelry. Bryant filed a complaint with the Connecticut state attorney's office, claiming Spears had attempted to blackmail Marcus into signing with him.

According to Bryant, Spears said that if Marcus refused to cooperate, he would go public with the fact he had been paying off Marcus's friends. Bryant said Spears allegedly had shown Marcus's mother a "fake lawsuit," saying 20 percent of Marcus's marketing assets and 4 percent of his salary should go to Spears. If Marcus were to be taken as one of the first three picks in the draft, the value of his contract would be far in excess of the $10,000 threshold for first-degree larceny by extortion.

I admit, the stories about Marcus came as a surprise. Marcus never had a car at UMass. He never lived off-campus. He never had the money to do it. He wore jeans and sweat suits most of the time. His mother lived in the same housing project on Garden Street she always did down in Hartford; she doesn't have a car. Was there a decision to make here? Probably not. He should have looked at this and said, "Hey, I can turn pro now. I'm going to have $3 million for my first three years, and hopefully be ready to re-up after two."

When the allegations came to light, I had to step back and say, "Wait a minute, I've got to make sure everything is in order because I'm not going to run from any situation." I never had.

I called Marcus Monday night. He was upset. He thought he had been used. Some other guy even claimed he was Marcus's surrogate father. I tried to tell him that the guy was using him. Newfound family friends were using him.

I felt good about what he said to me. I spoke to Bob about the situation and what had been written. When I learned John Loundsbury had denied everything, I felt that if Marcus had done something, it was after the season ended and that nothing was going to come back and haunt the university. I felt it was an isolated incident of bad judgment, so I was fine and we went forward.

Look, UMass has one of the best programs in the country in dealing with agents. They must register with the university. They have to check in when they come on campus. But what happens when a guy wants to deal with some friends off-campus?

Marcus made a bad decision, but that's not going to change anything. This is just a blip. But I am worried about the perception people are going to have of a great kid.

I am still bothered by the fact some people who were very close to Marcus were openly encouraging him to leave instead of letting him make up his own mind. They had ulterior motives. They were going to gain from him going with a specific agent, and that bothered me. I call those kinds of people scumbags.

While speaking about Marcus's problems, I mentioned the fact that I had heard about one National Player of the Year candidate who was driving a car. The Connecticut writers took that to mean UConn's junior All America guard Ray Allen, who they said was driving a Jeep last summer when he worked in sales at a local car dealer and then started driving one after the season for promotional purposes.

I didn't even know Ray's situation.

I called him on the phone and told him "Hey, Ray, you and I

are fine. I'm trying to protect Marcus. I'm not trying to hurt you. I was referring to a story in the papers where one of the National Player of the Year candidates publicly acknowledged he was test-driving a car before he had declared. I didn't even use the player's name."

Ray was great about it. I told him, "We'd better be good because I may try to trade up and draft you."

I left for Chicago that Tuesday to watch Donta Bright play in the NBA's pre-draft camp at Moody Bible Institute. I spoke with Bob Hill of the San Antonio Spurs. I talked with P. J. Carlesimo of the Portland Trail Blazers. I talked with Larry Brown of the Indiana Pacers.

They all said the same thing: "You've got to do this."

I stayed with Bob Hill and we went over the pluses and minuses. His attitude was, "It's different. It's hard. It's not what you think." He told me, "Look, you'd better get NBA people."

The negotiations with the Nets cut off that night. I called my wife, Ellen, and told her we were staying. Michael Rowe telephoned Craig on Wednesday morning to see if there was any movement. When Craig said no, Rowe told him he was scheduling interviews with other candidates Thursday. Three hours later, we were talking again.

I was sitting with Bob Ryan of *The Boston Globe* in Bob Hill's hotel room on Wednesday afternoon. We talked about everything. As we were about to leave, the phone rang. It was Craig. I got on the phone, and he told me the deal was on again. I was going from up to down to up to down.

As Craig was talking to me, I wasn't answering. I just said, "Uh-huh, uh-huh." Bob later told me he thought the phone call had something to do with Marcus Camby because I was unresponsive.

He didn't know we were going over clauses in the contract.

I got off the phone and we went downstairs to get a bowl of soup. After Bob left, I went upstairs and got on the phone with Michael Rowe. I said, "Michael, look, do your owners want me to be your coach or not? Because if they don't, I'm fine. Let's just not play games. If you want to do this, let's do this."

Craig called him. Boom. They got it done. And I'm the new coach of the Nets. I went to the Bulls game that night. It was the first time I had ever seen Michael Jordan play in person. Then I spoke to Larry Brown at length at the hotel. I finally called Brad Greenberg, the general manager of the 76ers, at one-thirty in the morning. I had been scheduled to meet with Pat Croce, their new president, the next day. I told Brad, "Look, this thing has gone too far with the Nets. And I'm going to meet with them Thursday and get this thing done."

He said, "Okay, if that's how you feel."

Philly was a whole different animal, a whole different ball game. I wasn't sure whether I wanted to deal with some of the personalities on that team.

It was late and I never got to call my wife, Ellen. That was a mistake. The story broke in New York Wednesday night on WFAN. I don't know where Mike Francesa got it. He obviously didn't get it from me. But it became a zoo. The next morning, there were media in our front yard. Ellen was upset. She told me later she had to find out I'd taken the job from Shawn Schilling, the wife of one of my assistant coaches, Ed Schilling.

I had no idea any of this was out. I'd flown back to Hartford and I drove to campus early. Bob Marcum called me and said, "So, it looks like you're going down."

I said, "Well, I've got to go down to Jersey and meet with some owners and make sure it's done. But I think everything is fine."

I didn't know that Craig had gone on WFAN Thursday morning and said we had an oral agreement. I wasn't mad at him, but we had a communications problem.

UMass was announcing the resumption of a long-dormant series with Connecticut at the Hall of Fame that day, but I was represented by an empty chair.

I had too much to do.

When I met with the UMass players, they were pretty disappointed. A couple of them said, "You know, we felt if Marcus had stayed, you would have stayed. What's that make us? We thought you would be here for us."

I told them, "Hey, if Marcus had stayed and this offer had been presented to me, I would have had to sit down with him and say, 'Look, I got to do this.' "

I remember the conversation I had with one of our starting guards, Carmelo Travieso. He told me, "Coach, this is our senior year and this is happening. We're pretty used to you." I told him everything would work out. And, if the program did the right thing and hired Bruiser, people would forget about me in four months.

In the end, they were happy for me.

Calling the recruits was hard, too. I talked to each of them and assured them Bruiser would be their coach unless something blew up, which I didn't think would happen.

The meetings took most of the day. I was scheduled to take a charter flight to Jersey for a press conference on Friday, but there were fifty members of the media camped out in the downstairs parking lot outside the Mullins Center. I had anticipated that, so I parked my car inside the arena.

The door opened. We shot out. I waved and took off.

I thought the press conference in New Jersey went well. The first question came from a woman reporter, who pointed out that

New Jersey had the highest percentage of Hispanic citizens of any state in the country and wanted to know if we were going to make any attempt to add Hispanic players to our roster in the future.

"Obviously," I said, "you haven't seen the backcourt at UMass," and went on to point out that our starting guards Edgar Padilla and Carmelo Travieso were born in Puerto Rico.

There were some tough questions and some negative stories about the fact that I had no previous coaching experience in the NBA. But the bottom line is, I've got a great contract and a lot of years and what someone writes isn't going to have a whole lot of bearing on how I do. I'm not going to be reading the papers anyway. I've got too much work to do.

This is a new chapter in my life.

At UMass, they hired Bruiser two days later. When he told his father, they both started crying over the phone. UMass held the press conference on alumni weekend. A number of alums as well as members of the Board of Trustees and faculty members were there and gave Bruiser a standing ovation when he was introduced.

Bruiser is only thirty-one years old, but he comes with great credentials. He was a standout guard at St. Joseph's and spent a lot of time with our guards. He had a lot to do with Edgar and Carmelo becoming the best backcourt in the country. Wichita State, Southern Mississippi, Drake, and Middle Tennessee State all contacted him after the season. And he was courted by North-eastern but turned the opportunity down.

Bruiser was loyal. He had been a member of my staff since 1989, my second year at UMass. He had replaced Roger McCready, who'd left to go into private business. Bruiser is a true friend, and not just a friend when it is convenient. He is a guy I feel I can count on and I think he'll be terrific.

As for me, I know I'll be coming in cold. I've got a lot to learn. When I first started at UMass, I was really dumb. Over the course of eight years, I got a lot smarter. I didn't waste any time getting into the job. There was so much to do. I was getting up at five-thirty in the morning and working sixteen hours a day.

I'm going to surround myself with people who are strong in areas where I'm weak. Believe me, I'm not coming in there with people who don't know what they're doing. It's going to be the hardest thing I've ever undertaken. But you know what? I'm going to be juiced. I'm going to be going twenty-four hours a day.

I did bring two of my assistants with me from UMass—Dave Glover, who was the assistant AD in charge of academics, and Ed Schilling.

I knew I needed NBA experience on our staff and right away I brought in John Nash, who had been the general manager with both the Philadelphia 76ers and the Washington Bullets, and Don Casey, a long-time assistant coach with the Boston Celtics. But, as a head coach, you can't do it all. You have to have somebody you can trust who can teach the way you want to teach. Eddie's young enough. He's got the energy I want. We'll be going at least sixteen hours a day, sometimes more.

I brought in Dave to be my right-hand man, someone who will be a buffer and act as my emissary when I'm not around. I told him if he wanted to become an AD someday, this would give him that much more experience. If not, I told him, he could be with me and move into the management of a club. I don't have the time to spend eight hours learning about something. He can do that and decipher it for me in a third of the time.

One of the first things we had to do was determine who we wanted to select with our first-round pick in the NBA draft, which was held in the Nets' home arena in the Meadowlands.

The Nets had the eighth pick overall and we needed perimeter help. There was more pressure in the day and a half leading up to the draft than there was in UMass's game against Kentucky in the Final Four. But it juiced me up.

Eventually, we decided on Villanova's 6′5″ guard Kerry Kittles, a two-year All-American. I went on a nice, long run the afternoon of the draft and thought this was what was best for the organization.

Kerry does things I like. He can play both guard spots. He shoots the ball. He is best in a wide-open, up-and-down-the-floor situation. He is a good anticipator on defense. He deflects balls. He's got long arms. And he had a great workout for us. He's wiry, strong, and his skill level really surprised me. Obviously, there are some things he has to do to improve, but every player in the draft is like that.

If Kerry was taken before we picked, I told the Nets' owners we would go to Kobe Bryant, a 6′6¹/₂″ high school player from Lower Merion, Pennsylvania. Some of their faces turned white. But this wasn't about immediate gratification. I was willing to pick a guy about whom some of the media might have shaken their heads and said, "Do you understand what you're doing?" because I felt that Bryant was the right pick for the franchise down the road.

But we got the man we wanted. As for Kerry, we want to let him feel success. He'll start the season coming off the bench, playing nineteen, twenty minutes a game. We want him to be a spark and a defensive presence, make open shots, play with some enthusiasm, and get the fans into it. He can afford to do that because we have a player, Kendall Gill, who can be an All-Star in a good year.

Kerry is not the answer to all the Nets' problems. We have a lot of holes, but he can help us get on the road to where we want to be.

I believe Isiah Thomas, the GM of the Toronto Raptors, feels the same way about Marcus Camby. A week before the draft Isiah had said that he would definitely take Marcus with the second pick, but there was some speculation he would change his mind after Shareef Abdur-Rahim, a 6′10″ freshman forward from the University of California, made a last-minute decision to re-enter the draft.

As it turned out, Isiah was true to his word.

I got a chance to speak to Marcus before the draft. He stopped by the Nets' war room, just to say hello. "I tried to trade up for you, big guy," I told him. He smiled. I was happy for him.

Sadly, Donta Bright, my 6′6″ forward at UMass, was not selected. I invited him to our free agent camp, which looked like a UMass alumni game.

I'm a big, big believer that coaching is about leadership; it's about inspiration. It's not about motivating. The players watch you, and either you inspire them or you don't. We've got to get the players excited about playing. We've got to improve the talent on the team. The first year will be just setting the tone. But we've done that before.

CHAPTER 2

MASS TRANSIT

Ground zero.

That's where the UMass basketball program was when I accepted the head coaching job there in 1988. It was ranked 295th among Division I programs and dropping fast.

Ten straight losing seasons will do that.

Our goal was to reverse gravity. I guess we did. The program has been in the Top 20 for five consecutive years. Bill Strickland, UMass sports information director, told me the Minutemen were the only team that had the distinction of getting better in the AP poll for five straight years. In 1992, our final ranking was 17, and we'd won sixteen games in a row. Our ranking the next year was 14, then 8, 7, and this year, 1. Kentucky has the most wins in the last five years—148. UMass has 146. When I held my first press conference, hardly anyone noticed. Yes, Julius Erving had played there—for two years in the early '70s, before he left to become a star in the old ABA. But there was little or no basketball tradition to speak of at this Atlantic 10 school.

I made the usual promises about taking the program to the next level, but few of the cynical sports fans in New England thought we could keep them. Their feeling was, "We'll believe it when we see it with our own eyes."

This past season, all they had to do was turn on the TV during March Madness. That was UMass warming up for a game against Kentucky in the NCAA Final Four at the Meadowlands on CBS. That was our center, Marcus Camby, the first player from a New England school to be named National Player of the Year.

The reality was UMass was the second-best team in the country.

It may have taken eight years, but we had arrived. We cracked college basketball's social register, which used to include only the traditional powers—like North Carolina, Indiana, UCLA, and Kentucky.

We didn't have their pedigree.

We didn't look all that imposing in the warm-up lines. Aside from Marcus Camby and Donta Bright, we didn't have any high school All-Americans out there. Just tough kids who were willing to play hard and who bought into our philosophy.

Now don't get me wrong.

This isn't brain surgery. You've got to have good players or you're not going to win. People act like we didn't have good players. We had terrific players. Lou Roe is in the NBA. Marcus will be in the NBA. Donta has a chance. Harper Williams, Tony Barbee, and Jimmy McCoy all played overseas. These are all guys who have made or who will make money playing professional basketball.

But there was no birthright to play for us. I told my team, "You deserve to play or you don't deserve to play. Potential loses basketball games. Performance wins games. You've got to defend, dive on the floor, take charges, and rebound. Those are the staples of how we play. Players who like to be cool on the floor have no place in our program."

We didn't have a deep team. We used only seven or eight players. Our five starters were co-captains Donta Bright and Dana Dingle at forward, Marcus Camby at center, and Edgar Padilla and Carmelo Travieso at guard. We had Tyrone Weeks and Inus Norville coming off the bench up front, and we were able to squeeze some minutes out of freshman guard Charlton Clarke after he recovered from foot surgery. Our other subs were seniors Ross Burns, Ted Cottrell, Rigoberto Nuñez, Edgar's brother Giddel Padilla, and freshman Andy McClay.

Most of our players came from East Coast cities. Three came from Puerto Rico and one was from the Dominican Republic. Most were black and Hispanic kids; some were the first in their family to go to college. All they wanted was a chance. And they were willing to fight for whatever they got.

UMass has always been a blue-collar team. That, to me, symbolizes New England. There were no silver spoons here.

But the players had inherited something better. An attitude.

I call it "Refuse to Lose": playing to win versus playing not to lose. Sure, we may get beat on the scoreboard, but when we do, it's not because we quit trying to win. We're not going to cave in; so if a team is going to beat us, they're going to have to play a helluva game. And when a team beats us, we never want to blame anybody. We never want to take away from somebody's win. We learn from our mistakes and move on.

It's an attitude that I explain to my team by using analogies: "If you were selling computers and your competitor got the sale you worked hard for, would you find the guy and punch him in the mouth? Or could you go to the customer who bought the computer from your competitor and find out why he made the sale? Was it because of his product—or his sales approach? Then could you walk out, smile at your competitor, and say that you'll see him tomorrow, knowing that you'll be better? In life, we don't win every time out, but we can learn and improve every day. And we can play to win 100 percent of the time."

We first talked about it in 1993. We were 6–4 and coming off back-to-back losses to Temple and Cincinnati. Harper Williams, our star center, had broken his hand, and we were ready to fall off the face of the earth. Our next game was at Rutgers, a place where we had never won.

We came in to prepare for the game, and I just wrote the words "Refuse to Lose" on the chalkboard. I told our players, "You have to figure out a way to win this game. Don't go down. I don't want to hear any excuses. Figure out a way to win." Well, we won that night and went on a fourteen-game winning streak, nine of them without Harper. When he came back, we won our second regular season title and our second straight Atlantic 10 tournament title.

In 1996, we were still talking about "Refuse to Lose," and this year's team embodied it. We were ranked No. 1 at the end of the season—the first school in New England to achieve that.

This was the team that defined UMass basketball. To me, it's five players on the floor, and eight to ten others on the bench, who have a burning desire to win and improve on a daily basis. They are excited about basketball and see it as a part of their personal growth.

I see selfless players who consider the success of the team to be more important than individual glory. The UMass players understand that a rising tide lifts all boats. As UMass wins, every player receives publicity and even glory. Last year, all five of our starters made the All-Conference team—the first time that's ever happened in the history of the Atlantic 10. I've never had a star system. We rely on all players to be part of our team success. During the time I spent there, we had ten guys who scored 1,000 or more points. That's a lot.

We had interchangeable parts, with a good point guard and post presence. We had kids who were warriors, who were unselfish, who had character. Championships are won with teams that have those traits.

I can coach that kind of team, and we'll win.

When the coaches are fighting for a young man to make him improve as a person and as a player—and he knows that—we create a bond. It's a great feeling when we've taught a group of players to rely on us for our advice. When we see the results—a team that's playing up to its potential—it's rewarding.

A lot of times people don't respect us. During the past two years, people looked at us like, "It's UMass. They're not that good. They shouldn't be doing that. They can't win this."

The media may have been surprised by our success, but our players weren't. They had given me a timetable.

When I asked the team what our goal should be this year, the first response came from Tyrone Weeks, a powerfully built 6′7″ junior who learned the game playing in the rugged Philadelphia Public League.

"Let's go undefeated. We can go undefeated."

I didn't know what to say. I didn't want to discourage him, but I wanted to make him understand that the first time we were to lose—and what if it's against Kentucky in the opening game of the season—our goal could be crushed.

So I came back with, "We can have a great season and still lose a game. If we lose to a better team, so be it. As long as we play our tails off."

"No. No. Let's go undefeated."

Incredible.

And contagious.

Marcus told me everything I needed to know about how far our program had come last November when we defeated Kentucky 92–82, the team that was ranked No. 1 in the country in every pre-season poll and would eventually go on to win the NCAA championship.

It happened during the final moments. We were on the verge of a huge upset.

But I was acting like we were down by 20.

At one point, I turned to press row and fumed to no one in particular, "Why don't they listen?" Then I screamed at Edgar when he made a careless turnover in the last minute.

That's when Marcus came up to me and told me to keep my cool.

"Don't go crazy. We got this one."

I admit it: he caught me off guard.

"Whatever you say, big guy," I told him. "Whatever you say."

Marcus had a better view of the future than I had at that time.

Well, we didn't go undefeated. But we went 35–2 and almost won the national championship. We achieved the greatest success this program and this university ever had because we chased a dream that was a little bit out of reach.

And we did it with players who were underrecruited by other schools that had questions about their scholastic and physical abilities. But they were better than people thought. I saw a lot of myself in them.

I inherited my attitude from my mother, Donna Calipari.

My mom was different. She talked about dreaming big dreams and not being afraid to feel special—to be unique and stand out.

She taught us to chase the dream, even if it seemed out of reach. She used to say, "You can be president of the United States if that's what you want to be." I was in fifth grade at the time. She still thinks that way.

I had thought about being a doctor or a lawyer, but my parents weren't college-educated, so it seemed as though those careers were out of the realm of possibility for me. Then I realized I wanted to be a coach. That seemed an uphill battle, too.

For years, I had people say to me, "A college coach. How are you going to be a college coach? Who do you know? You didn't play for Dean Smith. You didn't play in the NBA. What do you know that someone else doesn't know?"

I'd heard all that and replied, "I'm going to be a college basketball coach. That's what I want to do. That's what I'm going to be."

I wanted to be a major college coach by age thirty and win a national championship by the time I was thirty-five. At least, that's what I wrote on an index card when I was twenty-four years old and an assistant coach at Kansas.

I'd gotten an early start on my chosen career.

I used to practice all the time, and I was always figuring out ways of sneaking into the gym at Moon High School.

I discovered quickly that I could unlatch the windows. When I was in junior high, I officiated Pee Wee games on Saturday mornings; then I'd leave the latch open on the window. The next morning, I'd come back, push the window open, and climb in.

One day, I looked up and saw someone else climbing through the same window. I thought it was one of my buddies, but I wasn't sure. It looked like an older person. I put the ball up in the bleachers and I hid behind the bleachers. I just sat back there, watching. At first, I thought it was a maintenance person. It was a policeman. I thought, "Oh my God, I'm going to be arrested. But maybe he won't see the ball." He never did. He finally left. I stayed behind the bleachers for two hours. I thought it was a sting: the minute I'd come out, he was going to arrest me.

Finally, I was ready to go out the window. But I knew he was standing out there, just waiting for me to come out, right? I jumped down and stopped for a minute, expecting the worst.

The cop wasn't there, so I just ran home.

Before I graduated, I also learned to pop open the latch to a door with my comb. The school administrators caught on to that trick, so they put chains on the inside of the doors. But when I jerked the doors open, there'd be a gap. And as long as my head got through—I was so skinny—the rest of me would get through. There was no stopping me. I loved it!

I was lucky. Larry Brown saw the potential in me when he offered me a full time assistant's job at Kansas. So did former Pitt coach Paul Evans, who hired me in 1987. And Rick Pitino, who pushed me to get involved with the UMass job.

I saw the potential in UMass and our kids right away. It took the rest of the state a little longer. Nobody knew where Amherst was. Amherst is located only 120 miles west of Boston on the Mass Turnpike, but some of the Boston media still have trouble locating this town of 32,000 on the map.

Boston Globe columnist Dan Shaughnessy refers to our town as "Hooterville," and there have been constant references to UMass as a "cow college."

It has taken us a long time to get a foothold in Boston because people looked at anything beyond Worcester as farmland. There was nothing out there.

What people didn't understand was that there are 100,000 graduates of UMass living within a sixty-mile radius of Boston. These alums wanted to know what was going on. They would write to the newspapers, call the talk shows. That's why the Boston media started thinking our fans were paranoid.

But the truth is that the Boston media didn't want to drive all the way out here on the Mass Turnpike. If a writer got an assignment to cover UMass, he'd be upset. "Why did I deserve it? It's an hour-and-a-half drive." I know that drive because it's hard for me. To go to Boston, do my thing, and then have to drive home, it's a bear.

Eddie Andelman, who does a sports talk show on WEEI, had been the worst offender. He was constantly killing UMass graduates, poking fun at them on the air. What he said was, "Aw, they're all farmers out there. They're driving tractors. They don't make more than $18,000 a year." And get this: his wife is a UMass grad.

Our alums went nuts. They started calling in. Eddie Andelman got our alums to stand up and act. That's what his show is supposed to do, create controversy.

Four years ago, I called and asked him to speak at our banquet. People got upset, but I told them, "You don't understand what this guy's done for us."

Since then, he's been a big advocate.

At least Eddie knew where we were.

To the national media we were "UMass. Oh, yeah. They're in that place. You know, that place that's near Boston."

Amherst is a typical liberal college town—a lot like Berkeley— nestled in western Massachusetts. Amherst College has a strong, 200-year-old liberal arts tradition. Some alumni claim it was on their campus, in 1952, that a pie tin was first tossed, thus starting a new national pastime—Frisbee throwing. UMass, with a student population of 23,000, is Amherst College's relatively new neighbor. Now, I know our school didn't originate basketball, but maybe we did help to popularize it in the area.

UMass was founded in 1863 but most of its growth occurred in the late 1960s and early '70s. That's why there is such a hodge-podge of buildings on campus. Students began showing up quickly, accompanied by twenty-two-story dormitories.

Neighboring Amherst Center is filled with big Victorian houses and is inhabited by writers, professors, students, and time-warp hippies. Emily Dickinson lived here, and her house is now a museum situated in the middle of student housing. Bill Cosby has a home nearby. And Puffer's Pond, located northeast of campus, is still a picturesque place for undergrads to go swimming.

The outskirts of town are filled with bike trails—and large apartment complexes—but the local government has tried to maintain its rural character, prohibiting the construction of strip malls.

The town has also tried to keep the students under control ever since the school built up its "Zoo Mass" reputation for wild partying in the late '70s. The drinking age has been raised to twenty-one, and the bars close early.

Boston has the state legislature, Harvard, Radcliffe, and MIT. And like most big cities, the Boston fans are very pro-oriented. Unlike some big cities, though, they have reasons to be proud. There's a lot of tradition: the Celtics, the Red Sox, and the Bruins.

The last time Amherst had made headlines was when a young man set himself on fire to protest the Gulf War conflict. Overall, it seems a very unlikely place for a Top 10 basketball program to spring up. But it has worked, and the town seems fascinated by what we've accomplished.

———

After our win over Kentucky, we went on to beat Maryland. Then we defeated Florida, then Boston College, then Wake Forest. And that was just the beginning.

We won twenty-six straight games before we finally lost on February 24 to George Washington at the Mullins Center. We were 26–1 on the road. On the road! I don't think anyone's ever won twenty-six road games in NCAA history. We were 9–1 in our arena. We had four overtime games and eleven games when we were either tied or behind at the half, and we won them all. We hadn't walked through the season. We had to play every night. We had to be prepared to play.

To be No. 1 for ten weeks and have the pressure of also being unbeaten throughout that time, to have every team play us like it was their biggest game of the year—the highlight of their careers—we had to be ready.

Then we cruised through the NCAA East Regionals, beating Central Florida, Stanford, Arkansas, and Georgetown to reach the Final Four.

Right before the Final Four, the roof of a barn outside of town sported our logo, along with a message pleading for Marcus Camby to stay in school for his senior year instead of turning pro: "Go UMass. Please stay, Marcus."

I knew then we'd been accepted.

This was all new to our fans. At other schools, it is not enough just to win. You could win the national title but you didn't win by a big enough margin. You could win thirty games, but your season is considered a failure because you didn't get to the Final Four. But at UMass, there was an enormous outpouring of pride on campus and in the town.

We left for the Meadowlands on Tuesday night. While we were secluded in a hotel in New Jersey, Amherst was going crazy. Whitmore Administration Building was filled with UMass signs. Employees came to work dressed in UMass T-shirts and jerseys. There were giant letters, one on each window of the library, spelling out the words "Go UMass."

They even named a cheese steak after Marcus at D'Angelo, a local restaurant. "Steak with extra cheese, mustard, and ketchup," Marcus explained. "I like the flavor."

There was even a friendly bet between Pam Miller, the mayor of Lexington, and Barry Del Castilho, Amherst town manager. Miller wagered a blue denim shirt and a blue horse blanket for Amherst's new mounted patrol. Del Castilho wagered a book of Emily Dickinson's poems and a "Refuse to Lose" T-shirt. Officials at Lexington did turn down a request to fly the UMass flag in front of their town hall if we won.

Guess they didn't want the place torched.

The NCAA gave us 2,500 $70 tickets to the games. Of those, 800 went to the students by lottery and 800 went to 400 season-ticket holders, based on a point system of past support for athletics. The other 900 went to the team and the administration.

The NCAA also required UMass to take 500 hotel rooms—400 of which the season-ticket holders were required to book in exchange for their pick of seats—and 100 that the administration bought. Price for a hotel room for the weekend: $800.

Some of the students who won the lottery had no intention of attending the game once they found out what scalpers were paying for seats. After the students picked up the tickets, the scalpers were there to meet them as soon as they came out the door. One guy apparently didn't even bother to ask if the tickets were for sale. He plunked down $2,500 in a student's hand—took the tickets right out of the kid's fist—and then walked away.

Before our game with Kentucky, Bob Marcum took a walk into the student section. He returned to the floor, just shaking his head.

"We must have the oldest student body in the world," he said.

Everybody, it seemed, wanted to be part of the celebration.

Our secretary, Bonnie Martin, received a letter the week of the game from a UMass graduate who was set to get married at the same time as our game.

He wanted me to use my clout to move tipoff because so many of his buddies were UMass alums. I think he was serious.

He'd probably never watched a game in his life.

But Natalie Cole had.

When we first arrived in New York, the NCAA held a gala Salute to the Final Four at Radio City Music Hall. Natalie Cole performed. She had attended UMass as an undergraduate and got her start singing in the small clubs in town.

She wanted to make that perfectly clear. "I'm here to root for my school," she said.

Our chancellor, Dr. David K. Scott, was impressed enough that he insisted on meeting her after the reception. She wasn't just a fair-weather fan, either. She had followed our team and knew who the players were.

So did Rick Pitino.

I had only one thought while sitting on the bench at the Final Four: how we were going to win the game. We believed we belonged there. I believed my team belonged there. I believed I belonged there as a coach. I wasn't in awe. It was just a basketball court. When the game started, I didn't worry about TV or

Billy Packer or Jim Nantz. All I saw was the court. I coached the game like I coached every other game this year.

But I was a little bit nervous, and I think my team was, too—which was natural. I looked down and saw Rick, and said, "Here we are. We're in the battle again."

The campus just held its breath. The game was televised on two big screens at the Mullins Center. And the police had cordoned off the downtown area, just in case.

We were always trying to tell the kids, "Be ready for your opportunity. What is luck? Luck is where preparation and opportunity cross. You are so prepared, and the opportunity's there. Boom. You take advantage."

All season, we were able to put ourselves in the mind-set where we needed to be.

At one point late in the second half of the semifinal game, we were down 13 points. Carmelo got his fourth foul. Charlton Clarke was exhausted. I looked down the bench and saw Giddel Padilla begging me with his eyes, "Please put me in."

I looked at him and said, "Go ahead in. Go show them you can play."

Giddel had grown up in Puerto Rico and had come to this country two years before Edgar. He was a year older than Edgar and had helped teach him how to speak English. When we signed Giddel, he was a big star at Springfield Central.

Edgar wanted to follow in his brother's footsteps. He had always dreamed of playing with Giddel. But for the longest time, it didn't look like that would happen. Giddel rarely played as a freshman. He refused to play defense the way we wanted and started showing up late for practices.

Edgar started getting playing time as a freshman, and Giddel couldn't get off the bench. Giddel quit the team; he even left school briefly. Then he returned to UMass. He had watched Edgar develop, and he wanted to come back to the team. But he didn't know how to approach me. Finally Edgar came to me on Giddel's behalf. I told him we would give Giddel a second chance, but he had to show up at every practice, be on time, and be part of the team. He also knew there were no guarantees on playing time.

Now was Giddel's moment.

He had practiced hard all year. He had prepared against the best starting five in America. He had defended Carmelo better than any player we had played against all season. He came in, and Edgar finally got his wish. The two of them were playing in the same backcourt; and Giddel was giving Kentucky's All-American guard Tony Delk a lot of trouble.

Giddel sparked our comeback.

We made Kentucky work for its 81–74 victory.

If we had won, Giddel would have been *the* story because he was ready. He never let himself get beaten down. He never took "no" for an answer. He just said, "When you give me an opportunity, I'm going to show you I'm ready for it, and I'm going to show you how lucky I am."

There must have been new road maps printed in time for this year's awards banquet.

A sellout crowd was at the Mullins Center. Twelve hundred people paid $50 apiece to honor the team. It was carried live on Channel 40 in western Massachusetts. Our state treasurer, Joe Malone, was there, along with other dignitaries, including the school's new president, William Bulger.

Senator John F. Kerry presented the team's rebounding award

to Dana Dingle; and Senator Edward M. Kennedy presented Edgar Padilla with an award for being the team's assist leader.

It was good to hear Ted Kennedy's voice again.

Back in 1992, Bonnie had come in and said, "Coach, Ted Kennedy is on the phone."

"Yeah. Tell him to wait."

I was on the phone with Bob Huggins of Cincinnati at the time.

"Yeah," I said, "somebody's saying it's Kennedy. Don't worry about it."

I wasn't concerned. My friends from Pittsburgh were always calling the office and giving me different names: Jumpin' Johnny DeFazio. Dean Smith calling.

This time, it was Ted Kennedy.

Bob and I talked about five, ten minutes. After I hung up, Bonnie said, "John, Ted Kennedy's still on hold."

"Yeah. Put him through."

He got on, and I recognized the voice. It was him. I said, "Senator, I am sorry. I thought it was someone playing a joke."

He laughed. He told me that he and his mother had sat up in Hyannis Port and watched the Syracuse game. He said, "My mom really cheered for you guys and was really excited."

These days, we have some fans who are even farther away than Cape Cod.

Before we played at Louisville, we received a letter from an eighth-grader in Quincy, Illinois, who had adopted UMass after watching us on TV. He wrote a letter saying UMass was his favorite team and that he and his family were going to Freedom Hall to cheer for us. I asked Bill Strickland, our director of media relations, if he could find him. He did; the young man came down before the game, and the players signed autographs for him. After the game, the players gave him the game ball.

I received a letter from Bob Peck of Williams College who was on sabbatical and doing basketball clinics in Zimbabwe. He sent me a picture of a guy wearing a UMass jersey, along with a note: "Just thought you'd be interested to see how far your reputation has spread."

It didn't surprise me because we were finding out UMass is one of the hottest sportswear lines in the country. There's Notre Dame. There's Michigan. There's Georgetown. And there's UMass.

I guess a lot of people can relate to "Refuse to Lose."

Our staff assistant, Brian Gorman, first put the slogan on the back of T-shirts. The rest is marketing history.

So I got it trademarked. That idea came from Billy Packer, a CBS broadcaster. We were on a plane ride together and he said to me, "Have you trademarked that yet?"

"No," I said.

"You'd better," he said. "Because as soon as you get hot, someone will steal it and you'll have no control."

So I did.

Nebraska football picked it up. Boom. I told them, "You can put it on your butts or your pants, but you can't sell it."

The Seattle Mariners baseball team used it in the American League playoffs in 1995. Boom. Sat down with them. Jeff Gordon, the race car driver, used it. Boom. Sat down with him.

"Let's talk about how this works. It's UMass basketball."

And it was us.

CHAPTER 3

JOURNEY FROM THE MOON

My mom gave me the attitude. My dad gave me the opportunity.

I was raised in a two-story house in Moon, PA, a tiny suburb of Pittsburgh. We lived in a working-class neighborhood, twenty-five miles south of the city. It wasn't a big community—maybe 1,500 people at most. Many of the families worked at the airport.

My father, Vince Calipari, was a close friend of Ray Bosetti, the baseball coach at Moon Township High. They used to play softball together. Ray let me go to the baseball games with the team. I was the bat boy. Bill Sacco was the assistant baseball and basketball coach, and he asked me if I wanted to do the same thing with the basketball team.

I said yes. I lived real close to the school, so it was easy for me to get there. I used to sit on the bench with Skip Tatala, who was the head basketball coach of the Moon Tigers at the time, wearing my little red V-neck sweater and a clip-on bow tie, handing out towels.

It was a lot of fun.

A couple of times, I remember, they let me scrimmage with them. I was seven, eight years old. They let me score.

It probably gave me the basis for what I wanted to do. The people I looked up to were teachers and coaches because they were always nice to me, treated me with respect, and taught me. I wanted to be a high school basketball coach. The only time I changed my mind was when I went to college and saw that coaching college basketball wasn't bad either.

My grandfather had come over from Italy with his brother. Back then, the Irish were shipped one way—to the railroads— and the Italians another—to the coal mines of West Virginia. So that's where my grandfather worked until he died of black lung disease. He was fifty-eight.

My grandmother is from Coraopolis, Pennsylvania. Her neighbors were the Harleys, a black couple. That's how I grew up. Black and white never mattered. The railroad tracks were a stone's throw away. There was a Dairy Queen, my grand-mother's house, and the Harleys'. There were race riots in that area when I was very young. Below the tracks, there was a lot of trouble, and my father seemed really worried. I can remember Mr. Harley, who has since passed away, sitting on his front porch, looking at my dad, and saying, "Vince, you have nothing to worry about. Your mother is going to be all right. I'm right here."

That was my background in race relations.

My father worked at a steel plant for a couple of years. Then he was a fueler for Piedmont Airlines before it was bought by USAir. He's since been transferred to Charlotte, North Carolina, where he and my mother live now. I'm trying to get him to retire, but he won't. "What am I going to do if I'm not working?" he asks me.

My mom used to work part-time at the junior high school, selling ice cream in the cafeteria to help make ends meet. We never went hungry. We never went without. We always had food. We always had a home. It wasn't always the fanciest home, but we always had a place to live.

My mom had a dream that her children would get college educations and live in $100,000 houses. I think my parents paid about $13,500 for the house we grew up in; for us to live in a $100,000 house was a big thing.

I always had jeans, a couple pairs of pants, a few shirts, and plenty of sweat socks. But when I was growing up, I never had a whole lot of shoes. I wore one pair until they wore out. I can remember putting cardboard in my shoes to make them last longer. When I first started playing basketball, I wore tennis shoes, so I began to accumulate tennis shoes. Then I graduated to dress shoes. To this day, I like shoes, all different kinds. I have a dozen pairs . . . and counting.

When Ellen and I were dating, she looked in my closet and wanted to know why I had all these shoes.

"You have only two feet," she said.

I told her they made up for the few pairs I had the first seventeen years of my life.

I have two sisters. Leah is my older sister. Terry is my younger sister. Terry lives in North Carolina with her husband, Rick Geary, who is an executive for a food company. Leah's husband, Dennis Angelini, works for Microsoft and they live outside Philadelphia. All of us are college-educated. My parents were not. It was their goal to make sure their children got their degrees.

And they've achieved it.

I was always a football fan when I was younger. Growing up in Western Pennsylvania, what other choice did I have? We were bombarded with it on TV all the time. Friday night was reserved for high school football. The college games were on Saturday. Sunday mornings, I used to watch Notre Dame replays with Lindsey Nelson, followed by replays of the Grambling games. Then it was time for the Steelers.

I always rooted for the Vikings because Fran Tarkenton was their quarterback. He wasn't afraid to be different. He was six feet tall, didn't have the body, wasn't that quick and fast. He just got it done. He'd figured out how to win. People said he never won the Super Bowl. But he took his team there four times. Statistically, there are not many quarterbacks in the history of the game who accomplished more with less. He was an ordinary person doing extraordinary things.

So I kind of latched on to him.

I was a quarterback in seventh and eighth grades for our midget football team. I had to convince my folks to let me play—it was my first recruiting pitch. I weighed about 115 pounds with rocks in my pockets; my mom didn't think I was big enough. We'd be out there playing, putting pads on, and she would say, "You're going to get broken in half."

She was right, of course.

I finally got my parents to sign the permission papers the night of our first practice. I raced out the door. Within an hour, I was in the hospital with a broken collarbone. I played football just one more year. Then I had to make a decision whether to pursue my gridiron career in junior high. But by that time I knew I wanted to be a basketball player.

I guess you could say I was a gym rat as far back as I can remember. My family's property was located twenty or thirty yards away from the high school. I spent a lot of time there and looked up to many of the players. I always admired

Tom Richards, who went on to play at Pitt; and Phil Meanor, who's now working in North Carolina. Bob Davie, who is the defensive coordinator at Notre Dame, was a basketball, baseball, and football player at Moon. By the time I reached eighth grade, I used to play pickup games in the gym with the coaches at the school—guys like Skip, Mark Capuana, Ray Bosetti, Gary Brunette, Jim Boni, Tommy Haskins, and Bill Sacco, who was my high school coach. That's where I learned how to play rough and to be aggressive. These were men I was playing with, and they used to beat me up physically.

I had a good high school career as a point guard. In my senior year, we went to the state tournament for the first time in thirty years.

I was also the senior class president. Even back then, I was talkative. I ran for office because I felt our class was going crazy since we were going to school only half days. They were rebuilding the junior high school, so we went to school from eight o'clock in the morning until noon; and then the junior high went to school from 12:30 to 4:30 P.M.

I felt we needed some of the guys who were leaders in the school to step up and try to pull the students together. We tried to raise money for class activities so we could do things together and make our senior year fun. We arranged for a senior boat ride, but we made it reasonable so everybody could go. The same with the prom. Tickets were originally $30, but we cut the cost to $15, and the class treasury made up the rest.

I guess I've been a liberal my whole life.

I wish I could tell you the first two years of my college career were as much fun. I had gotten a scholarship to play at North Carolina–Wilmington. Mel Gibson, the coach there, found out about me through Five-Star camp. Five-Star is one of the best summer basketball camps in the country. It runs four weekly sessions every July at Robert Morris College in Coraopolis near my home. The sleepaway camp has always attracted many of the best players in the ninth through eleventh grade from the East and Midwest.

Mel came up and watched me. He needed a point guard and he thought I understood the game. When I played, I never wanted to come out of the game. I wanted to play every minute of every game. But I was backing up Barry Taylor, a junior college All-American whom Mel called the best point guard he had ever coached.

I was a kid. Barry was a man; he came in and could really play the position. He was a nice guy. But I wanted to play, so I decided to transfer. When I told Mel, he wasn't nasty about it, but he was matter of fact: "You're not going to play a lot of minutes here." When it happened, it was traumatic. I'd never had any aspirations to be an NBA player, but I wanted to be as good as I could be. To a nineteen- or twenty-year-old kid, it seemed as if someone had come in and taken away my dreams. I asked myself, "What do I do now?"

To this day, I've never told a kid he can't do something. I may have been hard with kids, but I tried to give them every opportunity to make it, even if they were going into their senior year. I wanted them to leave school with a good taste in their mouths about that university and that program. I wanted them to feel that we had done everything we could to help them as players, and as individuals. When they graduated, we helped them with jobs and helped them with their futures. We were there for them with anything they needed. I think that's very important in building a program and sustaining it.

North Carolina–Wilmington was not an all-bad experience

for me. It was an awakening. Maybe I couldn't play in a major college program, but I hoped to coach at one some day.

I got a lot of my self-esteem back playing for Joe DeGregorio at Clarion State, seventy-five miles north of Pittsburgh. Joe was always upbeat. I couldn't believe it. He had been an assistant at Niagara. Clarion was a tough situation for him, working at a Division II school that was always looking to do more with less.

The school was trying to run a champagne program on a beer budget. Joe was trying to do things right, trying to project a big-time image, but knew he couldn't. It frustrated him that he was beating everybody in the league, and doing it with less. He wanted more. And the school wouldn't do more.

Eventually, it drove him out of the business. Since that time, that program has not been the same. It's hard, when a coach is getting much less than everybody else, really to do more.

Joe had always been feisty. He'd had a confrontation with John Chaney a year before I arrived. Chaney, who is now the coach at Temple University, was still at Cheyney State at the time. He had come in with his "I'm going to intimidate you" attitude. And Joe, who's all of about 5'7", walked up to him and said, "This is my gym. You're not going to do this s—— in my gym." The two of them got into a shouting match and had to be restrained. The incident almost turned into a scuffle. Thank goodness there were enough people there to break it up.

But I learned more than how to deal with angry coaches from Joe.

Joe was very good about coming in, every day, excited about being at practice. When I felt like I didn't want to be there, he'd try to juice me up and get me going. So then I'd start thinking, "How the heck does he do it himself every day? How does he get himself excited every day?"

I learned a lot of basketball from him; we played motion offense every day. But the biggest thing I walked away with is the feeling that a coach has to have fun doing this, and that the kids have to have fun, too.

Joe left me behind on a bus trip. Clarion was the No. 3 team in the country. We were playing Textile in Philadelphia. Textile's coach, Herb Magee, is the greatest in the country for teaching shooting. There's no one better. And he can golf a little bit, too.

We were coming from Clarion, so we didn't fly. We got in vans and Joe's car, and we vanned all the way down to Textile. We got to the Marriott Hotel on City Line Avenue. We were four to a room. This was Clarion: we rode in vans; coaches drove; we stayed four to a room; we went to an IHOP for breakfast. I was the last one to get into the shower—because I was the smallest. I knew I was going to be the last one because the other three guys in the room were pushing me out of the way.

Well, I missed the bus. I had just gotten out of the shower, and those guys were yelling, "You'd better hurry."

"You jagoffs better tell them to wait," I yelled back. I toweled off. I threw clothes on. I ran down the hallway and saw the vans taking off.

So he left me.

They were just going to get something to eat; they weren't going to the game. But I had to get something to eat on my own. He didn't start me that night, and we lost the game.

That's why I say what I learned from him was that I always make sure that the top seven guys are on the bus before I get on, so I don't lose the game.

I got my first taste of coaching when I worked at Five-Star camp before my freshman year in college. I had been a camper there since tenth grade. I found I really enjoyed teaching.

After that, obviously, I worked at Five-Star every year. It set the foundation of who I am because here's what happened. I don't learn as much by watching as I do by doing. What some people learn from watching is "now let me try it." That doesn't work for me.

Five-Star was a laboratory where I could be myself and see if it worked. When I was there, I taught the best kids in the country and worked with them on basketball. I feel I'm a teacher of basketball, not just a coach. I think individual development is the most important thing I do in my job, and I've already seen it at work in the pros.

When I took the Nets' job, some people were really down on Yinka Dare, our backup center. But, since he started working out with us in the summer, we've been able to challenge him, to inspire him, and he's gotten better. He can see his improvement, too. The same goes for Khalid Reeves, one of our guards.

It's incredible, the coaches who went through there. At Five-Star, I saw all the great teachers—Hubie Brown, Rick Pitino, Chuck Daly. I heard the best lectures. I saw Bobby Knight. I saw Mike Fratello. I saw Dave Odom. They were all counselors or teachers.

I worked sessions at Pittsburgh and Honesdale, PA. I watched. I learned. I had an opportunity to carry over what I had learned. I got to teach and find out what worked for me and what didn't. And then I coached games. The biggest thing I did was coach ten games a week for five weeks a summer at Five-Star. I coached fifty games a summer. People could say it was only a camp game, but I had officials; I had a clock; I had a score. Those weren't just camp games. Let me tell you about some of the players I coached.

I coached Christian Laettner. I coached Danny Ferry. I

coached Grant Hill. I coached Troy Lewis, who went to Purdue; and Kevin Walls, who played for Louisville. I could go on and on. I was essentially coaching a college team, and I got an opportunity to learn what worked for me as a teacher. I learned that teaching basketball is more important than coaching.

Speaking of Danny Ferry . . .

While I was attending Clarion State, Howard Garfinkel hired me to be the youngest coach in the upscale development league at Robert Morris College, which featured the best rising sophomore prospects in the country.

I was coaching players as good as the players I coached this past year at UMass. It's funny. My contact with those kinds of players was a chance to learn about myself as a coach.

I met some good friends, people who have helped me in the business, people who could make phone calls for me. Obviously, Garf has been a close friend of mine, a guy who's helped throughout my career.

But Garf thought my career might have a premature ending one night when he saw me go off on Danny Ferry, who then was a young star with DeMatha Catholic.

As Garf remembers it:

"John would make a point of always getting on his best player," Garfinkel said. "It was about four-thirty in the afternoon and Danny did something John didn't like. John called time-out and proceeded to go nose-to-nose with this kid the whole time-out. John was screaming at him. It was unbearable.

"I turned to my right and there, ten feet away behind the fence, was Bob Ferry, Danny's father, the GM of the Bullets, and a friend of mine. I almost fainted. I'm thinking, 'There goes our contact with DeMatha. There goes my license. I'm dead.'

"I went over to Bob Ferry to try to make amends.

" 'Who's that coach?' Ferry asked.

"When I told him, Ferry just smiled. 'Give him a message for me. Tell him it's about time someone did that to my kid,' he said. 'That's the best thing that's ever happened to Danny.' "

Then he took my name.

"I wonder if Bob knew what the future would hold," Garfinkel said when he told this story.

Maybe he did know.

When I was in college, I also coached AAU ball for Irv Saracki of Buffalo for two summers. When I was in high school, I played for Irv. He had seen me and wanted to bring me in. He drove me up to Buffalo and I stayed in a church rectory. I was a point guard on the same team as Jim Johnstone and Mike Helms, who played for Wake Forest.

I got to coach Terry Williams, who went to SMU; Kenny Henry, who went to Connecticut; Tom Sheehey, who went to Virginia; Howard Triche and Greg Monroe, who went to Syracuse; and Gary Bossert, who went to Niagara.

When I went on to coach at Kansas, Pitt, and UMass, I used everything I used in Five-Star. Some of it was great. Some I couldn't agree with or didn't like. I learned so much about the game. Most assistants who get jobs have never coached their own teams. What makes you think you can coach? You don't know. You hope you can grab back onto past experience, watching your coach and seeing what he did.

I had an advantage because I'd coached the jayvees at Kansas.

Bob Hill, now the head coach of the San Antonio Spurs, got me my first break. He's my best friend. He's the big brother I never had. I've known him ever since I was in tenth grade and he was an assistant at Pitt, recruiting one of my teammates, Joe Fryz. He actually gave me my first brochure for Five-Star.

Bob was an assistant at Kansas in 1982 when he got involved with the head coaching job at Western Michigan. He came to Five-Star and asked me, "Would you like to get into coaching?"

I told him that's what I was trying to do.

He said, "If I get this job, I'm going to bring you along as the part-time assistant."

He didn't get the job. But he invited me to work at Kansas's summer camp. He persuaded Ted Owens, who was coaching there at the time, to bring me in as a volunteer assistant that fall. Bob told Ted, "We could really use him. He can help us in recruiting. He can help us with camp."

I went to Kansas right out of college. I wasn't on salary. Bob once told me he needed my social security number. I asked him why.

"I've got to take you off my income tax, I've been giving you so much money," he said.

Bob's a basketball junkie. I like Bob because he's into basketball—big time. He loves X–ing and O–ing.

At Kansas, we'd go for a run and come back to the locker room. They had the board in there. I'd say, "Okay. You have four seconds to go. You have the ball in the side out. Here's the chalk. You've got sixty seconds." He'd put up his men. Then I'd say, "Okay. I want a man-to-man. Go ahead. Tell me what you're doing." And he'd have to go through it.

And then he'd do the same to me—throw me the chalk: "Okay. You've got to go the length of the court. You've got eight seconds. You've got the ball down here. And I'm in a 2-2-1 press. Tell me what you do."

Then he'd come out, draw his Xs real big: "I'm in a 2-3 zone."

I'd say, "What the hell've you got, three seven-footers? Your Xs are too big. You have your Xs so big, this X is guarding four of my men."

And we'd laugh and throw chalk at each other.

We'd play one-on-one; people felt we hated each other. We'd end up throwing basketballs at each other. He's bigger than I am—he's 6′5″. He'd back me under. I had to physically cross-bodyblock him to keep him away from the basket. We'd end up fouling, throwing the ball, and laughing afterwards. But if you watched, you'd think, "These two are nuts; they hate each other." But we were really competitive, and he'd always say, "Don't blame me for your being so small. Blame your father."

I worked the Kansas summer camp, and Ted Owens paid me through the camp. I worked at the training table; that's how I ate. Calvin Thompson would be coming through the line, and I'd say, "Calvin, would you like mashed potatoes? We're shooting before practice; I'll be there at 2:45 P.M.," while I'm serving him. I was checking the players in, seeing who was there eating.

It was a fun time. I had no real responsibilities. I walked in the gym, showered, and thought to myself, "Phog Allen showered in this shower. Is this incredible?"

I still have strong feelings for Kansas, for the tradition of that program and being allowed to work in it.

I lived with Randolph Carroll, the part-time assistant, in a small house given to us by an alum named Ron Tebo.

Randolph played at Kansas for Ted Owens and was an imposing figure at 6′7″. He is now head coach at Yavapai Junior College in Arizona. We've stayed in touch. As a matter of fact, he ran my team camp at UMass for two summers.

We had a choice between renting furniture or getting ESPN.

We couldn't do both because we didn't have enough money. Randolph was paying for just about everything, anyway. We decided that we could sit on pillows. And we had crates. But we *needed* ESPN.

The only furniture in the house were the beds we had. And this was a major lifestyle improvement for me because I didn't have a bed when I went out there. There was a TV movie being filmed at the Allen Field House called *The Day After*, about a nuclear explosion in Kansas. The Allen Field House was the triage unit, so they had all these cots—I'm talking 500 of them—in there. When the filming ended, they were going to throw these things out because they were junk. So Randolph and I went down there and I said, "Let's see if we can find a big, double-wide cot." We found one that was three, four feet wide, with a folded-up mattress. We took it over to the house and put a sheet of plywood under the mattress—I would have folded up in it if I hadn't. And that was my bed for the year.

At the end of the season, Ted Owens got fired. Billy Whitmore of Vermont called me, flew me in, and offered me a job as the recruiting coordinator. I had the contract. I flew home. Then Larry Brown, who was the Kansas coach, called and said, "I want you to come back as a full-time assistant."

To this day, I'm glad I did.

If I could model myself after any coach, it would be Larry Brown. I like everything about him. He's a class individual. He's not as emotional as I am, but I'm just being me. I watched Larry and I said, "Boy, I wish I could be like him as a coach. I'd like to be a players' coach: a guy who teaches, is good in games, good with the media, and good with people. He's somebody I'd like to be like." I even dressed like him for a while.

And that's not all. One day, someone came up to me and asked, "Are you injured?" Association breeds assimilation if you like people and hang out with them. Larry wore preppy clothes at Kansas. I started wearing them, too. Larry had two bad hips and would limp onto the floor. So would I.

I probably learned more about coaching from Bob and Larry than from anyone else. On the court, I got my style of play and philosophy from Larry. It's the way UMass plays.

This is how it works.

I challenged my teams, but I wanted them to have fresh minds and fresh legs at the end of the season. Obviously Larry's teams did, because they played their best basketball down the stretch.

At UMass, we placed a premium on keeping practice going at a high intensity for a long period of time. Believe it or not, we didn't stop practice to shoot free throws or to take a break. We may have had managers sprint cups of water onto the court for a 30-second break, but we got right back into practice.

When we did shooting drills, they were high in intensity. Our free throw work was done at the beginning and the end of practice. We started practice with warm-ups and kept going full-tilt until the end with a minimum of stops. Obviously, the early-season practices required more explanations and stops than the ones later in the season. We would stop practice to teach, comment, and highlight good and bad plays, but these stops were kept to a minimum.

Because our practices did not have many stops, we were able to sustain our high intensity as well as any team in the country. We felt we could play hard for 40 minutes because we practiced hard for 90 to 120 minutes six days a week.

People wondered how our guards could play 40 minutes a game. We believed it was because they practiced for a lot longer than 40 minutes and were therefore prepared to play a full college game.

Even the day before a game, our practices were high in intensity. We simply went shorter in the length of practice. We never went light and we tried never to go at less than 100 percent.

Having said that, our teams at UMass were different from many college teams. We didn't shoot threes. We didn't make the game ugly. We didn't press the whole game. We'd press, but basically we played conventional basketball. I learned that from Larry, too. To me, the beauty of the game lies in the half-court: how you defend—together, and on offense, how you play together. It's in how the ball moves, how it goes from one side to the other, how you create shots for one another.

At Kansas, we called it "Buddy Basketball." Two guys working together, so as I come down the court, I'm looking for a buddy. There he is: "Jim, Jim, Jim." I back-screen for Jim, try to get him a shot. I don't get it. He posts. I cut off of him. That's "Buddy Basketball"—two of us working together, to try to get us a shot. And it breaks the game down a little bit easier.

At UMass, we wanted to be the best team from offense to defense and defense to offense. Our teams didn't give up many free baskets, but they got a lot of free baskets going on offense.

I think one of the things Larry's proudest of is that when he watched my teams play, he could see his teams and how they'd played in the past. More than anyone else, he's left his mark on how I coach.

In fact, one of my greatest thrills in coaching came when I taught one of our Kansas players, Cedric Hunter, a new move he used in a game.

Cedric was from Omaha, Nebraska. He jumped center in high school, but we were expecting him to play point guard, so I spent a lot of time with him before and after practice.

Larry coached the team during practice. When practices were over, there were individual instructions, and I taught Cedric an inside-out move. It's a fake crossover. I explained it to him this way: "You bring the ball in your right hand and you act like you're crossing over, but the ball never leaves your right hand, and you come right back and go down the right side." He loved it; he was going crazy. He said, "Give me something else."

So we added a palm move: he would drive down the lane now, beat that man, and ball-fake and shoot a layup.

To me, that's what coaching is all about—that and going to the NCAA tournament, which we did twice when I was at Kansas.

One more thing I learned from Larry. At UMass, I would get a thorough scouting report from my assistants. I studied it. Two days before the game, I went over it and we walked through it. Day before the game, we walked through. Day of the game, we walked through. I put it on the chalkboard game day, just so it was fresh in their minds.

The players never saw the scouting reports. They never looked at them. I wanted our players more concerned about how we were playing, not how the opponent was playing. I wanted them to worry about playing to win.

I did take the time to do some recruiting at Kansas, too.

Ellen Higgins, a small-town girl who had grown up on a farm in Missouri, was an attractive brunette working in the business office. I found lots of reasons to file expense accounts.

One of my friends said, "Why don't you ask her out on a date?"

I said, "Nah, she won't go out on a date with me."

I guess they had talked to her.

On our first date, I took her to a baseball game in Kansas City. The game was rained out, so we went to a movie and later had a chance to talk. She must have bought my pitch. We got married in June of 1986.

From Kansas, I took a job at Pitt as an assistant coach under

Roy Chipman in 1985. It was home. Larry was not real happy when I told him.

I tried to explain my reasoning: if you wanted to be a head coach—which is what I wanted to be—there were limited opportunities in the Big Eight Conference. In Kansas, you had Kansas, Kansas State, maybe Wichita State—three jobs; in Iowa, you had Iowa, Iowa State—two jobs; in Oklahoma, you had Oklahoma, Oklahoma State, Tulsa; in Missouri, you had Missouri, because St. Louis wasn't very much at that point; in Colorado, Colorado and Colorado State; in Nebraska, Nebraska. In a six-state area, there were twelve jobs.

"In the city of Philadelphia alone," I said to Larry, "there are six jobs. I need to get back East because an assistant is not going to get the Kansas State job. An assistant from Kansas is not going to get the Oklahoma, Oklahoma State, Colorado, or Colorado State job. You're kind of locked-in out here."

He said, "Hey, you can stay with me. I can get you a job." He probably could have.

I had been at Pitt six months when Roy called me into his office and told me, "I'm resigning." I thought he was joking. I had just left Kansas—I had just left Larry Brown—and he said he's resigning.

"You can't announce it now," I said. "Are you going to keep coaching the team?"

"Yes."

"If you're going to keep coaching the team, announce it at the end of the year. Don't announce it now. How are you going to coach these guys?"

He announced it anyway, and coached the rest of the year.

At the time, money was tight for me. We were invited to the NIT that year, and Roy said he wasn't going to go. My contract stated that I got $3,000 for any tournament. I said, "Look, man, we're going. I'll coach this team." We wound up having to go to Southwest Missouri State, and Charlie Spoonhour beat us.

After the season, Pitt hired Paul Evans, who had coached David Robinson at Navy. He kept me on staff. In my two years under Paul, I built a reputation as a recruiter.

But I've always considered myself overrated in that department. When I first came to Pitt, they were loaded with talent. Charles Smith was there. Jerome Lane was there. Curtis Aiken was there. Demetreus Gore was there. I did not recruit those guys. I walked in, and they were there.

It took me a while to network. The way I recruit is to get people to recruit for me. And, in the beginning, I didn't have great contacts.

The first two players I recruited were Rod Brookin and Chris Gatling. Most people had backed away from them because they felt they were academic risks. We thought they were good kids who would succeed. Both turned out to be outstanding players. Chris went on to an NBA career with Golden State and is still in the league.

Then we signed Sean Miller, a point guard from Blackhawk Area High near Pittsburgh. He was a great ballhandler who had once appeared on *The Tonight Show* when he was ten years old. Sean is like a cousin to me, even though he's not a blood relative. His grandmother practically raised my mother, so we always considered ourselves cousins. His uncle and I had played ball together at Moon High School.

Darelle Porter grew up in Pittsburgh and always wanted to play at Pitt. Brian Shorter was a tough one because he was from Simon Gratz High in Philly. He was on target to become the

Public League's all-time leading scorer as a junior before he transferred to Oak Hill Academy to try to get his grades up during his
senior year. He wound up sitting out his freshman year because
he failed to meet the NCAA's academic requirements. Under the
terms of Proposition 48, the NCAA required all athletic recruits
to earn a 2.0 grade-point average in high school and score a minimum of 700 on their Scholastic Aptitude Test. Brian helped us
recruit Bobby Martin from Atlantic City. More about him later.

We also landed Jason Matthews from Santa Monica, California, one of the brightest players we ever recruited. He works
in financial planning in Pittsburgh these days, and I'm one of his
clients.

During the next two years, we went to the NCAA tournament
each season. Paul Evans has been misconstrued by a lot of people.
He gave the impression that he was mean. He was tough on the
kids—there's no question—but he isn't mean.

And he knew how to win.

He told me, "If you want to win on the road, you need two
things. First, you must have a junior- and senior-oriented team.
You can't win on the road with freshmen and sophomores. I don't
care who you are."

He also taught me about structure. "You have to have some
structure in your offense," he said. "You can't just play motion
offense and let the players run up and down the court. They need
the structure to rely on when they need a basket so that they
don't feel the pressure."

We didn't have as much structure at UMass as Paul had. We
gave our players a little more freedom, but we did have enough
so that when we went on the road, we had something to rely on.

Pitt let Paul go in 1994. Then the rumor mill started grinding
again: "Calipari's up for the Pitt job."

I didn't feel comfortable taking it because they had just gotten rid of the guy I'd worked for. I finally called Paul and told him I didn't want his job. In the end, I think he saw that was the case.

I was hoping the school wouldn't contact me. But when they did, I talked to them out of respect for the people involved. We could never get past a couple of things—a new building and an admissions director rather than a committee—so we never moved any further. I recommended Ralph Willard, their current coach, heavily. I called and told him that.

I hope that Paul gets another chance to be a head coach. He has the best record at Navy and the best record at Pitt. I would say he helped David Robinson as much as anyone did. Maybe his personality rubbed people the wrong way; the minute he started to lose, they tried to fire him. The bottom line is, I think the guy can coach.

I tried to help him at UMass. I brought him into a game. I put him on my television show. I invited him to the Final Four this year. He turned me down because he just didn't want to be in the environment. I hope someone gives him a chance—the way UMass gave one to me.

CHAPTER 4

JOB HUNTING

I've never been a realistic person. That's probably why I took the UMass job.

In the spring of 1988, the trustees at UMass had decided their basketball program was an embarrassment to the school. They were tired of being the butt of jokes. They didn't anticipate winning championships but they didn't want to be 3–24 every year, either. They wanted to be competitive. They wanted a new coach. And this time, they were going to try to do it right.

And me? I was twenty-nine years old. But I knew I was ready to take the next step. I just didn't know where.

I'd heard the horror stories about the program, so I didn't really want the job. I thought it was a dead end. That's what most people had told me. But not Rick Pitino.

"It's a better job than you think. I think you should go for it."

So I did. Who was I to say no to Rick Pitino?

I went up to Amherst and interviewed. And when I saw the school, I became enthusiastic about the job. It was an hour from Hartford, an hour and a half from Boston. New York City was two and a half hours away, Philly, five hours away. North Jersey, three, three and a half. Wow. I felt I could recruit to this school.

And I felt the school had potential.

UMass is a good school. It has the programs that would give us some latitude for admitting students. The mission of this institution is to educate the commonwealth, so the admissions office could make exceptions for athletes because they made exceptions for nonathletes. There are programs for a wide range of students, including the engineering school and the business program. And there are some programs for students who would be the first college-educated members of their families. There are programs for inner-city kids; there are programs for junior college kids.

During my interview, I gave the search committee this analogy: "There are three shoe stores. There's a UMass shoe store, a West Virginia shoe store, and a Temple shoe store. You won't believe this, but UMass isn't selling any shoes. And the other two are selling shoes like they're going out of style, especially Temple. They can't even get them in quick enough, they're moving them out so fast. What we need to do is look in their windows and find out what they're doing—what they're doing with their admissions policy, what they're doing with budgets, what they're doing with salaries, what they're doing with their staffs. We have to say to ourselves, 'If we want to sell shoes, we have to do what they're doing, or we aren't selling shoes.' "

I told them, "Now, I'm not worried about what the bottom of the A-10 league's doing because that's where you are now. You're funded to be in the bottom of the league because that's where you are. If you want to compete with the top teams, you've got to put the money in to do it."

I'm also going to give Charlie Theokas some credit here.

People from UMass had gone to Charlie—who was then the athletic director at Temple—and asked him, "Well, what about budgets? We're spending as much as you are."

Charlie gave them a good answer. "Hey, we can drive everywhere. We can drive kids in. You can't do that. You need to increase your budget more than we do at Temple because you have no recruiting base. You have to fly everywhere and fly kids in to show them your program."

I've always felt that Charlie played a part in the resurrection of that program, and I thanked him. I appreciated it.

UMass started talking about increasing the budget—adding $300,000. They started talking about wanting to build a new arena. They started talking about X, Y, Z.

I said, "Wait a minute. You know what?" I looked around. "We can win here. We can do this."

I didn't know to what level, but I figured we could win. Then I got a little scared because I hadn't been prepared to discuss budgets and buildings. So I did some tap dancing. I had material with me about recruiting, about setting up a program, about what my goals would be. I gave them that—and ran with it for a bit.

The search took six weeks, and the field was finally narrowed from eleven applicants to two: Larry Shyatt, then an assistant at New Mexico, and me.

Here comes the "happily ever after" part, right?

Wrong.

Here's what happened—the real story behind the scenes. At this point in the search, there were some Big East coaches who had one goal—to wipe me out because of some past recruiting squabbles.

In most cases, the people who are making choices for head

basketball coaches don't know anything about coaching. They don't know any of the candidates because they haven't met them. And every once in a while, a guy will call the search committee and bury an applicant because he's trying to get his own candidate hired. It's kind of like recruiting.

In that region—New England—there are coaches who will kill you in recruiting. They're so negative, they don't spend time talking about their own system; they talk about you and your system. And guess what? They're not saying nice things about you. That's just how it is.

These Big East guys knew I was closing in on getting the job. They knew the committee people were saying, "Hey, this may be the guy."

During the interview process, I think the committee knew. I felt they were thinking, "He's the guy. But is there anything wrong with him?"

Now, I felt they were thinking, "Are we hiring the right guy?"

I knew how these campaigns work. Other coaches try to wipe out the front-runner. There were people saying about me, "Hey, this is not the guy. He's not a good guy."

Most of it stemmed from when I'd been an assistant at Pitt and we signed Bobby Martin, a 6'8" forward from Atlantic City.

Martin was the best prospect in South Jersey that year. He had verbally committed to Villanova in December of that year. Pitt had gotten into it before with the Wildcats over Doug West, a player we had both recruited. At the 1986 U.S. National Sports competition, West alleged that a dentist in his hometown of Altoona, PA, had offered him money to attend Pitt.

Nothing was ever substantiated. And the Pitt fans used to torture Doug West whenever he came to Fitzgerald Field House the rest of his college career.

This time, Villanova went in and bashed us over Martin. I honestly believe Bobby had wanted to come to Pitt in the first place. But his grandmother—whom I still talk to, to this day—became a little frightened by what she'd heard.

As it turned out, the Villanova staff outsmarted themselves. A week later, they started recruiting Perry Carter, a 6'9" forward from Maine Central Institute, who had shown a strong interest in their school. Originally, they had told Bobby they wouldn't go after another big man. Suddenly, they were calling Bobby and saying, "Do you mind?"

After that, his high school coach, Bill Devenny, called us and said, "Will you take him back? The kid is changing his mind. He wants to come to Pitt." I went in to Paul Evans and said, "We have to take this kid," knowing we would get some crap, and I would take some heat.

A week later, Bobby Martin changed his mind and announced he was coming to Pitt. Some people thought Lloyd Barksdale, an assistant at Atlantic City, had convinced Bobby to change his mind. But he felt Bobby wanted Pitt all along. He felt someone had gotten to Bobby's grandmother. Bobby made his decision the night we were scheduled to play Villanova. Rollie Massimino, their coach, went ballistic.

I went to Paul Evans, my head coach, and said, "Hey, you've got to protect me on this." Paul did a pretty good job of it, but it was hard because it got to the point where other coaches in the league were saying, "Calipari stole Bobby Martin. Pitt stole him. Paul Evans is a bum, Calipari's a bum. They're cheating."

The irony of the situation is Villanova never signed Carter, either. He went to Ohio State.

I did catch some heat, though.

Coaches are under incredible pressure to win. It used to be that opposing coaches would get together for a beer or some pasta after the game. I loved that. Today, newspapers, TV, and radio talk shows are out there, putting us under the microscope. Our profession has become so competitive that when someone asks a coach why he's losing, the coach says, "Well, that guy is doing this, that, and the other thing."

In those days, no one ever just signed a player in the Big East. Either you cheated, bad-mouthed another school, or stole him. People wanted to believe that I'd said this and that, that I was vicious and ruthless. But the right word isn't "ruthless." It's "relentless."

A few months later, rumors began to circulate that I had told a recruit, Marvin Branch, that St. John's coach Lou Carnesecca—a Hall of Famer—was dying. I still shake my head over that one. But when other coaches told Lou I'd said it, he was understandably upset.

It could have been a career-killer for me. It took Lou a while before close friends of his convinced him the rumors were ridiculous. "I never believed that John said that," Carnesecca later said. "First of all, it was allegedly said to someone who we were not recruiting. Why would he do that? I just wish he would have come to me and said, 'Lou, I didn't do it.' "

Here I was, a young assistant, and there he was, one of the great coaches in the country. I didn't know what to say. I've since learned how to defend myself against unfounded accusations.

And by the time I was involved with the UMass job, I had an idea of how to fight back. I did it on two fronts. I went to the Final Four in Kansas City. I got six of my buddies together. I don't want to name all of them, but Bill Bayno was one of them. Two of them are head coaches now. One is a head coach in junior college.

Their job was to go around to the main hotels, hang out in the lobbies, and say, "John's out. Calipari's out of the UMass job. He did a poor job of interviewing, and he's out. They've already called him to tell him he's out."

We started that at ten in the morning. By noon, just about every five minutes, I was approached by somebody who said, "Hey, you'll get a job, buddy. You'll be all right."

I knew it had worked when one of the other guys involved in the job had called a high school coach and said, "I got the job. Calipari's out. It's my job. Who's out there?" And that same high school coach had called a high school friend of mine who told me, "Yeah, I talked to so-and-so, and so-and-so had called him to tell him he's getting the UMass job because you're out."

But we knew I was the lead guy.

I think Larry Brown thought so, too. He made a call to Ron Nathan, executive director of the UMass Court Club, and the committee the day Kansas was getting ready to play Duke in the semifinals of the Final Four. Well, that was a big call. People on the committee said to me, "We're going to see him in a little while on national television, and he's calling us to recommend you for this job."

To this day, I appreciate the fact that he took time out of that day to call UMass on my behalf. He is a true champion—both on and off the basketball court.

In the week after the Final Four, everyone backed away from me. No one buried me.

Dave Gavitt, who was then the Big East commissioner, also went to bat for me. I think his call was very, very important. He told the committee, "Look, this guy will do the job. He's aggressive, and that has frustrated some people in our league. He gets after it, but he's doing it the right way, and I have a lot of faith that he'll run your program the right way."

But it was Rick Pitino who helped me get over the hump.

He told the committee, "If people are trying to keep you from hiring him, there's probably a reason—probably that he's going to be able to come in here, get it done, and be a pain in their sides. They know that. If they're telling you not to hire him, that's who you hire. I'm telling you, I know the kid. I've watched him coach. I've seen him in camp situations. He's got a great background with Larry Brown and Paul Evans. He's been in the Big East and has the vision. He's young. He's aggressive. He's who you should hire."

That did the trick.

Hopefully, I've made him proud that he did the right thing.

In the end, the committee was able to make a logical decision based on truth, and not on rumor.

And that's how I got the job.

When I first came to UMass, they offered me $63,000. That's what I made. That was it. When I signed the contract, I signed a deal to own the rights to the radio and TV shows.

They said, "Fine. You have that."

A shoe contract. They said, "Fine. You have that."

A camp. "That's fine."

All that stuff was worth nothing to them.

Ten percent of the NCAA money. "He thinks we're going to the NCAA tournament? Sure."

A percentage of season ticket sales? Well, there were none.

When I signed all those incentives, they were worth zero. When our program got going, they became a very high figure.

At the time, most people didn't know if we'd ever get it going.

UMass was operating in a black hole. The program had gone through ten straight losing seasons from 1978 through 1988. And the last three coaches—Ray Wilson, Tom McLaughlin, and Ron Gerlufsen—never sniffed a .500 record.

Ray Wilson lasted two seasons and won just five games, two

against non–Division I opponents. Wilson's successor, Tom McLaughlin, didn't fare much better, posting sixteen victories in two years before he resigned. Ron Gerlufsen could not produce a winner, either, coaching five years before departing with a 55–84 record.

"We went down to West Virginia for a game in the early '80s and at one point, we were down 25–0," says former sports information director Howie Davis, who is now a professor in the UMass Sports Management program. "I thought we were going to see the first shutout in the history of college basketball. Their players were literally throwing the ball to us so we could start fast breaks—and we still couldn't score."

The lack of commitment was matched only by the lack of respect for the sport on campus.

None of these coaches really had a chance.

They were just victims of an athletic department that treated the program like it was part of the physical education department. The school was not prepared to make the financial commitment necessary to be competitive in the Atlantic 10.

"When I was there, it was a low-budget program," says Bill Bayno, who played at UMass and was on our staff before he became the head coach at UNLV. "We were struggling and not a lot of people came to the games. My first year, we won three. My second year, we won seven.

"I can remember over intersession—we had a forty-five-day break between semesters—we had to stay in a dorm with the international students, who obviously didn't go home for the holidays. I can remember there was no hot water. We had a bed with a pillow, a couple of sheets, and a blanket. There wasn't a whole lot of heat in the building. We used to shower in the gym after practice. The pipes were broken, and it took them two weeks to fix them. For fourteen days, we never showered in the dorm."

At that time, too, the state was going through two bad financial periods. The first one occurred when the old manufacturing companies started taking off for better tax deals in other states. Later, with the help of then-Governor Michael Dukakis, Massachusetts began to attract a lot of high-tech corporations. There was a technology-based boom for five, six years, known as "The Miracle of Massachusetts." Then, all of a sudden, there were a lot of layoffs among those companies and things bottomed out a little. Some of them didn't survive, and the so-called "miracle" dried up.

The school suffered.

Massachusetts is so dominated by private education that people thought there was no problem cutting funds to public education. They cut everywhere. They cut staff positions. They cut maintenance. There is still $8 million in deferred maintenance on the campus.

The budget problems filtered down to athletics in a big way.

UMass won a national championship in women's lacrosse in 1982. Pam Hixon was the field hockey coach. She was coaching both sports at the time. She gave up the women's lacrosse. They put in a new coach and she just didn't have the clout to keep it alive. The school ended up dropping the program two years later.

The budget severely affected the way they did business in the basketball program, too. Brian Gorman, our staff assistant, worked for Gerlufsen in Ron's final year, and told me the athletic department would not even spring for money to exchange game films with upcoming opponents by Federal Express. He had to go to the assistant AD and argue the point. And that was maybe $1,000 over the course of the year, for everything.

Not that there was much to scout.

And the worst part about it was that nobody cared.

They used to get a crowd once, twice a year—for Temple, and for Northeastern, when they had Reggie Lewis. Otherwise, there'd be 1,000 people in the Cage, the old arena. You'd go to the local bank on Saturday, and they were handing out free tickets. You could get as many as you wanted. Obviously, tickets were not a hot commodity. You'd come out of the bank, and there would be six stuck under the windshield wipers.

Our fans longed for the old days, when Jack Leaman had been coaching UMass, and UMass was still playing in the Yankee Conference. Jack had been an assistant under Johnny Orr and became the head coach in 1966 when Orr left to take a job as an assistant at Michigan. Orr later became the head coach at Michigan.

Anyway, Jack, who does color on UMass radio broadcasts, still likes to tell the story about his trip to Philadelphia for the 1976 Final Four. He was heading for his seat at the Spectrum when he heard a page from the public address announcer.

"Will Jack Leaman please report to courtside."

"I didn't know what it was about," Jack recalls. "When I got to the floor, there was Johnny Orr, who was coaching Michigan against Rutgers in the first game of the semifinal doubleheader."

Orr wanted to do him a favor.

"Would you like to sit on the bench with me for the game?" Orr asked. "This is the closest you'll ever get to coaching a Final Four at Massachusetts."

But it wasn't for lack of trying on Jack's part.

Jack was the most successful coach in UMass's history, posting a 217–136 record in thirteen years from 1966 to 1979. He had given the school a regional tradition. He'd coached Al Skinner. He'd coached Rick Pitino. And he'd also coached Julius Erving, one of the greatest players of all time.

Julius came to UMass from Roosevelt, Long Island, where he had been a 6′3″ forward. He was recruited by Ray Wilson, Jack's assistant. At the time, nobody knew he was destined to become Dr. J.

But he was a big star up at UMass, averaging 26.3 points and 20.2 rebounds in his two years of varsity competition. Only once in fifty-two career games did Julius Erving fail to record a double double.

It's just that no one knew about him.

"The one thing I'll always remember about Julius Erving is that he played during an era when there was no dunking, and he never had the luxury of throwing it down," Leaman says. "He played varsity here for only two years, but if he had been able to dunk the ball, we could have had a new arena. His decision to leave set us back because the school didn't think we could win without him."

"Julius went to the Pan Am games and led that team in rebounding," Al Skinner says. "He played against different people and it was like, 'Wow, where did this guy come from?' He was more of a pioneer than I was. He laid the groundwork for me. He came out of nowhere.

"I remember we played North Carolina in the NIT. He played against Billy Chamberlain, who was a first-team high school All-American from Long Island Lutheran. He was considered the best recruit in our area, and was talked about being a first-round pick in the pros. And Julius just took it to him. He was something special. He just needed some exposure.

"I think we took a lot of pride in the fact it didn't matter if you wore a North Carolina uniform or a UMass uniform, you still could compete."

Jack's teams dominated the Yankee Conference, winning or tieing for eight championships from 1967 through 1976, winning twenty or more games six times in the '70s, and making five consecutive NIT appearances from 1973 through 1977. One year, six students decided to dribble a ball from Amherst to Madison Square Garden. They went through five basketballs before they arrived in Manhattan.

New England schools rarely, if ever, made it to the NCAA tournament. That's the way it was—everywhere but at Providence, which had a big arena and was recruiting players like Marvin Barnes and Ernie DiGregorio. Those two stars led them to a Final Four in 1973 and set a standard of excellence for the school.

"During the mid-60s, the six-member Yankee Conference had an automatic bid to the NCAA and, just before our good teams, they lost it," Leaman says. "UMass didn't fight to keep it. Connecticut was down, so they didn't fight to keep it. Rhode Island was in between. And Maine, Vermont, and New Hampshire were in another world. They couldn't win, so it wasn't that important. I think that eventually broke up the Yankee Conference."

UMass joined the Eastern Eight in 1976. Eventually the school became a victim of upgraded competition, first there and then in the expanded Atlantic 10. I feel bad for Jack because the school had moved to a better conference, but they weren't going to increase any budgets or salaries. No one can compete with mirrors. No one can do it—not even Jack Leaman.

Jack was not just a good coach. He was a great coach. He was the kind of guy who could get players to play together, turn them into a cohesive team. His biggest problem at UMass was he didn't have the resources to compete in a better league. The administration actually reduced his scholarships from twelve to ten. The reasoning was that "Jack is such a good coach, we can get by."

He needed more, not less. And they gave him less.

At the same time, the school was excelling in the classroom. *U.S. News & World Report* called UMass one of the best bargains in public education. And the school maintained Ivy League standards of admission.

When he first arrived, a recruit had to be in the top third of his class and needed a 1,000 on the Boards to get in.

"Those standards put us in competition with the Ivy League, but we were losing kids to the Ivies," Jack says. "I remember heavily recruiting one young man named Mark Donoghue, right up the road in Greenfield.

"UMass was a $12,000 scholarship. Tuition at Dartmouth was $20,000. He would have had to pay $4,000 to go to Dartmouth and nothing to attend UMass. I couldn't convince his parents we were offering a better financial deal. He went to Dartmouth for a year and a half, then transferred down here and played for two years."

Jack could see the end coming.

"For a while, we were able to hold our own," he recalls. "We had some good players—Derick Claiborne, Mike Pyatt, Jim Town. We even reached the finals of the league tournament my first year. But we were trying to compete against teams like Rutgers, Villanova, and Pitt."

And trying to recruit against them and the newly formed Big East without a budget.

"We did most of our recruiting in North Jersey, Long Island,

New York State in the Albany area, and New England," Jack said. "Anywhere you could go by automobile. We just weren't able to recruit with Villanova, Rutgers, West Virginia, Pitt, George Washington, and Penn State. I'm not sure whether we weren't good enough recruiters or whether it was just too tough to recruit. Driving to Pittsburgh, that was hard."

Driving to road games wasn't any easier. "For most of our road games, we'd get in the bus, play, and then bus back after the game," Leaman recalled.

Jack's last team in 1979 was 5–22 and 0–10 in league play.

"He wanted the school to make an investment," Skinner says. "They thought they could fix it by just making a change. So he said, 'Okay, fine. I'll step down. I don't need this headache.'"

When Jack resigned as head coach after the 1979 season, the school promised to make him an assistant AD. Instead, they shuffled him around. They assigned him to be the coach of Stockbridge School of Agriculture—a two-year school on campus that was the remnant of the old Mass Ag school—for a couple of years, and then made him an assistant on the women's team for a season.

"I actually enjoyed coaching Stockbridge," Leaman said. "The level of competition wasn't very good, the equivalent of a high school team. But the kids listened, and we were competitive."

At least Leaman didn't have to watch his old team play.

Jack has left his mark in Amherst. He has the most wins of any coach in UMass history. And he's been a great friend. Sometimes when you're the new coach at a school, the old coach is still on staff. He doesn't want you to win. He wants you to fail. But Jack was always one of my biggest supporters. He was always a guy I could count on when I needed advice.

He left this piece of advice for the administration: "You're not winning until you increase these budgets, until you make a commitment that you want to compete."

They didn't believe him. They went through one, two, three coaches in a ten-year period, and every one of them lost.

But I wasn't going to let history repeat itself.

CHAPTER 5

UNACCEPTABLE

Whenever I hear people say, "Gee, he got to the top quickly," I have to laugh. I feel like I'm fifty.

Actually, I'm only thirty-seven.

People think we turned the UMass program around overnight. It took eight years. I don't know how long eight years is in your life, but it's a long time in mine. And we did it brick by brick.

Only we'd inherited a crumbling foundation.

I had heard about the sorry condition of the program, but—believe me when I tell you—I still had no idea of what I was walking into when I took the UMass job.

It didn't hit home until the first time we entered our offices in the Curry Hicks Cage. The men's and women's basketball coaches shared one office. "You can't do that," I complained. "I've got to have my own space."

We were expected to share a secretary with the women's basketball program. "You can't do that. I've got to have my own secretary."

There was no air-conditioning in the building. It got so hot in August, I had to give my secretary time off.

And we had to do something about accommodations for our players over intersession. They were still staying in the foreign students' dorms instead of at the campus center hotel. UMass has the top hotel, restaurant, and travel administration program in the country, but we didn't stay in their hotel. We stayed in the foreign students' housing because it was cheaper. This saved $3,000 to $4,000.

My comment was, "Wait a minute. What are we doing?"

"Well, softball does this," I was told.

"We're not competing against our softball program. We're competing against Temple, West Virginia, and Rutgers. What do they do? Do they stay in the lobby of dorms or do they stay in hotels? What are we doing?"

The university still had rotary phones. First, you had to dial seven numbers, then you dialed the next ten; then you dialed four more. If you screwed up any one of those numbers, you started over again. How about if you did it right and you got through—oh, good—and it was busy. Hang up. Dial again. There's no redial when you're dialing a rotary phone. One day, I pulled the phones out of the wall and said, "That's it. I'm not spending two hours a day dialing. How can we get any work done?"

The team doesn't have box lunches anymore, but that's what they used to give the players on road trips. When we traveled, they'd give us a box lunch instead of paying for us to have a meal in a restaurant. You know, it'd be an apple, grape juice—or whatever—and a meat loaf sandwich. "You can't do that," I said.

I tried to get the administration to rethink how they treated prospects, too.

"You're not going to recruit big-time athletes and have them stay here if you don't house and feed them properly. You have to treat them like they treat them at North Carolina, at Syracuse, at

Pitt, unless you don't want to compete at that level. If you don't want to compete there and you want to go D-II, then do it." That was my comment.

I used the term "unacceptable" all the time. "Unacceptable" was a word that was used daily in those first years.

"Well, this is how we do it."

"It's unacceptable," I kept saying. "That is unacceptable. We can't do that here."

We demanded—and got—a $300,000 increase in the men's basketball budget. That included money for new equipment, travel, and housing players in the school-run hotel on campus during the semester break.

I knew we had to show progress in a short amount of time. There are certain advantages young coaches enjoy. Our energy level is higher. We're probably on a better wavelength to understand these kids. We know their music. We talk their language. We outwork people. And we play the game ourselves. Kids see that.

One more thing. We don't need much sleep.

I didn't get any my first few years at UMass. I spent a lot of time away from my family, just to get things organized. My first priority was to go out and hire a strong staff. I brought in Bill Bayno, Roger McCready, John Robic, and Dave Glover.

I had known Billy through Five-Star. He had played at UMass, so he understood the past history of the place. And he knew the players. Roger was a guy who had been recommended to me. I'd coached against him when he played at Boston College. He had strong ties in New York with Ernie Lorch of Riverside Church, a powerful AAU program down there. John Robic had been a graduate assistant who replaced me at Kansas and also coached the jayvees. He was an excellent scout, an X-and-O guy who had come highly recommended by Bob Hill.

I hired Dave Glover to oversee the academics. Dave was a high school coach in Connecticut, and I'd met him at Five-Star, where he was a counselor. He finished his undergraduate classes at Baylor in three years. He played four years of basketball. His fourth year, he was in an accelerated med school program for top undergraduate pre-med students. He was a guy who could coach but who wanted to be in the academic administration, so I put him in charge of our post players and had him organize the study hall.

We were all young. I'd thought about bringing in an older assistant coach to help, but I said, "This isn't about coaching at this point. We need players."

We'd inherited some—John Tate, Rafer Giles, Chris Bailey, Matt Anderson, Ben Grodski, Cary Herer, and Sean Nelen. But they weren't good enough to help us win in the Atlantic 10 on their own.

At one of our first team meetings, we had players fill out goal sheets. I wanted to know what they expected to accomplish that season.

One guy wrote, "Seven wins."

I exploded. "Seven wins! I hope we have that by December."

But that was ingrained in his mind.

We knew we desperately needed fresh talent, but we also knew we had to be realistic. UMass had no name and not much of a budget. When we'd go recruiting, we had to stay three to a room. An assistant and I would sleep in the same bed. We had only $12.50 per diem to spend. When we would go to New York City, we would eat at McDonald's twice and go hungry at night.

We couldn't get into the homes of any blue chippers. But we got lucky when we signed players like guard Jimmy McCoy, who was modestly coveted and eventually blossomed into the school's all-time leading scorer, and Anton Brown, a 6′2″ guard who became an All Atlantic 10 player.

Jimmy McCoy came to UMass from Pittsburgh Central Catholic. I had known him since he'd been in the ninth grade. His father, Jim, and his uncle, Julius, both played for Farrell High and later went on to star in college. Julius was a star in the old Eastern League.

We'd recruited Jimmy a bit when I had been at Pitt. But we already had taken Jason Matthews and Darelle Porter, both shooting guards. We were in a position where we couldn't take another off guard. I told him he could come, but we weren't going to give him a scholarship. If we hadn't had Darrelle or Jason, who had both signed early, he would have gone to Pitt.

Richmond had recruited him some, but they didn't think they could get him in school. When it looked like I was going to get the UMass job, I asked him about coming with me.

"I was kind of like, 'Oooh, I don't know.' UMass was not one of my top choices," McCoy says, looking back.

I told him if he came, he would get a chance to get some playing time. It was a gamble. But we were both from Pittsburgh, and his parents knew I would take care of him. I think they were impressed when I brought Ellen, my wife, with me on our recruiting visit. Jimmy was friendly with our player John Tate, who had grown up around the corner from him and had attended Penn Hills, one of Central's rival schools.

Jimmy ended up coming with UMass, and it was the right thing for him. We were a program that was building, and he was a player who was going to have to play small forward when he had been a two guard in high school. His father told him it didn't matter where he went to school: "If you can play, the pro scouts will find you." Jimmy's game really came around. From the time he walked in, he scored a lot of points. And we needed him to score points. That was the only way we could win. He got better every year. And so did we.

Jimmy was my first recruit, and the players always used to kid him about being my son. We had a father-son relationship and still do, to this day. Jimmy played overseas in Sweden, but he was in Pittsburgh when we played Duquesne this year and he came to our game.

"After the game, we were headed back to the hotel," McCoy says. "The coaching staff had two cars. I asked Bruiser which car Coach was going to take. 'Now, you know he's going to get into the car with his son,' Bruiser said."

After I got the UMass job, I got a call from Scott Rigot, a graduate assistant at South Carolina, who is now the assistant to Murray Bartow at UAB. I asked him if there were any guys around and he told me, "I've got a player for you."

I said, "Who is it?"

"Anton Brown."

"Aren't you guys recruiting him at South Carolina?" I asked.

He said they were, but they were waiting on test scores and had another guy in mind for that spot.

Anton was from A. C. Flora in Columbia, the same school that produced Xavier McDaniel and Tyrone Corbin. He was also being recruited by Arizona, but they seemed hesitant. I called Anton and invited him up. We signed him, sight unseen, but I had a lot of faith in Scott and knew he wouldn't lead me astray.

"I thought he was going to say, 'How about a week from now?'" Anton says. "But he wanted me to come up right away. I packed my bags. I went, and it wasn't what I expected. I expected a big campus, close to the airport. The ride from the airport to campus was between forty-five minutes and an hour.

"The whole time in the car, I kept asking, 'Are we there yet?'

"During that time, it was almost finals week, so there wasn't too much activity. I felt good about the players. I had a good time. But the key was Coach Cal. He was genuine from the start. He didn't promise me flowers and roses when I got there.

"He showed me the Cage. There were squirrels running around. I told him, 'My high school gym is bigger than that.'

"I went home. I was telling my father about the trip and he asked me if I wanted to go there.

"I said I'd take the chance.

"After I signed, everybody was asking me, 'Where's UMass?'

" 'That's the school Dr. J went to,' I said. I kept saying it over and over."

Anton was a shooting guard in high school—like Jimmy. On the advice of Jack Leaman, I ended up making him a point guard and hoped for the best. We decided to build this program around Jimmy's scoring. And also around Anton Brown doing his thing. I never promised a player playing time when I recruited him. Any time you start your relationship with a lie—'you're going to start and play thirty minutes'—you do damage to that relationship. We started six freshmen in my eight years at UMass. I did it, but they earned their spaces. In this case, we had no choice.

When I arrived in Amherst, I found a lot of stuff still under the carpet that I hadn't realized was there. The perception of the basketball program was awful. We had players beating up the pizza delivery man. They were viewed as thugs—who didn't belong. We set about to change all that.

But I was almost too late, and my career at UMass nearly ended before it began. Four months after I'd arrived, two of the players broke into a house. My senior co-captains, Duane Chase and David Brown, were arrested. They had burglary tools in their possession. I'd been on the job less than six months. These kids had been breaking into houses for three years.

I got a call at four in the morning: "You've got to come to the jail."

I'm thinking to myself: "What happened? Did they beat up somebody? Did they get into a fight in a bar?" Those are things I can deal with. Not burglary. I suspended the kids. That was the first move I made.

When the call came in, I asked my wife if she had unpacked all the boxes. She said she hadn't, and I told her not to because I was pretty sure I was going to be fired.

Fortunately for us, the chancellor at the university was concerned with how I was holding up and wanted to make sure the players got their day in court. At least, it was a sign of support.

I could have waited until the court case, which would have been after the season ended, and said, "Well, they're innocent until proven guilty." But I knew they were guilty, so I wasn't going to wait. I was going to do it right away. Again, you define yourself to your team through your actions—not your talk.

All we were trying to do that first year was to set the tone, to lay the foundation for how things were going to be: how kids were going to be treated, how hard we would work, how we would play, what we would strive for. That's what we were doing.

I told the players on that first team, "Look, you are *my* players now. I'm going to treat you differently than the other guys." I told them I would treat them like big-time athletes, but they were going to have to act like ones.

"That doesn't mean just around the court. It's how you carry yourself around the campus, how you carry yourself in the classroom."

I told the players things would change, but they didn't believe me at first. I remember saying to Ben Grodski, "This is how it's going to be. You're going to be treated like a major college athlete. You're not going to be wearing grays to practice. You'll have nice practice gear, a game uniform. You're going to travel right, stay in nice hotels."

You know what he said?

"Yeah, right. When I see it, I'll believe it."

I had trouble being treated respectfully, too. I had no prestige. When I first arrived, they didn't even give me a parking pass. I had to be on a waiting list. They didn't care if I was the new basketball coach or the new president. Everyone had to wait. I was parking in the lot away from the Cage. And my car was towed.

When I went to the campus security cop, I said, "You knew that was my car and you also knew they haven't given me a sticker yet."

He said, "Yeah, I did."

I almost choked the guy right there.

Another time, they gave me a dealer's car, but it didn't have a sticker. The cop pulled me over, told me, "You can't drive this car. It doesn't have a sticker." And they towed me again.

I tried to set the tone academically my first year. If a player missed class, the whole team ran at 5 A.M. The first time someone missed, I was on the road. It was late October. I flew back. Five o'clock in the morning, I met them at the football stadium. It was dark there. I pulled my car underneath the stadium and turned the lights on so we could see.

I had them running the stadium steps, doing hundred-yard dashes on the football field, and running three miles around the outside of the stadium. The cops came flying in, sirens wailing. They didn't know who I was. They thought I was wrecking the stadium. When I told them what I was doing, they laughed.

They said, "You know what? We need somebody like you around here because this is what these kids need."

I considered it a minor victory.

I don't know how the players felt at the end of that day. "During my whole four years, it was one of the worst drills I ever went through," McCoy says. "We had guys throwing up. The assistants set up a garbage can on the sidelines so we could puke in it and just keep running."

It was all part of our plan to give these kids some structure and self-esteem. We scheduled conditioning drills for six in the morning. We had mandatory breakfast at eight, and then the players would go to class. "When you're up and going, you feel better," McCoy admitted. "It was better than sleeping in until one, two in the afternoon. Besides, that's how the working world is."

There was plenty of work to do.

I told my staff we had three years to make progress. We had to show change. The school was investing big money and expected results. If we had continued to produce 9–18, 9–20, or 10–20 teams, I would have been in trouble. I was aggravating everybody because I was making them do more work; I was making them do things they had never done.

UMass did not have the luxury of belonging to the Big East. We had no tradition to play from, we had a limited budget to work with, and we were forced to play home games in the aging, near-empty 4,000-seat Curry Hicks Gymnasium, aptly nick-named "the Cage."

I went into the Cage and I looked at the bench. It was composed of metal folding chairs. You know what they had stenciled on the back of those chairs? "Property of the Biology Department." Those were the chairs we were using.

Unacceptable.

They had one banner, up over the scoreboard.

Unacceptable.

I said, "Where are the banners in here?"

"There it is. Up there."

I looked. I said, "You've got to be kidding me. That's it?"

I could barely see it. It had NIT (for National Invitational Tournament) on it, and it had years: 1971, 1972. So I took it down "to wash it" and threw it away.

I said, "We need new banners."

"What happened?"

"I don't know. We lost the banner that was up there."

We didn't go out and spend money to have the banners made, either. Brian Gorman's aunt, Kathy Theberge, did the original ones for season tickets. And they're still out there: maroon felt banners with NIT on them and the years. We got the white banners for winning the Atlantic 10 and participating in the NCAA championships. We did those ourselves, too. We didn't have them made for $400 or $500 apiece. Kathy still did them. And we still gave her season tickets every year to do all these banners.

The uniforms originally had "Massachusetts" printed on them—with the players tucking the "M" and the "S" into their shorts.

Unacceptable.

We went with "UMass" because the school had always been called that. I think what we were trying to do then was important. I still have the initial drawings for the practice gear and the game uniforms. I keep these images to remind myself of what we'd been able to accomplish.

We also went to baggy shorts, at the suggestion of the fashion consultants on the team. No more short shorts.

Back then, there would be a couple of thousand fans at the games; during intersession, there'd be 500. John Robic's wife had attended the games when he'd worked at Kansas. They were drawing 16,000 a game to Allen Field House, and you couldn't get a ticket. Here, she had an entire section to herself. She kept wondering where all the people were. "We couldn't even give the tickets away to our friends," McCoy says. "We had to beg people to come."

Bruiser Flint, who joined the staff during my second year, has a great story about our early days. He says when he was at St. Joe's and they came up here to play, if the ball went into the seats, the players had to go up and get it because there wasn't anybody up there to throw it back.

When I first took the job, one of the clauses in my contract stated I was to get twenty season tickets every year. They looked at me and said, "You can have Section C if you want it." Like, who cares? I wish I had taken Section C. It would have been worth a lot this past season.

The first time I realized we really had an uphill battle was in our pre-season exhibition game against the Swedish national team. We were at home and we had three hecklers behind our bench. They were in tie-dyed shirts and earth shoes. They had long hair and beards. These guys were twenty-eight-, twenty-nine-year-old professional students.

We weren't playing very well, and they started yelling, "I can't believe this. You're supposed to be different. This is awful. How much are they paying you? You can't be giving these guys scholarships."

Then they started chanting the names of my four assistants in unison.

"Billy and Roger and David and John. Billy and Roger and

David and John." It sounded like a chorus of "Lions and Tigers and Bears, Oh My" from *The Wizard of Oz.*

They were yelling it like, "What do you need all these guys for? My money's going to this team?"

I looked at the team and asked, "Does this happen at every home game? Is this how they are here?"

The guys said, "Yeah."

I just laughed. "You've got to be kidding me."

One heckler saw it as his duty to come and protest every game. The next game, I had a couple of big guys sit with them and talk to them aggressively about being true fans.

After that, they didn't say much.

But we had other problems.

During the first regular season game I coached at the Cage—against Southern Connecticut State—the old wooden four-sided scoreboard caught on fire. I looked up at the scoreboard, and it was smoking. They stopped the game. They took the scoreboard down and wheeled it away. We ended up having a flip chart with a little clock, like you would use at a camp game.

I said, "Can you imagine: the first college game I'm coaching, the scoreboard catches on fire?"

And we had to deal with pest control. I was coaching practice one day, and I saw this bird flying around in the gym. I couldn't believe it. It was eating popcorn from the floor. The food was left from the game the night before. I got a trash can and put popcorn in it. Then I lined up popcorn on the bench leading to the trash can. I was coaching with the lid to this trash can in my hand. The bird landed and my players said, "He's on the bench, Coach." It was following the trail of popcorn. All of a sudden, it jumped into the trash can. Boom. I put the lid on it. Rat, tat, tat, rat, tat, tat. I carried the trash can to the door, and that's how we got rid of it.

We also had squirrels. One of the managers' jobs was squirrel patrol. I'd throw balls at them in the rafters.

The players loved it. Anything to delay practice.

Some of it was lighthearted. Like we always said, there are things we have control over and things we don't. Let's make moves with the things we have control over. And that's what we did.

We played our first Division I game against New Hampshire. On the road. We were playing a team with the longest home losing streak in Division I. Gerry Friel is a great guy and a terrific coach, but he was up against it. His administration didn't do anything to sustain the program. They didn't give him any kind of commitment.

The game became a national story. New Hampshire usually drew 200 people for their games. That night, they got 2,000. ABC was there, taping what they thought would be the school's first win at home after thirty-five losses. When I walked in, I saw 2,000 people going crazy because ABC cameras were there.

The game came down to the wire. There were thirty seconds left, and we were down one. We took a bad shot. Two of their guys ran after it to win the game and they tipped it off each other. Now there were three seconds left, and we were inbounding the ball under their basket. We had no time-outs left. My players were yelling to me, "What do you want us to do?"

"Get it in. Get it in."

This was my first game at this level. We hardly had plays in place. Gerry called a time-out. The kids came over to the huddle. I said, "Okay, let's do this." The horn sounded. It was not a good play, and I knew it. I thought we had just lost the game.

Gerry called another time-out. The players came back over, and I drew up something different. We inbounded it crosscourt to the deep corner. Anton Brown made the shot, and we won at the buzzer. Billy Bayno jumped up, four feet off the ground, and carried Anton off the floor.

Billy had gotten a technical during the game, and I told him, "If we lost this game by one, I'm firing you."

I went down to shake Gerry's hand. His head was down because he had lost. I felt bad for him.

Believe me, I knew how he felt. We had to fight for respect every step of the way. And we didn't really have anybody we felt could get us over the hump. We were just trying to survive.

I'm sure it was hard for our players, especially Jimmy and Anton. "The first few days of practice, the coaches would put in a drill and a lot of guys couldn't do the fundamental stuff," Anton says. "You could tell that the coach who was there before didn't spend a lot of time on that aspect of the game. Jimmy and I were usually the first two to complete each drill. At night, we would go back to the room and talk to each other. 'We got to get out of here. Where are you transferring to? I'm about to call this coach. I'm ready to get out of here.'

"But we decided to stick it out."

I wish I could tell you we turned it around that year. We did win four of our first six games. We were picked last in the league. We finished eighth. I thought we'd had a great year. We won five games in our league. I couldn't believe we'd won any. Granted, we were 5–13; but we beat Rutgers and Rhode Island, two teams that went to the NCAA tournament. Maybe those five wins were the biggest victories of my career. We just didn't have the talent to play with anybody in the A-10. Those other teams were established. They had been there. Those other coaches had been there. I'm walking in, with a week of recruiting, starting two freshmen, playing two walk-ons—and we won five games. That was exciting.

Whenever we won a game in our league, we went absolutely

berserk. We would run off the court and into our coach's locker room and just laugh and say, "Can you believe it? We won a game!"

But we could take it only so far. Jimmy and Anton were freshmen, and we had sophomores and juniors who had never played before, even on the bad teams at UMass. We never lost close games because we were never in close games. We scored 84 points a game, but we gave up 90. You give up 90 points a game in college, you're not guarding anybody.

We gave up 100 points five times that season. We lost to Florida Tech, 106–87. We gave up 107 points to Penn State, 105 to Duquesne, 104 to Connecticut, and 103 to George Washington.

When we played Penn State at State College, they beat us so badly that Bruce Parkhill apologized after the game. I said, "What are you apologizing for? You played everybody. What are you supposed to do? Throw us the ball? Your bench wants to play, too."

Gale Catlett of West Virginia took it easy on us at home one time. I called him to thank him for not running up the score.

That's why I don't run up the score on anybody. I've been there. We didn't beat anybody by 60, 70 points. I know what that feels like. I've been in games where I'm cheering for the other team to score, to get it under 20. Johnny Orr of Iowa State came in. We were up by 38. I cheered for him. We were on the bench and my staff said, "What you you doing?" I said, "I'm cheering for him."

I went back over our practice plans trying to find out why we were so bad defensively and why we were spending only 25 percent of our time on defense. If you look at our most recent practices, we may have spent 65 to 70 percent of our time on defense.

It was an adventure.

Anton had no experience at that point, and I knew he was going to get stripped three times a game. You know the Earl Monroe spin move? He did the old spin where he switched hands behind his back, so opposing teams would look to see how he was spinning. He goes to turn the other way and they tip it. Boom. It's a turnover. After about five games, I stopped getting upset for the first three strips because I knew he was going to get that many. Then I got mad. I had three "screw it's" in my pocket. Every time he got stripped, I'd throw one out.

"Screw it."

"Screw it."

"Screw it."

After that, I'd start yelling.

I yelled at Jimmy and Anton, just so the other players would know I wasn't playing favorites.

"I remember one time we had practice at Temple," Anton says. "A couple of the older players thought Coach Cal gave Jim and me more leeway than the others. We were practicing. Jim had gone to the rest room, and I asked if I could go, too.

"He said, 'Sure. Go ahead.'

"So I went to the rest room, washed my hands and came out. Then the manager came in and said, 'It's time to go back to the hotel.'

" 'Oh,' I said. 'Is practice over already?'

" 'No,' he said, 'Coach just kicked you and Jimmy out of practice.'

"I walked back out and he was screaming, 'Put your stuff back on. Get out of here right now.'

"I didn't know what he was talking about. So we went back to the hotel and later he called us up to his room. Jimmy was almost in tears. I was frustrated. He told us, 'I did it for a reason. I have to show those other guys I can be hard on you, too.' "

I sure had my moments.

After we blew a last-minute lead to Duquesne at home, I punched a hole in the locker room ceiling. And our players still talk about the time I was so upset about their not diving for loose balls that I decided to show them how it was done. I wound up tearing the pants of my suit.

Then there was the incident at George Washington.

We were getting beaten badly. I didn't like the way the officiating was going, so I stormed onto the court and demanded a technical.

I told the official, "You're going to give me a T if I have to take my clothes off."

First, I ripped off my sports jacket and threw it to the floor. Then I took off my tie and undid four buttons on my shirt. Finally, I got my wish.

When I walked off the floor, I high-fived a GW fan who had come down to congratulate me. Looking back now, I wish I hadn't done it. But the officials were making a mockery of the game, so I did, too. It may have been immature, but I wanted our guys to know I was fighting for them.

My assistants said I was too hard on our players at the time. But I felt one of the reasons we were losing was that we were accepting losing.

Unacceptable.

My goal was to convince the players they'd work so hard, they'd expect to win, but the school still treated the team like an uncaring parent. We used to have one game program for every seven games. We changed that quickly.

But I couldn't change our personnel.

After I got rid of our two co-captains early in the season, I told the staff that we might not win another game because they were our best two players. But I've since discovered that you can give up a little talent and skill on a team and not suffer too much. If you have tough, hard-nosed kids with character, it can make a difference.

The rest were good kids. But they could take us only so far. We lost to St. Joseph's in the first round of the Atlantic 10 tournament. Five minutes later, I was off recruiting.

One of the local beat writers, Larry Silber, said to me, "John, the season just ended."

"Did you see the players we had on the floor at the end?" I asked him. "You'd go recruiting, too."

CHAPTER 6

CABLE READY

I've always felt a coach has all the security of a sky diver, so it was nice to have an administration that supported the program. Administrations win championships. Not basketball coaches.

There's not a whole lot of difference between coaches as far as knowledge of the game is concerned. Some of us can motivate a little better; some are a bit more personable; others can communicate better.

The big difference comes in terms of support. What's happening at UMass these days isn't happening at schools like Central Connecticut State or Buffalo. UMass has just built a new locker room for $100,000. They're building a weight room onto that locker room with a lounge for the kids, at a cost of $250,000. The program has new offices, and the $51 million Mullins Center to play in. They'll match that support with any school in the country.

Michael Hooker became the university president during my second year. He and Dr. Dick O'Brien, who was the chancellor at the time, were both committed to having a first-rate basketball program. One of the first things Michael did after his appointment was to hold a meeting with the athletic department to discuss some goals he had for us.

In the case of men's and women's basketball, he already had a timetable worked out. "I want one of you to get to a Final Four before the end of the '90s," he said.

I immediately turned to our women's coach, Joanie O'Brien.

"Good luck, Joanie. Hope you make it," I said.

We all laughed.

Then I fired off a note to Michael and told him, "I appreciate your raising the bar for all of us."

Michael Hooker and Dick O'Brien were fans. They and their wives came to every game. When they did that, it filtered down.

There are a lot of fiefdoms on a college campus. "I control this. Don't tell me what to do."

Some people make your job hard. But when the president comes in and says, "I want this to succeed," it makes your job easy. When your boss supports athletics, then it becomes the thing to do for the people who work for him. Suddenly, we didn't have problems with housing, admissions, financial aid, or parking. If there was a screw-up, I had somebody I could call.

Michael Hooker understood better than anybody the philosophy that even though our program was a small speck on a big campus, we were the front porch of a great institution. Our job was to get people on the front porch, so they'd go through the front door.

I felt pretty good heading into the 1989–90 season. We had what I thought was a very good recruiting year, bringing in five new players—6'7" center Harper Williams, 6'6" forward Tony Barbee, 6'7" forward Kennard Robinson, 6'8" forward Tommy Pace, and 6'3" forward Will Herndon—to go with our first class of Jimmy McCoy and Anton Brown. And Rafer Giles was back, along with John Tate.

Harper, Tony, and Will all wound up becoming starters for us. Each of them scored over 1,000 points during his career. And Harper was voted Most Valuable Player of the Atlantic 10 tournament for two years.

None of them had been Top 100 players when we recruited them. They were all in-betweeners. In fact, I almost misevaluated Harper completely.

Harper Williams is from Bridgeport, Connecticut, and he was one of those guys I could never get a good read on. I didn't think he was good enough when I watched him at a summer camp. I liked his high school teammate better because I felt he was a better athlete.

But I was convinced to go back and take a second look that winter when Harper played for his high school team. My reaction: "Oh my God, this is the guy who gives us post presence." We beat out Central Connecticut and Rhode Island to get him.

We beat out Evansville on Tony Barbee, who was from Indianapolis. I had coached him at Five-Star when he was a sophomore, and we were the first school in for a home visit.

We said, "Look, we're here first because you're our guy." I didn't know if we were in over our heads at the time. Tony was also being recruited by Purdue, Ohio State, Kentucky, and Evansville. His mother wanted him to go to Purdue, but they had given out their last scholarship to Rick Mount's kid, Rich. Rick had been a three-time All-American at Purdue and one of the best players ever from the state of Indiana. Purdue was hoping his son would follow in his footsteps.

Kentucky was in trouble with the NCAA at the time. And

Ohio State had decided to go in another direction. So when Roger and I went in for a second visit, he told me he was coming. He hadn't even visited our campus.

"When I signed at UMass, all I heard from my friends was, 'Why are you going there?' " Barbee says. "UMass was one of the worst programs in the '80s. It was so far away. During my senior year in high school, two of their players were arrested and charged with burglary. I knew it was a risk, but I also knew what kind of guys the staff were. I had gotten to know them all at Five-Star and so I went with guys I felt comfortable with and I felt cared about me."

Will Herndon is from Pittsburgh. He played for Taylor Allderdice High School and he knew Jimmy McCoy and John Tate well. In fact, he had lived very close to Jimmy's house. He had originally signed with Richmond, but they tried to play him in the post. I knew Will from high school. He had been a pretty good player. But he wasn't a post. He was a 6'3" power forward who played out on the floor.

He must have realized that, too. He started calling Jimmy and John every day. He was writing them letters: "I want to come to UMass."

I told our guys, "You've got to tell him we cannot talk to him unless he informs his school he's leaving." Will transferred to UMass after first semester in 1989 and was scheduled to be eligible at semester break the following season.

I was so confident we could now compete, I told our AD at the time, Frank McInerney, I thought we could sell out season tickets to the Cage.

"What are you talking about?" he said. "We'll never sell out season tickets. You forget where you are. You're in Massachusetts. They don't care about basketball here."

"Frank, let me tell you this. If I have to go door to door, if I have to get on TV, it will happen. All you have to do is tell the people, 'If you want to see our games, you'd better buy a season ticket because if you don't buy season tickets, you won't get in.' "

"John, that's a farce. I'll bet you $10 we don't sell out season tickets."

I jumped on it.

Before the season started, we'd sold out. Frank came in and put $10 on my desk, which I immediately had framed—with a note: "I'll bet you $10. Season tickets will never sell out." I didn't put his name on it, out of respect.

But when he walked in, he saw it. "You son of a gun," he said.

Our fans were calling me a lot of other names after our first game that year. We had scheduled what I thought was a tune-up against Lowell, a Division II team. My guys were going on TV, talking about beating them by 40, so everyone could get into the game. I had to tell them to tone it down.

We played before a packed house that night. The fans expected a blowout. Then the unthinkable happened. We lost to them, 70–69. We were down 10, with three minutes to play. The officials absolutely tried to cheat them and help us win the game. We were so bad, we couldn't even win that way. I got on the Lowell bus and told them, "You guys deserved to win this game. I want to wish you good luck and I hope you go on and win the national title."

I still have letters sent to me from fans and faculty members after that game. They were brutal. "I'll never come to another game. They're not what you say they are." It's shown me you never know how fleeting fame is in this business.

Tony was so upset after the game, he called his mother and talked to her about transferring. Just coming from the Midwest to New England was hard for him because the people were different. He said, "The guys teased me because I didn't come out of my room for the first two weeks. I was a freshman, a long way from home for the first time, and I didn't like it."

I got Tony's mom to convince him to stick it out. I told her it would pay off in the end.

The Lowell loss was a wake-up call for our kids—and our staff, too. We had to do a better job of getting these kids ready to play.

I didn't know what to expect when we traveled to Boston to play Boston University the next game. They had a pretty good team and they were coached by Mike Jarvis, who is now the head coach at George Washington University. Well, Jimmy McCoy went off for 32 points and we spanked them by 16 points at their place. Mike was so upset he kept his team in the locker room for two hours afterwards.

From that point, we did our thing. We went 17–14, broke a long string of losing seasons, and went to post-season play for the first time in thirteen years.

I knew we had something special going after Will Herndon became eligible that December. We were in Denver to play Colorado in the Mile High Classic. Colorado was a Big Eight team with some tradition, and the organizers wanted to set up a matchup between them and North Carolina in the championship game. We were supposed to be the sacrificial lamb.

Well, Colorado did end up playing Carolina.

In the consolation game.

We upset Colorado, 78–71, and Colorado State upset Carolina. Then they went on to beat us in the championship game. But our win over Colorado showed us we were good enough to beat a big-time team. And it gave our players confidence to win our first six league games once we came back. We were 6–0—and No. 1—in the Atlantic 10.

And we got votes in the CNN/Coaches' Poll for the first time ever. I can still remember a guy carrying a sign that said RANKED 31ST AND COUNTING.

It brought tears to my eyes.

I looked over and said, "Can you imagine? Our second year and we're in the Top 50."

It was a sign of respect, one that we didn't get the night before we played Colorado. We had gone to watch the Denver Nuggets game. North Carolina was also there. They sat behind the bench. We sat out in nosebleed heaven.

I made sure I pointed that out to our team.

We were always talking about respect in those days.

We came back to earth quickly. We ended up losing five games in a row—four road games and UConn at home—but that's because we were very young. To win on the road, you have to be a veteran team and a talented team. But we were still in a position to receive an NIT bid if we finished up strong in our league tournament.

All it took was a little luck.

Larry Brown of Kansas is a very superstitious guy and some of it must have rubbed off on me. We stuck with this one: you don't get your hair cut on the day of a game. If you were on the team and you did, I wouldn't play you. If you were on the staff and you did, I wouldn't seat you on the bench. Why? I have no idea. But we did it at Kansas, and I've done it ever since. If I get my hair cut, it will usually be four or five days before the game.

Ask Ted Cottrell, who was our team barber.

And I could write my own version of "Three Coins in a Fountain."

I would go walking on game days if we were on the road. If I found a penny heads up, I knew we were going to win. We were getting ready for the 1990 Atlantic 10 tournament. I felt we had to play three games in order to have a shot at post-season play.

I found a nickel heads up before our first game against West Virginia. We won, 78–55.

I found a quarter before our Penn State game. Another guy came in and said he'd found a half-dollar. I taped the coins on the blackboard, and I said, "We're all right, guys."

And we won that game, 64–58.

When we came out to get ready for the championship game against Temple at McGonigle Hall, there were coins showered all over our bench and the floor. It was as if our fans were saying, "Good luck."

Our luck ran out that night. Temple defeated us, 53–51, but the NIT selection committee must have seen how competitive the game was. I still owe Jack Powers, the executive director of that tournament, and the selection committee, a debt of gratitude for giving UMass a chance to play in post-season. That was big. The NIT is an invitational tournament. That's all it is. You could win twenty games and not be invited.

One thing I should point out here: we got there without Anton, who had fractured his leg midway through the season. We plugged in Carey Herer as our point guard, and he did a great job.

Carey was one of the kids I inherited when I took the job. He was overweight and I told him so. I made him lose twenty pounds. I told him it was going to be hard for him to play here, but that we did need him. All those kids, I think, thought about how we did things. We really challenged them. We really pushed them. In the end, Carey was like the success story of the century. Here's a kid who had been here for three years and wasn't going to play. He was our third guard. Then after Anton went down, Carey stepped in and ran our club.

He couldn't shoot. But guess what? He led the league in assists and was second in steals. He was an unbelieveable defender. Like Giddel, he was a guy who was ready for his opportunity. At some point in time in our program, there was a good chance a player would have an opportunity to show what he could do. Most of the guys took advantage of that opportunity.

The great thing about the NIT is that it gives upstart programs like ours a chance to feel what it's like to play in the postseason. I told the team I didn't care where they sent us—it could have been to California. We would have flown the red-eye out there, just for that shot.

As it turned out, we were sent to Maryland and had no chance to win the game. They had Walt Williams and Jerrod Mustaf. I mean, they had some pros on their team. We ended up getting beat, 91–81. But we were in the game. We were up 7, 8, at one point. The game showed we belonged and we were going to get better.

If the NIT was the linchpin for our success, then television has changed our image forever. I've never been one to stay up late and watch TV, except when HBO is showing my favorite movie, *The Godfather*, but I quickly realized that television could be the great equalizer in college basketball because of the exposure it offered.

I did *CBS at the Half* last winter. I stepped into the studio and sat down. Guess what Pat O'Brien said to me? "Do you know why you're here? Recruiting. If there's a young man out there who sees you, who likes you, who wants to come, this is all worth the trip." What TV did for our program—the image and perception—is important.

People ask me why I did that TV commercial with Degree deodorant. It didn't have anything to do with money. I really wasn't going to do it until the last minute. After I did it, I'm telling you, every home that I went into to recruit, you know what they said when I walked in the door? "Do you have any of that Degree deodorant?"

I was at an AAU tournament and Kevin Garnett, who skipped college and went to the NBA, said to me, "Coach Cal, do you have any of that Degree deodorant?" Now I don't know Kevin from the man in the moon.

So guess what? It wasn't a bad deal.

It wasn't always that way. Recruits ask and ask: "How many times will you be on TV? How many times will you be on TV?"

I used to cup my palm over my mouth and go like this . . .

"Once, on SportsChannel."

Everything about our program was changing. I wanted to make sure the rest of the country noticed our progress. People wanted to see change with their own eyes. In New England, people are skeptical. I could talk about things and say this or that is going to happen, but they had to be able to see it.

At first, I was actually naïve enough to think our league could help us in that area. The first time I attended an Atlantic 10 coaches' meeting, Ron Bertovich, the commissioner at the time, got up and started talking about our TV package.

"We have three games on network TV and three more on ESPN," he said.

Everybody in the room applauded. Then he started to reel them off. Temple vs. Georgia Tech on CBS. Temple vs. Notre Dame on NBC. Temple vs. Louisville on ABC. On ESPN, the only teams that were on were West Virginia, St. Joseph's—and Temple.

"What about the rest of us?" I asked.

It was obvious UMass wasn't ready for prime time in their minds.

My first year, we were on television once. We played St. Bonaventure at 4 P.M. on Super Bowl Sunday in the Atlantic 10 package, which didn't even reach into all of the league cities.

You can just imagine how many people tuned in to watch that one.

I decided to promote our program myself. I was constantly on the phone with Tom Odjakjian and Dave Brown of ESPN. I begged and pleaded for a game. I really believe ESPN has brought parity to college basketball. The networks weren't going to help anybody get started.

ESPN had a policy. A school had to make post-season play— at least the NIT—to get on. The only exceptions were if a school belonged to a major conference, like the Big East, that had a contractual requirement with the network to put everybody on the air. If a school had great tradition and possibly had a down year, it would get on. Or if a school had a great freshman, like Jason Kidd, coming in, it would get on.

Our third year, we finally got on ESPN. Against Boston University. But there was a stipulation.

Here's what happened: I had called and pleaded with Tom Odjakjian, the program director of ESPN at the time, for a game on the all-sports cable network.

"How about you play at midnight," Odjakjian said.

"Where?" I asked. "Out west and play it at nine o'clock?"

"No," Odjakjian said. "A home game."

I asked, "What are you going to do? Run a tape delay of the game?"

"No," he said. "We want you to tip it off at midnight."

"What?" Then I said, "We'll do it, as long as it's on a weekend and nobody's missing class."

The whole midnight game concept had started with Jim Delany of the Ohio Valley Conference. One year, many years ago, the league got two teams into the NCAA tournament instead of one and they suddenly had double the money they expected to have. They invested it in a local television series at 11:30 P.M. weekends and they produced their way on after the local news.

I guess it was somewhat successful.

Then, through Bray Cary of Creative Sports, the Ohio Valley came to ESPN and said they would like to give some free games to ESPN after SportsCenter. People had already done Midnight Madness practices, so ESPN said, "Okay, only if it's Friday or Saturday, and as long as everybody knows this was your idea."

"We didn't want people to think, 'Gee, big ESPN is forcing people to play at midnight,' " Odjakjian recalls. "They knew they weren't going to get on in any other appearance, except championship week.

"It was a novelty. It got a lot of publicity. We did six games. Now people in other leagues caught this and told us they were interested, too. As the network became more successful, quality control became more important, so we became more selective and we told them, 'It's one thing if you're giving us your top two teams but we don't need your bottom teams even if you're giving us your games for free.' When we did a second contract with Creative Sports, you'd be surprised how many teams wanted in. It got to be a cult thing.

"We usually wait for teams to volunteer.

"UMass kept volunteering."

I remember one thing I told Odjakjian: "You send a kid the videotape of a local telecast and you send a kid a tape of ESPN. What's the difference? When the kids see our style on an ESPN tape, it has more of an impact."

We were willing to play anyplace, anytime, anywhere, as long as it was fair. In other words, if it was a program that was much better than ours, we'd play two games at their place and one at ours. But they had to be a Top 10 team.

A lot of teams want to play cupcakes before they go into a league schedule. We felt that if we ever wanted to be thought of as one of the best, we had to play good teams. We didn't necessarily have to beat them. But we had to play them. After a while, we said, "If we want to be No. 1, we've got to beat No. 1." We're not going to be voted No. 1. We're not the champ. We've got to knock out the champ to be the champ. We knew we were the underdog. A lot of guys aren't willing to play the champ. They'd rather be on the undercard. I was tired of being on the undercard.

My team was, too.

I agreed, as long as the game was scheduled on a weekend. It was, and UMass played BU in that late-night time slot that season.

I got some grief from Mike Francesa and Chris "Mad Dog" Russo on WFAN radio in New York. They said, "How could you do this? Don't you care about academics?"

"Mad Dog," I said, "You went to college at Rollins, which meant you didn't go for an education. You wanted to go to school and hang out. I'll tell you what your weekend was like. If you went to class on Friday, you had dinner, then you took a nap, got up at nine o'clock, had a shower, looked in the mirror, and at eleven P.M. you were going out. And you came home between two-thirty and three on Saturday morning. Am I right?"

"Yeah," Russo said.

"That's what we're doing on this game," I said. "Except there's no drinking, no partying. The students are going in there to cheer, and it's going to be a fun atmosphere. Instead of being in a bar, they're going to be at a basketball game. We're doing it only once a year. It's not like we're killing our kids."

We played the BU game in the Cage just twenty-six hours after we had beaten Rhode Island, 70–67, on a three-point shot by Rafer Giles at the buzzer in overtime during an emotionally draining Atlantic 10 game.

The midnight game was a sellout and the students came dressed for the occasion. Some wore pajamas, nightgowns, bathrobes, and hair nets, which played well to the ESPN cameras. They had begun working themselves into a frenzy two hours before game time. We were in the midst of the Persian Gulf conflict at the time, and many of the signs reflected that. On one was printed, ESPN: ELIMINATE SADDAM HUSSEIN PERMANENTLY NOW. There were chants of "USA, USA," and several students carried American flags onto the court when the pep band played the national anthem.

A far cry from the '60s.

For the most part, the crowd was well behaved. We did have four injuries when students who were waiting to get in a side door broke ranks when the lights on an ESPN truck went on and they thought the game was about to begin.

We presented Rafer Giles with a basketball for scoring his 1,000th career point before the game, but he said he didn't need any special ceremony to get ready for this game. Rafer shot seven for eleven and scored 24 points as we blew by Boston University, 82–65, to complete a three-game sweep of the New England schools on our schedule. And Harper Williams added 21 points, making up for the fact that Tony Barbee had missed both games with mononucleosis.

The only players who looked like they were sleepwalking were Will Herndon and Jimmy McCoy. Will finished with only 6 points and fouled out. Jimmy, who admitted he had slept sixteen hours between Friday's game with Rhodey and the time he got up to go over to the Cage, shot just one for five in the first half before he went off for 16 of his 18 points in the second half as we improved our record to 14–6 and set ourselves up for post-season play.

That was the defining moment for our program. The school made $15,000 from ESPN. The money had to be split with the conference. More than the money, though, the school got the type of national exposure that UMass felt would make us attractive in future TV scheduling. The game ended up being unbelievably electric. The next year we did it again, against Siena.

Eventually, we did a third midnight game, against Southwest Louisiana. The reason I did it was because it was the last game in the Cage and ESPN had been good to us. They needed the game. To get a highly rated team on at midnight was good for their ratings. It also helped the local economy. The restaurants and bars in town loved it because they did business all night rather than just having people come in for a pre-game meal and leaving.

We did our last midnight game two years ago, against Manhattan. Then ESPN sat me down and said to me, "You've outgrown it."

I felt good and bad about that.

We became the Midnight Marauders. We held Midnight Madness. In 1992, we played in the Great Alaskan Shootout, and every game was played at midnight, East Coast time. We're undefeated in midnight games. That's why I always said we were a late-night team.

"UMass earned everything they got and they were willing to play, but the fact is, they performed," Odjakjian says. "I remember when they first got on, people came to me and said, 'Gee you're on this UMass bandwagon.' But how many teams— as they got better—remained just as cooperative?

"Temple and UMass both got a lot of appearances because they were willing to play strong opponents. Also, they did not have home arenas that sold 20,000 tickets. If you are selling out a big arena, particularly against Little Sisters of the Poor, it's tough to go on the road. If you have a smaller building like the Cage, you aren't taking a financial hit by traveling."

That was always a major part of our scheduling philosophy. The Big East wasn't a whole lot different from the Atlantic 10 a few years ago, when St. John's, Seton Hall, and Georgetown were all playing in campus arenas. Then those teams started moving into big buildings. Our league didn't have a big arena. We didn't have a Landover or a Meadowlands or a Garden. So Bob Marcum allowed me to schedule us into big arenas around the country. We played in Anaheim, St. Louis, and the Meadow-lands. We played before big crowds.

It helped spread the word.

By my third year, 1990–91, our students jumped at the chance to watch us play. They had become mesmerized by Will Herndon, who some folks think was the most exciting player to play for UMass since Julius Erving. Will could jump out of the sky. I saw him get above the square on some of those alley-oop passes Anton used to throw.

Not only did he have great jumping ability, but he had great hands. You're talking about a guy who could not only jump, he could jump three times in a row and hit his head on the rim. He was one of those guys who could run the floor, and someone could just throw it to the rim and he'd dunk it. He was an unbelievable athlete. We never again had anybody like him, with the possible exception of Marcus Camby. Marcus could do it, but not like Will Herndon.

We were selling out consistently. Attending a game in the Cage was a wild experience. The place reminded me of St. Joseph's Field House, in Philly, with claustrophobic seating, a tiny balcony, and no glass windows up high. Capacity was 4,500. No one told the fire marshal. There were games when students were lined up three deep in the corners. "When we got it going, the Cage was like our sixth man," Anton Brown says. "A lot of people asked me if I felt bad about not playing in the Mullins Center, but the Cage was so much better as far as a college environment. Teams were scared—or hesitant—to come in and play us."

They still talked about students sleeping out all night for tickets when Julius played there. When we got it going, general admission tickets were on a first-come, first-served basis. Just bring your I.D. They would line up during the day in the middle of campus and pack survival lunches until the doors opened at 6 P.M. I wonder what the profs thought as they walked by on the way to class.

No matter how cold it got outside, most of the students wore T-shirts to the games because it was like a sauna inside. Temperatures must have flirted with the hundred-degree mark and claustrophobia undoubtedly set in.

There was bench seating, but nobody in the student section sat. They stood on the benches the whole time, sweating it out and screaming themselves hoarse while the public address speakers blared the song "Rage in the Cage," by the J. Geils Band, a local Boston group. They used to play it nonstop, maybe ten times a game, the way they do "Rocky Top" down in Tennessee, and the students would always chime in during the chorus.

For the 1995–96 season, Peter Wolf, the lead singer in the band, wrote a song, "Sky High," dedicated to our team.

Even the season-ticket holders stood. At least that way they could see. The press was seated in the four corners of the balcony and half of them couldn't see the entire court. Don Henderson, who does the Temple games on radio, came to Howie Davis in November of '92 and asked, "Where's our game going to be played? In the Cage or in Mullins?"

When he was told it would be the last game at the Cage, he said, "Great, it gives me one more chance to prove to people I can call a game without seeing it."

The ceiling was so low that the noise bounced off it. It was so loud, you left with your ears ringing all night. It was nuts. But it became the thing to do on campus. And kids would do anything to get in.

Brian Gorman told me he used to let his buddies in through a side door. We had more managers on our gate list than we actually had working for us. It got so crowded, officials had to move the kids back just to inbound the ball from the baseline. Eventually, the school caught on to the scam and posted a campus policeman at the door.

"You had people falsifying media credentials to get in," Howie Davis says. "One game, we had two guys saying they were from *The Hartford Courant*. I walked down and saw two guys in three-piece suits. I said, 'I can't remember the last time I saw a reporter coming to a game in a three-piece suit.' "

It didn't take long for the enthusiasm to overflow onto the floor. When Rafer Giles made a three-pointer at the buzzer to beat Rhode Island in 1991, a thousand fans stormed the floor. And we were only a .500 team at the time.

We were 10–8 in the league that year. Paul Franklin wrote in *Eastern Basketball* that we were the most disappointing team in the Atlantic 10. Again, we had lost a lot of close games. The kids still didn't totally believe. And there were still some second-guessers.

That Christmas, we played in the Abdow's Classic at the Springfield Civic Center. They gave my dad seats thirty rows up. The guy sitting next him was just killing me: "Calipari, sit down; you're a bum! The guy can't coach."

It was one of *our* fans. That's how they were in those early days.

My dad started to get upset.

Then the guy struck up a conversation with him; "Where are you from?"

"Charlotte."

"What are you doing *here*?"

My dad said, "My son's the coach of the team."

"Oh, he's a great guy."

When my dad got up to leave, he overheard the guy say to his friends, "That wouldn't be his dad. He wouldn't be sitting up this high."

We were 17–12 after we lost to GW in the first round of our league tournament. But the NIT gave us another invite, and it proved to be a shot in the arm for the program.

We defeated La Salle and Fordham in the first two rounds, then we beat Siena, 82–80, in overtime to advance to the Final Four at the Garden.

And guess who made the basket to force overtime?

Tony Barbee.

We didn't play well and neither did they. It was an ugly game. We were down one, 78–77, and they were shooting fouls. They made two free throws with 2.6 seconds to go. I thought it was over. We were down three and had to go the length of the court. We got the ball to half-court and Anton called a time-out with 2.1 seconds to play.

As we broke out of the huddle, their P.A. announcer came over and said, "Tickets for the NIT Final Four will be on sale tomorrow morning. Buses will leave Knickerbocker Arena to the Garden at this time. . . ."

He must have forgotten the game wasn't over.

We threw it in, and Tony hit a three at the buzzer. And it went to O.T. Then Jimmy McCoy hit a banker from the wing and that was the only 2 points scored in overtime.

Our persistence had paid off. We lost to Stanford, the eventual champion, by a deuce in the semifinals and they had a good team—including center Adam Keefe, who was a lottery pick. After the season, Massachusetts state legislators, as a final gift to their cancer-stricken colleague William D. Mullins, appropriated funds for a new arena.

We were going to have a new home.

CHAPTER 7

BREAKING OUT

Go ahead, call me a Rick Pitino clone.

Everybody else does.

People are always making comparisons between the two of us. But the truth is our team didn't play at all like his. His suits are much more expensive than mine. And so are his shoes. He wears Gucci. I wear Itchy. Rick is always saying we both have big noses. My wife gets upset. She says I'm much more handsome.

But seriously, I've always had the greatest respect for him. I've always felt that he was the premier coach in the country at any level because he taught the kids how to play. He taught individuals to be better players before worrying about the game. His philosophy has always been that as individuals get better, a team's potential to improve increases. That's what he believes in. That's what he's worked on.

Rick has done a lot for UMass. In 1992, he even offered to play us in an early season game at Rupp Arena and threw in a guarantee. We needed a payday, and he needed a name team Kentucky could beat. I knew he knew if he scheduled a really bad team, his fans would go crazy, so he invited us.

It all sounded good.

I just wish the timing had been a little better. We opened the season in the Great Alaskan Shootout in Anchorage, then had to fly all night to get to Lexington after the championship game. That's the price you pay for working on a shoestring budget.

I had really liked the idea of playing three extra games when we were first invited. But we had no money, and I couldn't tell our administration we had to spend thousands of dollars. I called Rick and told him we would come to Lexington, but I needed a $22,000 guarantee.

He agreed.

We were scheduled to fly to Alaska, then fly to Kentucky, then return home. We told Alaska they had to book us twenty-two triangle flights between Hartford, Anchorage, and Lexington, supply us with three days in a hotel, three days of food, and arrange for our transportation while we were up there.

Our school would pay for the remaining hotel nights and food in Kentucky. But I felt with the $22,000 from Kentucky, we would come out even, or even a little bit ahead. I thought we'd have a $4,000 or $5,000 surplus, so our AD went for it.

Now, here's the funny part: the bus. I called Ron Petro, the AD at Alaska. He gave us the school ski bus. We called it the "correctional vehicle" because it was green and looked like the buses they used to transport the inmates to prison. The bus seated only about twenty because it was made to hold ski equipment. Sean Ford, our administrative assistant at the time, was the driver.

One night, about ten of us piled into the bus to go out to a club. We parked it across the street at a gas station. We stayed about an hour at the club. I was tired. We came out, and the bus was gone. My first thought was, "The bus was stolen. Someone stole the University of Alaska's ski bus from us." You know what happened? Sean had parked in front of a sign as big as a wall that said NO PARKING.

The police had towed the bus. The next morning, the guys had to go to the compound to pick it up. The next night, we were getting ready to go to the arena for a game and the bus wouldn't start. *Ooom, ooom, ooom, ooom.*

Oregon State had just left the hotel, and they had a luxury bus, with a video box and all that. But you know what? Despite our transportation problems, our kids enjoyed it. At that point, we were just happy to be there.

And guess what? We won the tournament, defeating New Orleans 68–56. I wish I could tell you this story had a completely happy ending. But our flight to Lexington took twenty-two hours. That's right—twenty-two hours. We missed shoot-around. Anton had shin splints. And we lost 90–69.

After the game, Rick came into our locker room and talked to our kids. Then he took our AD, Frank McInerney, and our staff over to his restaurant. I'm sure he thought he'd never see us again.

"The only way I thought we'd meet them in the NCAA tournament was if we were the No. 1 seed and they were a 16," Pitino admits.

If only he had known what I'd suspected. This was a breakthrough team. "Everybody knew we had made good strides in the past year," Anton Brown suggests. "But they looked at us as just a mediocre team. It was important for us to show we were not overachievers."

During your fourth year, you find out what you've built. You become a little bit more sure of yourself and you become a little more comfortable. You put things in perspective. You want to work hard, but you don't want to drive yourself nuts. You work smarter, and so does your team.

And we were working toward March.

We had kids who were finally reaching their potential, and we achieved so many firsts during the 1991–92 season.

We defeated a nationally ranked team, Oklahoma, in Springfield.

We finally defeated Temple.

We won our first Atlantic 10 regular season championship.

We won our first Atlantic 10 tournament.

We won thirty games.

We went to the NCAA tournament for only the second time in school history.

We went to the Sweet 16 for the first time in school history.

It was rewarding in other ways, too. We had lost eight games by 3 points or less the previous year. It was ridiculous. But in '92, we weren't just winning those games, we were blowing people out.

It was like living a dream. That team will always be viewed as the one that put UMass in the limelight. If it weren't for the 1995–96 team, the 1991–92 team might have been the best team ever to play at UMass. I say that because of the competition both teams played and how they played in big games. The balance. Both teams had five players who were double-figure scorers.

Jimmy McCoy was a 2,000-point scorer. No one I've ever coached had the first step he had. He could get by anybody and then elevate over them. He had an uncanny ability to score. We were running offenses that would break down, and we'd just give him the ball in the open side of the floor. We didn't even need a screen on the ball. He was unstoppable. We're talking about a kid who's probably in the Top 30 scorers in the history of college basketball. And we're talking about a guy who did it with one or two dribbles. He'd catch it. He'd break you down. And he'd kill you. Harper Williams, Tony Barbee, and Will Herndon all scored over 1,000 in their careers. Anton Brown would have done it, too, if he hadn't gotten hurt in his sophomore season.

Some programs subscribe to the "buffalo mentality," meaning there is one buffalo—a single high scorer—who leads the herd. The lead buffalo may lead the others to green pastures—or off a cliff. If the lead buffalo goes to the green pasture, all the buffalo eat well. But if the lead buffalo jumps off the cliff, all the buffalo follow.

Conversely, UMass basketball had the "geese mentality," meaning we flew in formation. When the lead goose got tired, he dropped back into formation while a different goose took the lead. We didn't know who was going to make the big play in a given game. The opportunity was available for any player on any night. It didn't matter who stepped up and made the play, as long as someone did.

Although anyone could step up on a given night, we did clearly define roles that helped players play to their strengths and away from their weaknesses. Every year, before the first game, we sat down, and I told each player his role in front of the entire team. I specifically told each individual what we needed from him, where his shots should be taken from, and where he stood at that particular point.

Jimmy, Anton, and Will were all seniors, and Harper and Tony were juniors, so we had great leadership. Anytime you have guys together for two or three years, you're going to have a good team if they're good people. We had good people. Each of them sacrificed a little bit of his game for the good of the team.

We got on a run that was similar to the one we had this past year. The only differences between the two teams were we didn't have a seven-footer like Marcus in 1992, and the '96 team had more speed. Talk about the guards—Anton and Jimmy were different from the two guards we had this past year, but they were terrific. Tony, Harper, and Will: that was our front line. They were 6'5", 6'7", and 6'3". And we had Lou Roe coming off the bench.

Our game with Oklahoma was one of our first steps into the big time.

Their coach, Billy Tubbs, and I had agreed to play two games at Oklahoma and one at UMass. But we insisted the first game be played at home and the third game come with a paid guarantee.

Oklahoma arrived with a 10–0 record. They were ranked 14th in the country and were averaging 103.6 points.

The game was played before a sellout crowd of 8,469 at the Springfield Civic Center. And ESPN was there to record the moment.

Our guys stepped up in a big way that night, especially Jimmy, who had missed most of the week's practices with the flu. He scored 20 points and we won going away, 86–73. We broke the press early and charged out to a 13–4 lead.

I'm not sure if Oklahoma knew what hit them.

This was the first time we had ever beaten a Top 15 team, and it ranked right up there with the greatest wins in UMass's history—even bigger than the school's 81–79 overtime victory over Providence in 1976 or the 86–85 victory over Seton Hall in the 1977 NIT.

Why did we play so well? Because we were scared. The players were scared they were going to be blown away on national television.

Back then, UMass could beat a team like this and people

seeing just the score thought maybe Oklahoma hadn't played well. But people saw this game and knew we played well. The voters in the wire service polls must have watched the highlights. They gave us our first national ranking ever in the CNN/Coaches' Poll, voting us 25th.

It was a big win, a defining moment. People got to see it on national TV. You believe what you see. People are skeptical when they're reading something that is hard for them to believe—which is UMass beating Oklahoma by double digits. We were up by 25 with a couple of minutes to play.

After the game, Billy was great to me and my team. He didn't make excuses. He wasn't mad. He was terrific.

In the return game in 1993, we were up 7 with about eight minutes to play. They ended up winning by 8 or 10. I walked over to shake his hand and he said, "You know what's great about this game?"

"What?" I asked.

"You've got to come back here next year," he said.

In 1994, we went back, rallied from 15 down, and won the game on a buzzer beater.

I went over to shake his hand and said, "Billy, where's the check?"

These days, if you want to play UMass, it's home and home.

If our win over Oklahoma seemed big, you can imagine how much it meant—particularly to the seniors—when we finally defeated Temple—after twenty-one straight losses—on February 16, 1992. It was a huge win for our fans, too. They had been talking about the game all year and they camped out Saturday night for the Sunday afternoon matchup. In the past, it was festival seating for the students. But this was the first time we actually handed out tickets. The university didn't want the students waiting outside most of the day in mid-February weather, so they opened the doors to the Cage early and we brought the kids pizza.

I remember we were down at the half. Jimmy went in and just blew his top. "This is it for me," he said. "I'll never get a chance to play these guys again."

I just sat in the back and listened. Jimmy didn't want to go through his whole career saying he had never won a game against Temple. I knew after his speech we weren't going to lose.

At one point, the referees stopped the game, and we thought they were going to give us a technical. It looked like the fans were throwing debris on the court. But it was so hot, the ceiling was starting to peel and paint chips were falling onto the court.

We won big, 67–52. Will opened the game with a thunderous dunk, and Jimmy went off for 18 points. "I had a headache after that game," McCoy remembers. "The heat, the pressure, people screaming at me."

He didn't mind having to take a couple of aspirins, though. From that point on, we knew we could play with Temple. They knew it, too.

We showed we could play with a lot of people that year.

When we played West Virginia in the Atlantic 10 championship at our place, security caught three kids hiding out in the bathrooms at three in the afternoon. And thirty-four kids showed up at the gate, claiming they were there to sell popcorn. They were never on the gate list. They just wanted to be part of it.

I don't know who was more excited that night—our fans or our players. We won easily. We were up by 30 at the half.

Thirty!

We knew we were going to win the game, so we just played it out. I subbed everybody.

It was fun.

Qualifying for an automatic bid to the NCAA tournament was a statement of what we had done and what we had worked for. I remember sitting around our house with the players the day of Selection Sunday, knowing we were going to be somewhere in the brackets. As it turned out, we were seeded third in the East, in the same region as Kentucky and defending national champion Duke. But it also meant we would get to play in a subregional at the Worcester Centrum, just an hour away.

The players all looked upon this as their time to prove they deserved to be there. A lot of people still thought the NCAA had just *given* us our seeding. "I don't want people to think they gave you anything," I told them. "You've worked hard for what you got."

Worcester had been like a second home to us since I'd been at UMass. They bleed maroon and white in that town, and we had tried to schedule a game there every year since 1993.

"We all came from winning high school programs," Tony Barbee said. "As we learned how to win in 1991—suffering through a lot of close losses—we became even closer. Nobody was going to stand in our way. We had been to the NIT Final Four. We thought we should have been in the NCAA tournament. We wanted to prove we belonged."

We came in, wanting to make a statement in front of our home fans. And we did.

We blew out Fordham by 30 in the first round. Then we took out Big East champ Syracuse, 77–71, in overtime. We took it right to them. We're talking about Syracuse, which was a good team. We were up 72–71 in overtime. We came out of a time-out. They changed defenses, and we didn't do a very good job adjusting. Will wound up dribbling the ball outside as the shot clock wound down.

Fortunately, Harper saw that and yelled to Will to get him the ball. He caught it at the top of the key and immediately shot a three with just one second to go on the forty-five-second clock. It went in. We were up by 4 with thirty seconds to go and the game was over. Before that shot, Harper had made only one of five three-pointers all season.

That is not to say he hadn't practiced from that range. We had a six-minute shooting drill. For the first five minutes, we made Harper stay inside. But, in the final minute, we allowed him to shoot threes—just in case of emergency.

Those were crazy times.

A lot of people had played this up as a confrontation between Atlantic 10 and Big East powers. Until the game was over. Then, suddenly, it wasn't that big a deal because we'd won. If the Big East had won, it would have been headlines, especially if they had won big. I never worried about the Big East. I told my staff, "If you worry about them, it's wasted energy."

A lot of coaches live with that paranoia, and I think that's why they fail to succeed. You've got to worry only about what you can change. I couldn't change the fact that UMass was in the Atlantic 10 and another program was in the Big East. I couldn't change the fact that someone else was in a higher-profile league than we were. So why worry about it? What good does that do?

The Syracuse win put us in position to play a rematch against Kentucky at the Philadelphia Spectrum.

After we got by the jitters, we played them the same way we did in the Final Four this year. We were right there. Kentucky forward Jamal Mashburn had scored 28 points when they'd defeated us in December '91. He had 30 this time. But we made the game hard for them before finally losing, 87–77.

We fell behind early, 37–16, but rallied to cut the lead to 70–68 when Anton hit a 3-point basket with 6:15 to play. It was the first time I really saw that "Refuse to Lose," never-give-up attitude from the team.

At that point, I thought the game could go either way. Kentucky came down the floor and Deron Feldhaus attempted a three-pointer. The ball sailed off the rim and Anton went up to pull it down, but Kentucky guard Sean Woods came up behind him and tapped it back to his team.

I began motioning that Woods had gone over Anton's back and made contact on the play. Then an official, Lenny Wirtz, hit me with a technical—for being out of the coaching box.

I was stunned. Richie Farmer made both technicals, then Feldhaus scored on the possession and we were never the same. Afterwards, I was flooded with questions from the media as to whether I had actually stepped out of the box. I decided not to make an issue of it.

My high school coach, Bill Sacco, was there, staying at the hotel with me. We walked the streets of Philly. When I got back to my hotel room, I wasn't taking any calls. But then Sean Miller called and said, "Hey, look at it this way. If you had beaten Kentucky, Duke was going to beat you by 30."

That was a good way of looking at it.

In retrospect, Lenny Wirtz had thought I was out of the box because the Spectrum had different lines. I wasn't. I didn't blame Lenny. I didn't take away from Kentucky's win.

I said, "If I stepped out, I deserved it."

I knew what had happened. There was nothing I was going to gain from burying Lenny Wirtz, so I didn't need to jump in on it.

I will say this, though. Lenny and I did a trip that was put together by Billy Packer a year or two later. Lenny was the official. I was the coach. Billy had forgotten.

He said, "Do you mind him coming?"

I said, "No. I have no problems with it."

He said, "All right, I'm going to bring him with us."

I was fine with it.

Hell, life's too short. It made me more human because all the Philly people had been going by what Rollie Massimino had said about me. Then they saw me respond in that way. Again, your actions define who you are.

And so, in a stressful situation, where it looked like a guy took our season away, I didn't blame him because I was trying to show my kids that's what "Refuse to Lose" is.

I told them, "You're not going to win every game. Things aren't always going to go your way. If someone's going to do something that he shouldn't and you don't win, don't blame anybody. Learn from it."

I learned I can't be so hyper in the NCAA tournament.

Our success that year opened up some doors for me professionally. I signed my first contract with Nike. I had gotten my initial sneaker contract during my first year at UMass. It was with Adidas. A guy came up to me and saw I had a UMass basketball shirt with "Adidas" on the sleeve.

He said, "You're with Adidas? I didn't know that."

"They don't either," I said.

I didn't get any money. They just gave us forty pairs of athletic shoes. Eventually I went with Nike in 1993.

It was neat for me and neat for the program, that they wanted us to be part of their program. But, here's a great story. It was the first time I had gone to the Nike suite at the Final Four in New Orleans. I was very excited. I got off the elevator. I looked down the hallway, and who was coming toward me? Phil Knight, the CEO of Nike. He had running shoes, shorts, a shirt, and sunglasses on.

I looked and I thought, "Oh my gosh, Phil Knight. I'm going to meet Phil Knight."

I said, "Hello, Mr. Knight."

And he said to me, "Do you have the key to my room?"

He thought I was the bellman.

I started to walk around the corner with him and told him who I was. He just burst out laughing. Later he sent me a book with the inscription, "To one of the great bellmen of all time."

I was a marketing major in college, so I can appreciate what Phil Knight has accomplished. I was constantly looking for ways to promote our program. We started a coach's TV show in 1992. It went statewide three years ago. The crazy thing is that, in Boston, our show ran Sundays at midnight, and its rating was equal to Saturday and Sunday afternoon basketball there, including pro games.

The show rated high in Amherst, but it rated higher in Boston. It was getting a 25 percent market share. That was important because it gave great credibility to our program in the Boston market. UMass had become the commonwealth's team.

No other coach in Massachusetts had a show that was broadcast statewide. The good news is, it also went into Connecticut. Are you ready for this? It was seen in Philly on SportsChannel, so all the people there got to enjoy my show once a week. They watched it, too. I know that.

I wanted more people to know about our success, but I was still having problems getting any of the local merchants to carry UMass apparel. They didn't think there was a market, and they didn't want to spend the money to find out. I didn't want to open up a store. But I said, "You know what? I'll open up a store and the other merchants will sell it then because they'll see I'm making all the money."

We got a spot uptown and opened a small store. We called it Coach Cal's Closet.

I convinced Champion to put out a line and took some sweaters and hats from other people. At the same time, I approached Champion about putting satellite shops in the JCPenney stores across Massachusetts. I wasn't making any profit from these shops; that was Penney's. But they put my name on them: Coach Cal's Corner. We thought we'd open up four, but thirteen JCPenney stores had Coach Cal's Corners. We're not in the Collegiate Licensing Program, but Champion is talking about selling over $3 million in UMass apparel. I hope they can find some room in the Mullins Center to sell the apparel.

Yes, the Mullins Center became a reality.

Finally, I had another door opened for me during the 1992–93 season when the university completed work on the Mullins Center. It had been a long time in the making. I'd first heard about the blueprints when I was being interviewed.

That following April, I saw Johnny Orr and we talked about the program. "Hey, did they show you the model, you know, where they take the top off?" he asked me.

"Yeah."

"I saw that son of a bitch back in 1960," he said.

That made me wonder if we were ever going to get this thing done. Sounding like my players back in 1988, I never believed it would happen until they started digging.

We were fortunate. People think I had a lot to do with it. But what happened was the horse farm across the road from the university went under. Our school was the only one that could buy it. When it was purchased, the administration moved our agriculture school into the horse barns across the way. That opened up the space we needed. If that hadn't happened, UMass might still be playing in the Cage.

I used to go over there all the time. I was inside the building five times a week. The construction workers used to laugh. I would go over there and dream. I would see it, feel it, watch the guys build it. I brought recruits over. I was excited, like a little kid, because this was the fruition of all our hard work. Obviously, it was one of the last pieces of the puzzle we needed to turn this program into a national power.

The minute we could move in, our stuff was in there. Boom. The doors weren't even on yet.

There were some kinks to work out. We dedicated the William D. Mullins Convocation Center on February 4, 1993, with a game against West Virginia. We won 64–59, in overtime. But the game was almost postponed at halftime when construction workers discovered a leak, and they were concerned enough to shut off the water. Trying to flush the toilets was an adventure that night.

Once the plumbing was fixed, the Mullins Center became the best on-campus arena in the Northeast. It seats 9,434. I was happy with the size. Some people wanted it to be for 15,000. But our program wasn't there yet. They wanted to build luxury boxes. Now, yeah. The school can still do it. If they want to expand it, they can. But back then, we wanted to create a demand for tickets that was so heavy that, even if we faltered a little bit, it wouldn't go away.

Tickets cost $15, if you can get one. It's always sold out.

Mullins is like a big Cage. It's louder than any building of its size I've ever been in. The kids go nuts, and the fans are right on top of you. Four thousand of our tickets go to the students. More than five thousand go to season-ticket holders. We make sure our students are close to the action. We give them good seats on three sides of the court—both baselines and behind the opposing team's bench. The other side and the corners go to the season-ticket holders. But the students are there. And they still stand throughout the game, just like they did at the Cage. They're active and they feel a part of our program.

Our overall record at Mullins is 39–2 and we won twenty-eight straight games before losing to GW in February of 1995.

We went on a fourteen-game winning streak in 1993, and nine of those wins came without Harper Williams, who was out with a broken hand. When Harper was hurt, we posted up Tony a lot more. Kennard Robinson played well. We just kind of made do. This was who we had. This was how we were going to have to play. We were just going to have to survive. And we did.

I learned a lot about myself in those days.

I was talking to a reporter once about legendary UCLA coach John Wooden and I told him, "You know, I wish I could be like Coach Wooden—just sit there with the rolled-up program."

"He wasn't always like that," I was told. "For the first couple of years, they said he talked too much."

"That's beautiful. Maybe there's a shot for me."

You know what's amazing? Any time I've backed off and tried to be somebody else, it hasn't worked. I watched Lute Olson of Arizona coach one game and he rolled up his program and just watched the game. I thought I would try to do the same thing. Well, all of a sudden, my team wasn't playing as hard or with as much emotion. They were starting to look at me and were saying, "Wow, this must not be that important to Coach."

The players actually came to me during one team meeting and told me to change back. So I did. I'm an emotional coach—and that's never going to change. I started getting into the game, challenging the kids, and it led to a very aggressive, emotional style. As a staff, we had a burning desire to win the game—every game. Sometimes, I got into it with officials because they didn't always know what I do. I may be jumping up and down, stamping my foot, just trying to get the team going. In Colorado, I was stamping my foot, telling a kid to rebound the ball. An official came across the court and called a tech.

A lot of officials might not like a coach being animated on the sidelines. And the moment you say something—boom—technical. And you think, "What are you worrying about me for?" But most of the guys who know me know how I am. It's a good thing.

The players feed off what we are.

The night Harper came back, we were playing Temple in the next-to-the-last game at the Cage. He was wearing a big bandage on his right hand. I can still remember the electricity when he came into the game. The people just went crazy. I can remember when he made a basket, he ran by the bench, and I just slapped him on the back. Harper scored 17 points and gave us the emotional lift we needed during a 52–50 victory that ended with Tony tipping in the game-winner at the buzzer.

Harper eventually came back and won his second consecutive A-10 tournament MVP after scoring 20 points and grabbing eight rebounds as we defeated Temple, 69–61, in the championship game.

Harper Williams was good to this program.

He gave us the post presence we needed, the warrior mentality close to the basket. And this guy could really shoot it from fifteen, sixteen feet. But, in tight to the basket, he was such a fierce competitor, he was exactly what we needed to get over the hump. As much as any player was important to our program—Tony Barbee was a guy who could do everything; Jimmy McCoy was a scorer; Will Herndon was an athlete—Harper Williams was the guy who got us over the hump.

He was such an incredible worker. Practice would be dying down, and I would do competitive drills. He would be the guy who took over. When everybody started fading, he would start stepping up. I just kept saying, "This is why he is who he is. He just steps up and takes over. The rest of you, if you could just step up like him, imagine how good we could be."

He just had so much more heart and desire than most human beings.

I temporarily forgot that during the NCAA tournament; it was probably my biggest turnover in coaching. Harper was playing what proved to be his final game for UMass against Virginia in the second round of the tournament.

Some of the players had gone out the night before. But I thought we were still good enough to advance to the regional semi's against Cincinnati and see what happened. I was angry, looking at guys not playing. Tony played great. Mike Williams had a broken hand, but played well.

But Harper couldn't even get up and down the court; late in the game, with four minutes to go, he was beaten deep. Their center, a 280-pound guy named Ted Jeffries, outran him and scored on a breakaway layup. Then Harper didn't dive for a loose ball.

I yanked him. I said, "That's it. Get out." I sat him down and never put him back in. What a mistake. Here was a kid who had given his heart and soul, who had played with a broken hand, who had done so many things to help our club win. He deserved better. Even though we were going to lose, I should have been a little more mature. He had had a bad day. He had been out all night. Hopefully, that experience taught him what this was about.

Well, I learned.

Three years later, Lou Roe had a bad day against Oklahoma State. At that time, Lou was more concerned about agents, going to the NBA, making money. He just wanted the season to be over. Now he's wishing that the season had gone on longer.

I took Lou out. I put Tyrone in. I thought we had a chance to win. He kept saying to me, "Give me another chance." I did, and he kept hurting us. In the end, I subbed Lou with twenty seconds to go when I knew the game was over. I hugged him and said, "You had a great career."

I did the same with Derek Kellogg and our other senior, Jeff Meyer. Derek came up to me and told me, "Coach, I'm sorry."

He had nothing to be ashamed of. He made the All Regional team.

CHAPTER 8

WHISPERS

I was watching Duke coach Mike Krzyzewski on TV a few years ago and heard him say, "A lot of people don't like me—and they don't like Duke—because we've beaten a lot of people."

I jumped out of my chair and said, "Thanks, Mike."

That's what a lot of this is about. We won a lot of games, and I am not the shy, retiring type. That makes a lot of people mad. There have been plenty of whispers, suggesting our success might somehow have been tainted by illegal recruiting.

We had nothing to hide at UMass. We ran a clean program. If you don't run a clean program, usually you keep a lid on it and don't let anybody in to observe it. But we had good kids, bright kids who were well-spoken. I wasn't afraid to let people come in and be with the kids, to walk to class with them, to watch them to see how they are.

I had been through this before at Pitt. I'm sick of hearing trash talk about our recruitment of Marcus Camby and Lou Roe— two guys we supposedly cheated to get.

Nobody even knew about Marcus until his senior year in high school in 1993.

Marcus grew up in a Hartford housing project, just a short walk from the Civic Center where Connecticut plays some of its home games. He once waited outside to ask for an autograph from UConn star Cliff Robinson. He also admits that after Tate George hit a jumper at the buzzer to defeat Clemson in the 1990 NCAA regional semifinals, his whole neighborhood rooted for the Huskies. Everybody wanted Marcus to go to UConn. But as I said, he was still a relative unknown until late in his high school career.

A lot of the credit for who Marcus is today goes to his mother, Janice, a single parent who raised Marcus and his younger sisters, Mia, now seventeen, and Monica, sixteen. When Marcus was in first grade, Janice enrolled him in Project Concern, a voluntary program of school desegregation. Marcus would get up every day before dawn and bus to the mostly white suburbs. During his freshman year at Conrad High School, he grew an amazing ten inches. But he played varsity for only five games during his junior year before transferring back to Hartford Public, his neighborhood school. State high school athletic regulations force transfer students to sit out a year, so Marcus missed another year.

We first heard about Marcus by reading the recruiting publications that listed him among the top ten prospects for his age in the region, despite the fact he had hardly played in high school. We had no idea of Marcus's potential, but we kept sending him letters.

Then we saw Marcus play for Jackie Bethea at the Hartford Boys and Girls Club the summer after his junior year. Jackie is now the director of female services for the Boys and Girls Club in Hartford. They call her "Miss Jackie" down there because she's done so much for the kids in that neighborhood. She looks after them and has never asked for anything. She's got some presence because the kids say, "She helped me get where I am."

Jackie first met Marcus when he wandered into the Kelvin D. Anderson Recreation Center off the streets in North Hartford as a skinny ten-year-old kid. She didn't see greatness in him at the time, except for a love of basketball. But once he began to grow, he started dominating play on the outdoor courts at Waverly.

Marcus played in a program called Athletes for Excellence. His traveling team was the Untouchables. They didn't have a national reputation like the Gauchos or Riverside Church in New York. But they were never afraid of competition. The team would pile into vans and play in tournaments throughout the East, the Midwest, and Canada.

Jackie took Marcus—and many other kids—under her wing during his formative years and reinforced Janice Camby's ideas about education. The Boys and Girls Club Jackie works at is just a gym and a couple of classrooms. The sad fact in this country right now is that if the money runs out, the Boys and Girls Clubs, the YMCAs, the outdoor courts, the soccer and football fields, and the summer programs are the first things to go. She's one of the best reasons I know why we should invest in young people.

Jackie helped sell Marcus on the idea of using basketball as a vehicle for college. She didn't have to sell my assistants on his potential. They came to the office and they were salivating. They thought they'd found the next Bill Russell.

There was some question in their minds about whether Marcus was going to have to sit out his senior year because he had transferred. But Jackie assured us that wasn't the case and

she went on to say that Marcus would be eligible his freshman year.

I was a little skeptical about all these rave reviews about
how big and fast and athletic Marcus was. I wanted to see how
he would do against better competition, so I had Bruiser
call Sonny Vaccaro and get Marcus into the ABCD camp in
California. We went out there. Marcus was running up and
down the floor, dunking, blocking shots. He was a little raw
and wasn't in great shape. But when he played hard, he was
dominant, and you could see he had the potential to be a
great one.

I was standing there, bumping Billy and Bruiser like I couldn't
believe what I was watching. Then I turned to them and said,
"Who told you to get him to a camp? Now everyone is going to
recruit him, and we'll never get him."

When Marcus got back home, his mail box was filled with a
stack of more than a hundred letters from recruiters around the
country. In reality, we had a big lead because of our relationship
with Jackie.

UConn didn't pick up the recruiting until after they'd seen
Marcus at ABCD, but, as you might expect, they tried to come
after him hard. It did get a little crazy when they had the mayor
call Jackie. They also got the governor's assistant and a local judge
involved.

UConn had arranged to meet with Marcus the first day of official contact that fall. But when their coach, Jim Calhoun, arrived
at the school at 8 A.M., he discovered we had beaten him to the
punch, having called Marcus and his mother at home at midnight and talked to them for an hour.

Jackie was strongly in our corner. She was down on Connecticut, too, because she felt they had screwed another Hartford

kid, Shawn Ellison—her first "baby"—who played in Marcus's AAU program. She didn't want Shawn to go to UConn because she thought he might not play. She was right. He had been told some things by Connecticut; they didn't follow through, and he ended up being asked to leave. In Jackie's mind, if you're going to do that to one of her kids, she's not going to send you another.

When UConn came back again, she said, "You screwed us once."

In Marcus's case, it came down to the fact that he wanted to stay close to home. He liked the idea we had been in on him from the start. He stayed loyal.

And he wanted to be a part of building something special. He wanted to be in a program where he could play right away. He wanted to be somewhere he could be brought along at his own pace. He didn't want to have to carry all the weight, and he wanted to play for someone he really felt was good enough.

In his mind, he'd made the right decision. Jackie helped him make that decision. She didn't make it for him. He made it at the end.

I must admit, I had to do some fast talking during one visit. We were in his home. Marcus is seven feet tall; after I saw him play, I knew he'd be the difference. When I went to see him, he told me he wanted to be a two guard. I looked at him and said, "You're seven-feet tall, and you want to be a two guard?" I paused for a moment. "Okay," I finally said. "You can be a two guard, but I have to tell you one thing: we post up our two guards."

Interestingly enough, if Marcus hadn't come to UMass, I think he might have gone to Providence. Everyone in New England

wanted him. It was funny. People missed on him and then suddenly they couldn't get him in school. That's all I heard from
UConn fans.

Marcus just laughs when he hears those sour grapes. "Let me
tell you," he said, "they wanted me."

After watching Marcus lead Hartford Public to a 27–0 record
and its first state championship in thirty-one years and then
dominate play in the Capitol Classic and the Olympic Festival, I
can see why.

Lou Roe was our first Top 40 prospect. He was Bobby Martin's
cousin and, like Bobby, he'd played for Atlantic City High.
Bobby told him to go to UMass. Bobby's mother told him to go
to UMass. Most people saw Lou's tenth-grade transcript and
said, "He'll never make it."

I'd heard all that. But a prospect didn't really need a 2.0 cume
overall. He needed a 2.0 in the core—eleven Cs—which he
could get in his junior and senior years. Lou earned good grades
his junior year—and very good grades his senior year—and
became eligible.

A lot of people backed away from him because they had heard
about his transcript. But Lou had a coach, an AD, and a math
teacher who really cared about him. They drove him to school
every morning just so he could get tutoring help.

Lou also had felt loyal to us, but we had to fight off Syracuse at the end. They were really on him. One of their assistants told him, "You're going to be playing New Hampshire,
and you're going to turn on the TV and see us playing Georgetown on CBS. Do you understand that?" I couldn't get mad
because, at the time, it was true. Another school down

south told him, "Why would you want to drive a Volkswagen when you can drive a Cadillac?" The analogy was not about giving the kid a car, but playing in an established program.

Lou told us he was coming in the spring of 1991. I was at the Hall of Fame Dinner in Springfield and I called him.

"What's up?" I asked. "Did you sign the papers?"

"I did, Coach," he said. "I'm going to Syracuse."

"What?" I was flabbergasted.

"I changed my mind," he said. "I had to. Syracuse was just too big a school."

I thought he was serious. Then he burst out laughing.

"You son of a bitch," I said. "Wait until I get you."

Roe had a mischievous side to him. The day he got his score, he called me. He told me, "Coach, I've got some good news and I've got some bad news."

"Give me the bad news," I said.

"You know that test I was supposed to take Saturday," he said. "I slept through it."

I went crazy. "What, you slept through the last test, the last opportunity you had to pass this test? Are you nuts?"

"Coach, stop it," he said. "I passed."

Lou had made it. Not by a wide margin, but he'd made it. He told me when he first opened up the letter, he looked at the numbers and thought he hadn't made it. Then he looked again. He went from "Oh my God" to "I made it."

During the entire time I spent at UMass, we recruited only one McDonald's All–American—Donta Bright, who signed with us in 1992 from Baltimore Dunbar. Donta was a center on a team that also featured his cousin, Keith Booth, who plays for Maryland, and former Syracuse guard Michael Lloyd. Dunbar cruised to a 29–0 record during Donta's senior year and the No. 1 ranking in the *USA Today* poll.

Donta was a center in high school, but we knew he might not be the same type of player in college. But he had such pride. He outplayed everyone he ever played against in his senior year. And that included Rasheed Wallace. They played the best schedule in the country and he was the MVP of every tournament he played in during high school."

Donta grew up in violent, drug-infested East Baltimore and still carries the scars of his childhood, especially the ones he suffered after two thugs tried to mug him at gunpoint when he was thirteen. Donta had only $2 in his pocket, so he took off and slipped, scraping his arm against a tree.

The scars still remain from that incident and from a divorce that occurred when Donta was only ten years old. His mother, Patricia, tried, as a single parent, to raise him, but Donta was struggling badly in the classroom and actually dropped out of school the summer after ninth grade. His coach, Pete Pompey, tracked him down and talked him into coming back.

His mother never gave up on her son, although she did have to practice some tough love, preventing him from going on a trip with his team to Germany when his grades fell. She made him stop playing basketball for a week and got him to deal with his problems.

Ohio State was in early, and he visited St. John's late. A lot of people tried to say the only reason he came to UMass was because he didn't have his grades. But that's not true. He had until June to get his last test score—and we were going to sign him anyway, even if he was Prop. 48. The decision seemed to suit his mother, who desperately wanted him to earn a college degree; she knew we could help him do it because UMass has one of the best learning disabled programs in the country.

Billy, Dave, Bruiser, Ed, and I all got our start at the Five-Star basketball camp as counselors. A lot of people think that was an enormous advantage when we first started out.

But take a look at the starting five on our 1992 team that reached the Sweet 16. Tony Barbee did go to Five-Star.

But did Jimmy McCoy attend Five-Star?

No.

Anton Brown?

No.

Will Herndon?

No.

Harper Williams?

No.

Besides, how many of those players were considered high-profile recruits? They were all legitimate players, but they had been overlooked because they had kinks. Maybe they weren't big enough, maybe they didn't run fast enough, or maybe they didn't jump high enough. But together, they won thirty games. And nobody knew who they were.

What we sold early on was a vision of what we were going to build. It was a dream. It had nothing to do with what we had done.

It was hard at first.

During my first year at UMass, I recruited a player from

Indiana named Matt Waddell. He was a point guard. I told him he reminded me a lot of Sean Miller, the point guard I'd coached at Pitt. I told him he could come in, run our club, do the things that I wanted him to do, help us get to the NCAA tournament, win a national championship, blah, blah, blah.

Matt really liked me personally. We went into his home and he had his grandmother there, his mom, his dad, his girlfriend, a couple of buddies. They all wanted to meet me. I'm telling you, I hit a home run. The chemistry was there between the family, the kid, and me. I spoke about an hour and a half. I knew we were going to get this kid.

Finally I asked, "Are there any questions?"

His mom said to me, "You're not going to be at UMass."

I almost fell out of the chair. "Now, why would you ruin this day by saying that? What do you mean? Where am I going?"

"Well, you'll get another job," she said.

"What do you mean?" I said. "We were 10–18. Who would hire me?"

In the end, Matt went with Gene Keady at Purdue and had a great career.

He came to our game when we were getting ready to play Georgia Tech at the Meadowlands just before Christmas in 1995. He was sitting in the end zone. He knew Ed Schilling and he knew me. He came up and said, "I never thought you'd be at UMass this long."

I'd been there long enough to see things change. At first, it was hard to get a player of the caliber of Lou Roe, Marcus Camby, Donta Bright, or Dana Dingle. They would look at a college's program and say, "You've got to be something;

you've got to show me something because I can go where I want to go."

After our breakthrough season, we started building a reputation. When we recruited Lou, Marcus, and Donta, we sold our vision first, our results next. Then we were selling results. We walked in and were able to say, "One, you'll get better as a player. Here's why. Look at our players; every one has gotten better. Two, you'll be taught life skills. Our kids have all done well. You will be able to get your degree if that's what you want to do. Over 80 percent of our kids have. Besides that, twenty-two of the players who have gone through our program are either playing professionally or have jobs in the field of their choice. That's the key: preparing kids for life after basketball."

Lou was our first drafted player. He was selected early in the second round of the 1995 draft by the Detroit Pistons. Now UMass has another one, Marcus Camby. I told recruits, "You can come here, get a great education, have fun, and be comfortable whether you're black, white, green, or gold. You can become an NBA player. You can be Player of the Year. And you can win a national title. You can realize all your dreams here because it's been done—except for the national title—by somebody. So why can't you do it?"

When we recruited a player, we looked at character traits as much as we looked at basketball skills. As a college coach, my job was to teach skills. I've been told, "Your kids play so hard. They're warriors. They play with emotion." Well, guess what? We recruited that. If a guy was a warrior, and he had a burning desire to win and improve above all else, we really looked at him hard. He was somebody we wanted in our program.

We were always looking for guys who played bigger than their size, guys who accepted their teammates. All the players we recruited have been that way.

People say I didn't recruit shooters. When I looked at a player, I was looking for toughness. Was this kid tough enough? I wanted guys who wanted to get after it when we were in a hostile environment, with 13,000 fans screaming at us. A great shooter wouldn't have helped us if he didn't have toughness.

We wanted a guy who was selfless. The problem with a basketball team's chemistry occurs when one guy worries about someone else's success. Some players not only want to be successful, they want everyone else to be a failure. Or they want to be the only guy who has success. It's a problem. I've had guys in the UMass program who couldn't deal with others' success. They didn't last there very long.

In college basketball, when a team has unselfish kids who buy into a coach's philosophy, they can all be successful. All five of the UMass starters this year—Marcus, Donta, Dana, Edgar, and Carmelo—made All Conference. It was the first time in the history of our league that happened. That's because we did well enough that they all got their just desserts.

For a player's stock to rise, the NBA wants to know he's a winner. You know what they're saying about Donta Bright in Phoenix, what they like about him: "Heart, man. This kid knows how to win. He's got heart and character. He won a national title in high school. And he took a team to the Final Four that had never been there before." Bad teams in the NBA need to get a lot of people who know how to win and can get that across to the other players. This kid has won 90 percent of his games.

Kids with mental toughness who do not waiver when things get tough are a must. We had a controversial situation with a prospect named Mark Blount, a 7'0" blue chipper from Summerville, South Carolina. Mark had attended two different high schools—Summerville and Oak Hill Academy in Mouth of Wilson, Virginia—as a sophomore and junior—and was scheduled to enroll in Sacred Heart of New Rochelle in the fall of his senior year.

He visited our campus a couple of times and I had a chance to speak with him on the phone. I liked him as a kid, but I didn't like his track record. I came down hard on him. I told him, "If you come here, you *have to get your act together.*

"If you leave the school you're enrolled in again, UMass is out."

"I'm fine with that, Coach."

"Do you understand this is the way I do things? If you change schools one more time, I cannot—I will not—honor this commitment."

He got himself into a jam because he was living in the wrong town, and he had to enroll at Dobbs Ferry.

I told him, "Mark, we are such a high-profile program that if you come with us, not only are you going to be killed, we're going to be killed. You know what? It's not worth it. It's not fair. You changed high schools. You knew what I'd told you. And now we're done. I'm not going to be able to take you."

He cried. His mentor, Mo Sangeniti, tried to explain the situation, but I'd have none of it.

"You may not understand how I am," I said. "But when I say something, that's how it is."

I did get on the phone with two coaches—Ralph Willard of Pitt and Denny Crum of Louisville—and told them he was not a bad kid. This was not about drugs or stealing. This was because he left a high school after he'd made a commitment. He finally signed with Pitt. It was an unfortunate incident, but I think I did the right thing.

We had been able to get involved with more and more good players up and down the East Coast, even in Philly, where I thought we'd never have a chance because of the Bobby Martin incident. Rollie Massimino hurt me in Philadelphia. The provincial writers there believed everything he said. He was pretty vicious, but he'd been that way. At this point, I would say he and I are on the right track. We've talked about it. He's done some of our Atlantic 10 games, and I'm fine with him. I don't hate anybody. I've said, "Hey, let's move on," and he's fine with that.

The one person who helped us combat the negative publicity was Bruiser Flint, who grew up in Philly, played for Episcopal Academy and St. Joe's, and had been on our staff since 1989. I knew Bruiser from Five-Star. I'd watched him work there and knew him as a player. I liked his ability to teach, coach, and relate to the kids. I thought he was a classy person, aside from basketball. Again, I was looking for those traits. He was competitive as a player. He always did more than people thought he could do. Most important, he was loyal.

Bruiser had coached in the Sonny Hill League, which was a magnet for the best players in Philly. He helped ease the way for us to recruit that city when he invited Tennis Young from the Hill League up to work our summer camp. He came with two other coaches—John Hardnett and James Flint, Bruiser's father—for a weekend to catch some of the games and hang out with us.

"They had some questions when I decided to come here as an assistant," Bruiser says. My dad said, 'It's your career. If that's what you want to do, go ahead and do it.' But John Hardnett and Sonny Hill really didn't trust John, and they knew the situation at UMass was pretty bad. They told me, 'We don't want you to go up there and then be out of the business in a couple of years.'

"But I got them to know John. I sent John down there during recruiting, without me, just so they could get a chance to know him. They gave him the cold shoulder for a while, but they eventually came around. They started to realize our staff worked pretty hard. I told them, 'John is a good coach.' They knew I really enjoyed myself up here and that is pretty much it. Then we started winning."

Bruiser tried to get into Philly immediately. He knew the city had produced a lot of Division I players and felt we should try to establish a strong foothold there. His attitude was, "Who knows? We might pop up and get one of those good ones who can get us over the hump."

Actually, we got two—Tyrone Weeks from Franklin Learning Center and a 6'10", 270-pound center, Lari Ketner, from Roman Catholic.

Tyrone was a 6'7" rebounding machine in the Philly Public League. He grew up in North Philadelphia, just around the corner from the late Hank Gathers, who was an All-American at Loyola-Marymount. Hank Gathers was like a big brother to Tyrone. "We used to hang at Father Dave Hagan's (halfway) house," Tyrone says. "Hank was my role model. He used to come home and give me sneakers. He used to tell me I should keep playing ball because I was growing. I was 6'4" then.

"He was headed for the NBA," Tyrone said.

Then, one day during Gathers's senior year in 1990, those

dreams died when his heart stopped. Gathers collapsed at mid-court during the WCAC Conference championship game. He never got up. Tyrone was stunned. "He was the guy who got me into the sport," he said. "He told me if I worked out I could be the next guy from the 'hood to make it big."

Tyrone played in Philly at the same time as Rasheed Wallace, Jason Lawson, and Alvin Williams. Wallace went to North Carolina. Lawson and Williams went to Villanova. And Bruiser convinced Tyrone to come up to UMass.

Of course, he had help.

"Tennis Young used to be my assistant coach in the Sonny Hill League when I first started out," Bruiser says. "He once told me, 'Look, if you ever get to a place, I'm really going to try to help you out.'

"He was very close to Tyrone. So I called in my chit and said, 'I want Tyrone.' We were a perfect fit for him. He needed to get away from the city and some of the things that could hold him back. One of the reasons I had Tennis come up and work the camp was that he could see this was a good program for the kid. He knew I was going to look after him, and he knew John was going to push him."

Lari Ketner came out of nowhere. He was a late-bloomer. Bruiser called John Hardnett, asking if Temple was involved. He was stunned when John told him they weren't interested.

We were.

His mother was interested in us, too. Bruiser told me that a week before he visited us in April, Lari had been robbed right in front of his house in West Philly. His mother wanted him to attend school outside the city. When he visited, he wanted to sign the papers and get it over with. He said, "This is the place for me."

His mother actually started crying because she knew he wanted to come to UMass. They were so tight. She kept telling me she was losing her baby. But his mother told him, "Hold up." She didn't want him to commit right away. She wanted him to make absolutely sure this was what he wanted. She felt he had an obligation to visit La Salle, which had recruited him hard.

We told him, "Hey, sign them. We won't turn them in until after you visit because we can hold them for two weeks before we have to turn them in to the NCAA office." Those papers were not turned in until after he came back from his official visit to La Salle.

If he had told us that he wanted the letter torn up, we would have done it. I'm not going to name the player, but I have done it before. He was one of the top players in the country. He'd signed the letter with us. His grandmother signed it. He visited two other schools, called me back and said, "Coach, I want you to tear up the letter." I asked him why. He told me why, and I said, "Fine." And I tore up the letter.

The problem came up when our league office announced Lari had signed, and released the date he'd signed. La Salle coach Speedy Morris went ballistic. He came down pretty hard on the kid and his mother, saying the school wanted its money back from Lari's official visit. The school had thought it was over and done with, that Lari was going to sign with the Explorers. In fact, during the Atlantic 10 tournament, a story broke in the *Philadelphia Daily News* that quoted Lari's saying he was "90 percent sure" he was going to La Salle.

But that same night, his mother had called us with a message:

I learned a lot from sitting next to Bob Hill and Larry Brown at Kansas in the early '80s.

As an assistant to Coach Paul Evans at Pitt in the mid-'80s, the camera caught me in a rare moment with my mouth shut.

February 24, 1994, Temple coach John Chaney
and I put our differences behind us in the first
UMass-Temple game after "the incident."

Lou Roe's loyal fans whoop it up in the Mullins
Center in '94.

The First Fan visits our locker room after the game at George Washington during the '94-'95 season.

Carmelo Travieso puts the ball on the floor.

Edgar Padilla came through for us all year.

Diagramming a play during a timeout.

Marcus Camby visits with a couple of youngsters in the playroom of the UMass Medical Center pediatric unit. Camby spent four days in the hospital after collapsing on January 14, 1996, but doctors were unable to find any problems.

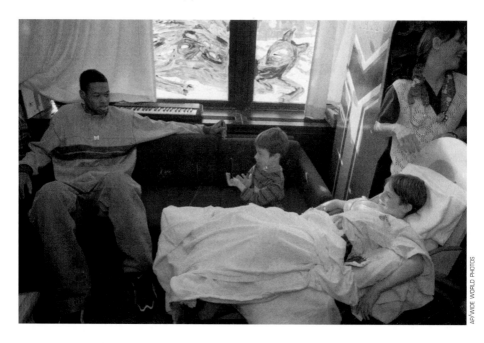

Marcus Camby slams
one home.

Giddel Padilla, shooting over Tony
Delk and Antonio Walker, waited all
year to spark our almost-comeback
against Kentucky in the Final Four.

On the Jumbotron in New York's Times Square during the 1996 Final Four. Little did I know at the time that I'd soon be making the Meadowlands my new home.

1995-96 UMass Minutemen. *Front Row (left to right):* Ross Burns, Charlton Clarke, Donta Bright, Dana Dingle, Edgar Padilla, Giddel Padilla, Carmelo Travieso. *Back Row (left to right):* Head Coach John Calipari, Assistant Coach Ed Schilling, Andy Maclay, Tyrone Weeks, Ted Cottrell, Marcus Camby, Inus Norville, Rigoberto Nuñez, Assistant Coach John Robic, Associate Coach James "Bruiser" Flint.

At the press conference naming me as the new coach of the Nets. Michael Rowe, seated on the left, and Willis Reed, seated on the right, look on.

I asked for it—the intense pressure of coaching the Nets became very apparent on NBA draft day.

Erin Sue, me, Megan Rae, and Ellen.

"Do not worry about the article that was written in the *Daily News* today. Please call immediately."

I think one of the reasons Lari didn't want to announce was that he was concerned there might be backlash from the Roman Catholic people because Speedy Morris used to coach there.

La Salle's reaction didn't surprise me. Speedy is under the gun. He's in a position where he has to win. That situation looked like a dagger to him. But I'm still disturbed about all the flak we caught from a new member school. Here was a league team burying us and trying to make us look bad after we had voted them into the league. If you had a choice between La Salle and UMass, where would you go? There is no choice. You've got the No. 1 team in the country and the 250th team in the country. Where would you go? One team is on television twenty-five times a year, and the other team is never on. Where would you go?

We'd gotten enough exposure that we were able to spread our wings in recruiting. Last year, we signed two players out of talent-rich North Jersey—6'9" center Ajmal Basit of St. Anthony's of Jersey City and forward Winston Smith of St. Patrick's of Elizabeth. I think it was just a fact that people liked the way we played. We had been on television so much that we were very familiar. Winston Smith, a bright young man, has a learning disability, and UMass and California have the two best programs for dealing with that.

To be honest with you, Winston's guardians, Mr. and Mrs. Jack Sapp, brought it up with us. The kid wanted to play good ball but he also wanted to graduate. Because UMass has that program, he can make it through. That makes a big difference. Winston's whole attitude is, "I do want to graduate from college. I know I have a learning disability. I want to go to a school that can help me out." The Sapps did a good job. They really recruited us.

Ajmal was someone like Lari. He was a really late bloomer. At the beginning of the recruiting, his coach, Bob Hurley, Sr., didn't even know if he was good enough to play for us. He said, "I don't know if he'll be good enough to play for you, but I must say this, the kid just keeps getting better and better." I was the first person to call Ajmal on the first day you could recruit and the kid always remembered that. When we went in on a home visit, his mother reminded us of that.

We told him he didn't have to come right in and be a star. The kid was just starting to get good and he didn't want to go anywhere there was a lot of pressure. He wanted to go somewhere he could learn. We told him if he came with us, we would make him better.

That's why we were able to go into St. Raymond's of New York. Gary DeCesare, the coach there, says, "How did he do with my last guy?" Dana Dingle was recruited by Texas A & M and Western Kentucky. No one else in the East recruited him. So when Charlton Clarke was out there, he chose UMass over the Big East.

I think it will help the program at St. Anthony's of Jersey City in the future, too, because Coach Hurley will be able to see growth in Ajmal.

The same in New York. "Everybody doubted how good Dana Dingle would be," Bruiser says. "A lot of guys said to me, 'I can't believe that kid is playing like that.' One coach told me, 'You get these guys that I say, there's no way you can win with them when you recruit them. These guys are hitting shots, doing things that I can't believe.'

"And I say, 'That's one of our big things—individual instruction. Making guys better. Improving their confidence.' "

And it's worked.

CHAPTER 9

FIGHTING MAD

In many ways, Lou Roe mirrored the UMass program. He had to fight for everything he ever got, too.

He grew up on the backwater streets of Atlantic City. He once said half of the guys he hung out with were dead of gunshot wounds. Fortunately for Lou, his mother, Madeline Henderson, who was working days and taking college courses at night, gave him enough to do around the house to keep him out of trouble. Lou was responsible for cooking and caring for his twin sisters. Once in a while, though, he would sneak out of the house and hang out with his friends. That ended after one scrape with the law. Lou's mother had to go to City Hall to get him out.

"I got scared straight," he said.

Lou never had much interest in basketball until he got to junior high, where the coach, Bernard Reynolds, convinced him to try out for the team.

It was the best decision he ever made. Lou was the best player in South Jersey his senior year.

Mike Williams had the same type of talent when he played for Weaver High in North Hartford. He came to us from the Blue

Hills section, just across the street from the public housing projects. He once said half of his friends were in jail. Mike escaped that fate, but not without scars.

Lou started making plans for his future the minute he met Mike Williams at an AAU tournament. Lou and Mike decided they wanted to go to the same school and make headlines. "We had big dreams," Lou said. "We wanted to put UMass on the map."

Five years later, Lou had his jersey number retired in the rafters of the Mullins Center. And Mike had been dismissed from the team after an exciting, but rocky, career. In between, they helped take the program to the next level.

And put us on the map.

If Harper Williams had been our original warrior, Lou Roe seemed like a natural to follow in his footsteps. He was a powerful 6'7", 230-pound forward who did not back away from anyone. Whenever Lou was challenged by either the coaches or an opponent, he was unbelievable. He always had that little chip on his shoulder—because he hadn't been selected for the McDonald's All America game, or he wasn't thought of as one of the best players in the country.

He was always ready for the big game. And he would get himself up emotionally every time. He wanted to prove he was as good as anybody in the country.

He did that against North Carolina.

North Carolina had won the national championship in 1993. They had four starters back, the best recruiting class in the country, and three future lottery picks—centers Eric Montross and Rasheed Wallace and forward Jerry Stackhouse. And they were everybody's pick for pre-season No. 1 when they arrived in New York for the semifinal of the pre-season NIT.

We were their opponent, but we arrived with a little less fanfare. We had beaten Towson State to advance to the Garden, but Carolina was a double-digit favorite and the subject of all the pre-game hype. The media felt our game was nothing more than a preliminary for the championship game between Kansas and North Carolina.

But I had guys who had confidence and took great pride in their games. They felt our team was not being given any respect nationally. None of them, except for Donta, had played in the McDonald's All America game. None of them had been recruited by North Carolina.

"A lot of guys talked about being a big-time program, especially Mike and myself," Lou recalls. "We always talked about playing a Kentucky or a North Carolina on national television and beating them with Mike and me being the center of attraction. But those were only dreams.

"When we arrived at the Garden that night, it was like a dream come true. We didn't care about just making a good showing. Derek, Mike and I all talked about winning the game. I wasn't in awe. I felt it was just another game, and I wanted to make the younger guys—Edgar and Carmelo—feel the same way, too."

I told the players before that game I'd heard every reason why they couldn't win. North Carolina was the defending national champion. The Tar Heels had five pros on their team. They had size, guard play. They had a great coach. Then I made them tell me why they thought we could win.

They began ticking off the reasons.

"We've got better guards."

"We've got Donta Bright—and they don't."

"We've got Marcus."

"We've got Lou Roe."

Roe was unstoppable that night, going for 28 points as we stunned Carolina, 91–86, in overtime. Mike Williams, who had suffered a sprained ankle a couple of days before the game and had been questionable up until game time, made some big shots, too.

It wasn't as easy as it looked, though. Carolina jumped out to a quick 11–0 lead, and Dick Vitale had all this filler material he was ready to use. He was talking about his all-airport team, his all-name team.

I called a time-out at that point. The fans behind our bench must have thought I was crazy. I was hollering, screaming. But I wanted our team to be more afraid of what I would do to them than what North Carolina could do.

I used the Rick Pitino method: a little bit of fear. I wanted each of our players to think, "If I don't dive on the floor for that loose ball, he might punch me when I walk into the locker room." I got that from Rick Pitino. He goes crazy if his kids don't play all out. The enthusiasm and passion on the sidelines are emotions that carry over to the players.

The strategy worked.

Lou went off for 17 points the rest of the half, and we rallied to within one point, 40–39. The second half was tight and Vitale was thinking, "Oh, my goodness." But he still said UMass had no shot. The whole game was about North Carolina.

But we actually benefited from Carolina's incredible wealth of talent. Dean Smith had twelve high school All–Americans, and he had to play everybody. We were playing six or seven guys, because our chemistry was better when we did that. Everybody knew exactly where they were supposed to go. We weren't as good when we were trying to play nine, ten guys; then the other

154 JOHN CALIPARI WITH DICK WEISS

team was going to make us play half-court. When we went out there with three guys who'd never played together, it was harder.

It was a physical game. Five players fouled out, including their two big men, Eric Montross and Kevin Salvadori; our starting guard, Derek Kellogg; and two of our key subs, Donta Bright and Jeff Meyer. Late in regulation, Carolina had a 3-point lead. But with twenty seconds left in regulation, Mike worked himself free and hit a three-pointer to tie the score. The overtime brought more concerns. Just sixteen seconds in, Marcus went down with a knee injury. But Dana Dingle poured in the first 6 points, and then Mike hit another clutch three-pointer with 13.2 seconds to play to send us up 4.

When the game ended, I walked down to shake Dean Smith's hand. I was almost embarrassed. I had my head down; I didn't show any emotion. I would never, never pump my fist or go nuts. We had just beaten a Dean Smith–coached team. The first year I had the UMass job, he saw me at the Final Four. I didn't think he even knew who I was. He said, "Hey, you helped my man, John Kuester." Kuester was the coach at George Washington at the time. They had gone 1–27 that year, and their lone win was against us.

I wanted to celebrate, but I was concerned about Marcus, who was icing down his knee in the trainer's room. At the time, it didn't even register where we were: in New York City, in Madison Square Garden. I just remembered that Marcus got hurt. I kept sending our manager into the locker room to see how he was. I thought it was a torn anterior cruciate ligament. I was sick to my stomach because I thought it could be the end of his career. If it were an ACL, I knew he'd never be the same because what had set him apart was his athleticism. He was a seven-footer who could run and jump.

The doctors reassured me he would be able to do both again.

Marcus missed the next two games. We lost to Kansas in the championship game, but we had made a point. Our win over North Carolina and Boston College's win over Notre Dame in football the week before had given college sports a niche in our pro-minded state.

I couldn't sleep. I walked the streets until five o'clock in the morning. Carolina had five No. 1 draft picks, and here we were, little UMass, hanging around, giving everything we had. I didn't expect the euphoria to last for long, though.

When you travel through Kentucky and North Carolina, all you see in the papers are stories about UK, Duke, and UNC. Back home, we had to fight the pro mentality in our state that filters down to the fans. I realized that as soon as the Celtics or the Bruins played again, we'd be off the front pages.

And we were.

"I think a lot of people thought it was a fluke because we came back and lost to Kansas," Roe says. "They really weren't sure about us. But as the season went on, we picked on a lot of folks, and a lot more people jumped on our bandwagon."

Everyone but Temple, that is.

Temple had dominated the Atlantic 10 in the '80s because they had better players. Temple, West Virginia, and St. Joseph's always had the best players in the league.

We were the new kids on the block. We chased Temple my first four years at UMass. There's no question: we set our sights on beating them. Every year, that was our goal: to beat Temple. At first, our goal was to get John Chaney and Jim Maloney—the two who coached the team—to uncross their legs during the game. You have to understand: for the first two games we played, they never uncrossed their legs. It was like a day off for them, so loved playing UMass. Well, we got them to uncross their legs. We got them to be active.

And we ruffled some feathers.

I guess you could say my problems with Chaney began during my second year, during the 1989–90 season, the day we took Temple to triple overtime in an 83–82 loss at the Cage. We had lost seventeen straight games to them at that point. In this matchup, we'd had a chance to win in regulation, but Jimmy McCoy missed a twelve-footer as time expired. He had the ball at the end of the first overtime with the score tied at 71–71, but we couldn't get off a shot. Later on, in the third overtime, we took an 82–80 lead after Rafer Giles made a pair of free throws. But then, Temple guard Michael Harden—who had been averaging only 7 points a game—made a three-pointer from twenty-one feet to give his team an 83–82 lead.

Jimmy still had a chance to win it for us, but he missed a jumper with five seconds left, and we were forced to foul. Temple forward Mark Strickland went to the line but missed the first part of a one-and-one. We grabbed the rebound and pushed the ball up the floor, finally calling a time-out with a second left. We inbounded the ball to Tony Barbee, but his shot went up after the buzzer.

As exhausting as the game was for our players, it also took its toll on me. Late in the second half, Temple had scored a basket after the shot clock had expired and I went up to protest. The Cage was so loud, I was banging on the horn, just to get the officials' attention. The protest was upheld after the scorekeeper confirmed what I'd seen.

I was in a huddle with my assistants, and they spotted Chaney talking to the officials. He was questioning the clock. NCAA rules state that one coach is not allowed to be with an official unless the other coach is there. A coach cannot huddle with officials.

I walked down to them, and Chaney said, "Get away from here," as though I didn't have a right to be there. But I did. He said something to me and I thought, "I'm not backing down to anybody. Don't act like you're going to bully me. I'm not going to be intimidated by any human being. I'm not saying I'm beating up the world. There are those kinds of guys. But you're not going to come in and scare me. If I have to fight you, I'll fight you. I'm not saying I'll win, but I will get some licks in."

We had words. And then he shoved me. The officials broke it up. Chaney later said he was wrong to have gotten involved, but the game was so close and so intense, he just exploded. "It wouldn't have mattered if it was my mother," he said. "I would have reacted the same way."

It was an omen.

At the A-10 banquet that year, Chaney got up and said, kiddingly, "We got a guy at UMass who coaches his team and runs the clock at the same time."

The Temple rivalry started on our campus, not theirs. Their people could have cared less about UMass—until we started giving them some tough games. Then they said, "This is a big-time game."

The fires that fuel this rivalry run deep. But I hadn't known how deep until that season. Mike Williams had a habit of always sticking a dagger in the Owls' heart. He slid past Rick Brunson and floated up a game winner with three seconds left to give us a 56–55 victory over them at Mullins on February 13, 1994. At crunch time, everybody knew who was getting the ball.

I'm sure that just frazzled John Chaney.

But at the time, I didn't know how much.

I was giving my post-game interview when Chaney stormed into the press room after having heard from one of his assistants that I had berated an official in the hallway.

"Could I say this to you, please," he said. "You've got a good ballclub. But what you did with the official out there is wrong, and I don't want to be a party to that. You understand?"

I told him he hadn't been there, so he didn't know what had happened. But he persisted.

"You got a game given to you earlier by officials right here with GW on three bad calls," he said. "Then you send your kids out there pushing and shoving. You had the best officiating you could ever get here. And for you to ride them, I don't want to be a party to that."

I tried to calm him down, but he would have none of it.

"Shut up," he said.

Then he lunged forward and had to be restrained by Mike Williams. In the end, he threatened to kill me. He also said his players "would knock your kids in the f——ing mouth" when we played them again—on February 24 in Philadelphia.

It was ugly. And the TV cameras were there to capture it all. By eleven o'clock that night, it was national news.

I lost a lot of respect for John Chaney when he did that. I was always the guy who tooted Temple's horn.

I think he was given bad information about what had happened in the hallway.

I'm still surprised at the outburst. We were close to rolling around on the floor. Then who would have looked bad? Me. Because I would have been rolling around on the floor with a sixty-five-year-old man. But you know who I thought about while it was unfolding?

Woody Hayes.

The Hall of Fame football coach at Ohio State had lost his job when he lost his cool and slugged a linebacker named Charley Bauman during a 17–15 loss at the 1978 Gator Bowl.

People think I came away from the incident looking very classy. But the bottom line is, I was involved in a very ugly event. When the skunk sprays, it hits everybody. And I was a part of it. People say, "Well, it didn't hurt you." Being a part of something that hurts another coach doesn't do me any good. I wish it hadn't happened, for Chaney's sake. John Chaney's behavior in this case was on national TV, across the world, and has marked his career with an asterisk. In all honesty, if I had done what he had, I probably would have been fired.

Did he have more chips in the bank than I have?

Yes.

Did he deserve to make a mistake and not be ruined by it?

Yes.

He deserved to make a mistake and recover from it. What he went through afterwards was enough of a punishment.

The scene affected me, too. Both of my daughters cried. "Why would he do that to my daddy?" Usually they see that everybody likes their daddy. We're in the mall, and people say, "Great job. Can I have an autograph?"

I tried to explain to them, "Not everybody likes your daddy." I said that if we have a losing season, I don't want them to be confused if someone comes up to them and says, "Your dad's a bum. He's being overpaid. He can't coach."

So when I say to them, "Not everybody likes your daddy," they say, "Who do you mean? Coach Chaney?" I know it is still in their minds. It's not something that goes away. My wife sees that side of it and says, "Wait a minute, now."

The Atlantic 10 slapped Chaney on the wrist, suspending him for one game against seventh-place St. Bonaventure. He did have to make a public apology to me, the students, the fans of both schools, and anyone else who witnessed "the incident," but our administration thought the league should have done more.

I'll tell you what bothered me the most about that incident. I think everybody knew who was right, who was wrong. Mike Jarvis, the coach at George Washington, went on radio in Boston and said John Chaney had done the right thing; John Chaney was right. I'll be honest. My relationship with Mike hasn't been the same since then because I started thinking, "Oh, so the jealousy has kicked in." I don't know why Mike said it, and I've never asked him about it.

The second thing that happened was that Joe Burris of *The Boston Globe* went down to Philly and did a puff piece on the other side of John Chaney. I didn't speak to Joe for a year after that. And you know why? He has a right to do that, but if the same thing happened to me, would the Philadelphia writers come up and do a story on me, talking about my feelings, or would they absolutely whack me, day after day after day, saying I should be fired, I shouldn't be in coaching, and that I teach these kids the wrong things?

Joe is a good guy. He just got caught in the middle. But why go down there, trying to get people to understand why John Chaney went off and attempting to humanize him? They saw Chaney on TV. I didn't see anyone from that paper coming up and doing a piece on what my family had to go through.

We had to go back to Philly the next weekend for a game with St. Joseph's. My two young daughters said to me, "Are you going to be killed in Philly?" I tried to explain that Chaney had been just talking.

When we landed, a flight attendant offered to sneak me off the plane when she learned there was a group of Philadelphia reporters waiting for me. I told her, "I'm not Tonya Harding . . .

I'm Nancy Kerrigan. I haven't done anything." Still, the media were painting me as the bad guy. One reporter even wrote that I'd instigated the problem. But across the country, other than in Philly, the media had seen the tape on ESPN and said, "What is going on?"

Well, the next day, I did my worst job of coaching all year, and we lost to St. Joe's. It was the only time since I'd been at UMass that we were a prohibitive favorite and lost. I don't want to take anything away from St. Joe's; they played well. But I took the blame and told our guys, "This will be the last time I think about John Chaney and what he did to me, Temple basketball, and all these Philly writers. I'm going to coach you, and I apologize."

Then we moved on.

There had been some concern on the part of Bob Marcum and Michael Hooker about our ESPN game at McGonigle Hall, Temple's tiny campus arena, the next week. We held discussions about game security, and they threatened to pull our team off the floor at the first sign of trouble.

I had a fifteen-minute conversation with Chaney, too. He told me this was an issue about him, not me, and that he felt bad. He did not want my team to feel threatened in any way. On February 24, a Thursday, we played Temple at McGonigle Hall. Mike Williams banked home a twenty-eight-foot shot at the buzzer—and we won, 51–50.

It was the first time we had ever won at McGonigle Hall, and it clinched the regular season title for us. So there was justice.

Ironically, I had always been the guy who said we were following Temple's lead, promoting Temple's program. We used to say we wanted to model our program after theirs. But there were still tensions.

In the fall of 1994, the American Diabetes Foundation held a roast for me at the Meadowlands and I invited Chaney, hoping we could smooth things over.

My wife was upset. She didn't care about P.R. She wasn't interested in showing the public that things were okay. She asked me, "Why are you letting him off the hook?" She didn't believe that I should; to this day, she doesn't believe I should have. After all, this guy attacked her husband.

"Because it's the right thing to do," I told her. "Look, if I let everybody know this is okay by me and I forgive him, then what problems could anyone else have?"

Some people were telling Chaney, "Don't do it." But he was smart enough to know it was time to move on. Jim Maloney told him to do it: "Come on, come on, come on. You had the upper hand. Now he has the upper hand. Go do this." It was right because it was for the American Diabetes Association. John Chaney's mother had died of diabetes, so this was a great cause.

When Chaney showed up that night, he had a piece of tape over his mouth.

It was a way to show everybody I'm fine with him. And he's fine with me. I'm not looking to punch him in the face or for him to punch me in the face. Temple and UMass are two competitive basketball teams, and this is a rivalry that ranks up there with any in the country. And now UMass has the upper hand.

We chased Temple—and went by them. We were the only team to beat them three times in a season in the history of their school. And we've done it twice. In the spring of 1996, we produced a T-shirt that said, "One for the Thumb" to commemorate our fifth A-10 tournament title.

We started zeroing in on Duke about three, four years ago. The Blue Devils went to the Final Four seven times in nine years.

If UMass does that, the next goal is to catch UCLA, with their eleven national titles. Obviously, that's unrealistic. But, then, everything we've accomplished here has been unrealistic.

The major benefit of playing against a John Chaney–Jim Maloney–coached team was that they made my staff and me better because we were coaching against their matchup zone. Chaney and Maloney coached the best matchup zone in the country, and we understood how to break it. It may not happen every time, but the team has a good understanding of what works against it.

After that, any time we played a zone, my team was comfortable. Syracuse played us man-to-man when we played them in Hawaii this year. No one made the Orangemen come out of the zone this year except us. They came out of the zone with eighteen minutes left to play against us and went man-to-man.

Ironically, I think I extended John Chaney's career, just because we played in the same league. It gave him something to play for. Coaching was no longer just coming out, crossing your legs, and the game's over. Now he was in second place.

When we defeated Temple 69–61 to win the 1993 Atlantic 10 title at Mullins, Chaney made his team sit and watch us receive our championship awards, just so they knew what it meant to be champions.

Some of our players needed to learn that lesson, too.

Mike Williams was as talented as anyone I had ever coached, including Lou Roe and Marcus Camby. He didn't have Marcus's ability because he didn't have Marcus's size. But his skill level and his potential were tremendous. He made big shots his entire career, including six game winners. In a lot of those games, he hadn't played well, which is why the games were close to begin with. He would shoot two for twelve, one for eleven. But he just had a way about him. He knew he could win the game, and he liked to be in that situation.

But one of the most dramatic games—I think of it as his comeback after his academic suspension—occurred in January 1995 when he made a three-pointer with 16.5 seconds in overtime as we rallied from an 18-point deficit in regulation to defeat West Virginia, 97–94, before a near-record crowd at Morgantown.

We had been struggling to hold on to our No. 1 ranking, and I thought this game might be difficult, especially since Derek Kellogg was out with a groin pull.

I didn't know how difficult.

When the Mountaineer mascot shot off his musket, Dana Dingle made a point of saying it felt like he was back in his old neighborhood in the Bronx. He was kidding, but I knew how he felt.

I thought we should run for cover after we fell behind 80–62 with 4:48 left in regulation. During a time-out, I said, "Hey, guys, why don't we try to win this and have fun? Let's do some crazy stuff and try to win this."

This was one time we threw out the playbook and just played with reckless abandon. Four minutes to go and their students were surrounding the court. Every UMass player—it wasn't just one guy—made a big play. That was the defining moment of what "Refuse to Lose" is all about: if you lose the game, fine, but you go down swinging.

We outscored West Virginia, 24–6, to force overtime. But it still took some last-second heroics. We were down 86–82 with nine seconds left in regulation when Cyrus Jones fouled Mike on a 3-point attempt. Mike made his first two free throws, then missed the third. But we regained possession. He tried to win it with three, but the shot didn't come close. Fortunately, Dana was there to tip it in just before the buzzer.

The one thing I liked about that game was the fact that no one ever pointed fingers when we were down. And we kept playing like a team.

Sadly, Mike didn't always buy into the philosophy and it eventually cost him a spot on the team. When he was a sophomore, we were coming off a frustrating game against Holy Cross and he suggested that he, not Lou, should be the focal point of the offense, and then indicated he might transfer. He later apologized.

But worse times were coming. The beginning of the end for Mike Williams occurred when we went on a road trip to Southwest Louisiana in early February 1995. We defeated them in the afternoon. That night, we watched LSU play Alabama on TV because I thought Alabama—with Antonio McDyess— was the type of team we might have to play in the NCAA Tournament.

When the game ended, I told our staff I thought we had a chance to win the national championship. We called a team meeting in my suite, and I told the players they had a chance to do something special; but they would have to dedicate themselves to a common goal and give 100 percent for the next six weeks.

Lou Roe and Derek Kellogg, our co-captains, got up to speak, and they got everyone to pledge not to party until after the tournament.

No sooner had the meeting broken up than Mike Williams went outside and got into a waiting car. An hour later, he came back and got Andre Burks, our freshman guard. The two got in at five-thirty the next morning.

The rest of the team was mad. I had no choice but to suspend them both.

Then, Mike went AWOL for a couple of days. He went back to Hartford. That was it. I told him he was off the team. I told him he could come back and finish his education and that we would pay for it. I told him I would try to get him a look from pro scouts and an invitation to the Portsmouth Invitational, a post-season showcase for college seniors. But I told him we would go on without him.

The players agreed with me.

Mike Williams could be the funniest, most charming person I've ever met. But there was another side of his personality that didn't care about anybody else. I had worked with him for three and a half years. When I dropped him from the team, it was the toughest decision I'd ever had to make because I didn't want to make a decision that would hurt a kid's future. Here was a twenty-one-year-old kid with twin sons. His mother pleaded with me to keep him on the team. But this wasn't a personal thing. It was about, "You're not doing the right thing. You've had plenty of time to change and you refused to do it."

So we did it.

I make decisions, but it takes me a while. People asked me why I waited so long to throw Mike Williams off the team. Because it's the way I am. I give a player the benefit of the doubt as long as I can. Always. Until . . .

Until I say, "That's it." But when I say that's it, then that's it.

And the players knew that. They knew I'm a softie at heart. They knew that freshmen always had the benefit of the doubt, that they'd have screwed up three or four times before I came down on them. I'm not saying I let them get away with things. They were disciplined, but not in a harsh way, or in a way that anyone outside our basketball family knew. I gave them time to grow.

I looked at the older players and said, "Don't be upset. You were given the same benefit of the doubt that these freshmen are getting now. Correct?"

"Yeah."

Sometimes somebody said, "Well . . ."

"Wait a minute now. Don't you remember your freshman year?"

"Enough said. You're right."

I have always leaned toward the player—not myself, not the school, the player. I wasn't worried about making a point so that the school benefited.

What bothered me more than anything else is if a kid got into trouble and the school immediately attacked the kid and said, "That's it. You're out. You're off the team." Why? Because the administration wanted to make a point. Don't make a point with an eighteen- or nineteen-year-old kid and try to wreck his life so you or the institution looks better. The school is not going to be hurt immensely by one person. We've all made mistakes. But I still think schools sometimes act quickly because of politics. They act quickly because they want to make a point at the expense of a young kid. I've never done that. I didn't do it with Mike Williams. I didn't do it with any other player that I've disciplined here.

I look at it this way: there is a cliff. A player and I walk toward it—together. But I stop. I'll go as far as I can go. And he keeps walking right to the edge. And when he takes one more step, it's a long drop. But, on the other hand, he'd walked a lot of steps before he got to that cliff.

It's like former NBA coach and pro basketball TV commentator Hubie Brown says, "Don't say hello when it's time to say good-bye."

And that's what Mike Williams did. The bottom line is, I also had to think about our program and the other players. If they hadn't agreed with me, I couldn't have done it. I've never made a decision without consulting my team.

People asked me if I should have gotten rid of Mike earlier because then Edgar and Carmelo would have had a chance to play with Derek—and we would have had an unbelievable back-court. My answer: "No. I wanted to give Mike every opportunity to turn it around, which I did."

In the end, did it hurt our chances to get to the Final Four? We won another Atlantic 10 title and we advanced all the way to the Elite Eight before we lost to Oklahoma State, 76–63, in the regional finals. We would have gone to the Final Four if Edgar Padilla hadn't gotten hurt in our regional semifinal game against Tulsa.

And our rotation was all screwed up. I tried to play Donta Bright at guard some, but he didn't play very well because he had never played the position before. Lou Roe didn't play well, either. Nor did Marcus Camby play well; he got thrown around by Bryant "Big Country" Reeves. Neither did Dana Dingle; if you remember, he missed three layups.

So, all of a sudden, Carmelo and Derek were trying to carry our team, and we weren't good enough for them to do that. For us to win, we had to play good basketball—but we weren't. And we still were up by 5 on Oklahoma State at the half.

I walked into the locker room and said, "We are going to Seattle. We're not going to shoot 29 percent in the second half."

I was wrong. We shot 27 percent, and the next thing I knew we were down by 14. We just caved in because we had never been there before. We had a lot of guys on that team whose minds were elsewhere. They were thinking about where they were going to be in another year and not thinking about the Final Four. The minute you do that, you're gone.

I felt the 1994–95 season was a good one. I knew 1995–96 would be better.

CHAPTER 10

MAKING THE GRADE: ACADEMICS AT UMASS

While I was at UMass, I had my own experience with "global" warfare.

The Boston Globe set off a firestorm there in the fall of 1994 when the paper printed a series of articles on the academic standards of our basketball program. They were written by Dan Golden—an investigative news reporter, not a sportswriter—who claimed four of our players were on academic probation with grade point averages below 2.0 from the spring 1994 semester. The *Globe* reported three other members of the team were in danger of joining them. Golden had based his story on illegally obtained student records.

I was livid about this invasion of our athletes' privacy. It is against federal law to make public college transcripts and to identify the students whose records were published. When the paper chose to trample on the Buckley Amendment, colloquially known as the Student Privacy Act, it created the perception that black kids were dumb—that those kids whose grades were published were dumb. And that was unfair.

I had known it was coming, but it still hit like a bombshell. And it left scars that may never heal.

Here's the way I feel about the media.

We both have jobs to do and I try to be accessible. But the moment I see a guy who's not being fair or who has an ax to grind, I won't spend time with him. I don't give him any access unless it's in a general forum.

Will McDonough, who writes a column for *The Boston Globe* and works for NBC, called and suggested I meet with Dan Golden. I didn't want to talk to him because I'd heard he was going to do a hatchet job on us and that the *Globe* editors had put him up to it. I'd gotten that from sources at the paper. Some people there had said, "John, be careful because this guy is coming after you."

But Will McDonough is a guy I really trust and I really like. His son Sean, who works for ESPN, and I are good friends. If Will gave me advice, I would take it under consideration because he's very connected and streetwise.

When Golden came into my office, the first thing I said to him was, "Look, if you have the story written already, why don't you leave?" The second thing I told him was he had stolen information that wasn't accurate.

The paper knew that. We had told them before they printed it. They decided to print it anyway. The paper may argue this fact, but Bill Strickland, the UMass assistant AD for media relations, had been sitting right next to me at the time and heard what I'd said.

I let Golden go to the training meal and meet with the kids. I told him he could go to classes with them if he wanted. I opened up to him. I said to him, "Do what you want because what you think is at odds with the way our program is."

I also gave him a list of our twenty-two players, past and present. At that point, 75 percent of the kids I'd recruited had graduated, and a couple who hadn't graduated were back in school working on their degrees. For the most part, these were black kids who had graduated. We're not talking about kids from suburbia who got degrees. We're talking about kids who came in as average students, and who were doing well.

All of our players without degrees have good jobs. They're either playing professionally or are in jobs in their chosen fields. We've taught them life skills. We've worked with them. The program could have a 100 percent graduation rate in three to four years.

That's better than at many schools. Heck, at Duke, Mike Krzyzewski decided not to hang some of their championship banners because a couple of kids on those teams haven't graduated yet.

I didn't want Golden to drill our academic support staff, so I said, "Well, maybe I slacked off." At that, he sat up in his chair and started writing. "I want you to know, I've done my job," I told him. But he had the quote he needed: "I slacked off." Within two days, the story was written.

The campus was outraged when the story came out. Some administrators came to me, wanting me to apologize.

I said, "I will resign before I apologize."

The school didn't know how to handle my adversity—they had never been this big. They wanted to print a two-page rebuttal in the *Globe*.

"No. You have a one-sentence statement because it wasn't true."

The kids were the ones who were really upset by it.

Donta Bright came into my office and cried. Tears. He was sitting in a corner when I came in, his fists balled up in his eyes like a little baby.

"Why did they do this to me? It took me a year to get by being called 'Not-so-Bright' because I had to sit out. I did all the right things. I've done my work. Why have they done this to me?"

What could I say? What could anyone say?

Marcus Camby was hurt, too. He said the paper was trying to make him out to be stupid.

Lou Roe came to me and said, "Coach, I'm going to graduate. I had a 2.7 GPA before the term started. They've made me look like a dummy."

I said, "You know, Lou, you're right." They could have printed that Lou had done well all along and had had a bad term. But they chose not to.

They really stuck it to Dana Dingle, who was a great student and graduated on time without having to attend summer school. The paper claimed he had a 1.5 GPA. That was way off base. As I said, we told them they had misinformation on some of our players and they went and printed it anyway. Gary DeCesare, Dana's high school coach at St. Raymond's in the Bronx, was so mad, he went on WFAN to dispute the allegations.

The *Springfield Union News* and *The Hartford Courant* were quick to run with the story, too. *Sports Illustrated* named our program "UMess" in their "Scoreboard" column.

I was livid about the backlash that followed.

When we played Kansas in the Wooden Classic, in the second game of the season, the Jayhawks had two honor roll students in their backcourt. After they beat us, a columnist from the *Los Angeles Times* wrote a piece called "Smart Guys, 81—Team Thick as a Brick, 75."

Nice, huh?

And I still remember the students at St. Bonaventure chanting "You can't read" at our team when we played at Olean.

When someone questions my integrity—someone who doesn't

know me, who hasn't talked to my family, or talked to the people who really know me—it bothers me. Sure it does.

Treat me like that and I'm not going to be nice to your newspaper. Or invite your writer into my home. The day the 1995 NCAA championship pairings were announced, we had a party for the media at my home and we barred a *Globe* reporter. That set off some sparks.

The editor talked to me and said, "Do you understand we have a circulation of 500,000 on weekdays and 800,000 on weekends?"

"Do you understand, I don't give a shit?"

I think anytime you experience adversity, your actions define who you are. And our players' actions defined them. They didn't make vicious statements in the press. They hired a lawyer, and they sued the school in December of 1995 because of the unauthorized release of confidential information.

I don't blame them for that. The university is the protector of the records. If a parent of a UMass student asks for his or her child's grades, the parent can't get them unless the student releases them. Our players' records were released without the students' consents. UMass's theory is that Golden got copies of preliminary grade forms from tutors, not university transcripts, and that whoever did it had access to a lot of areas, including the registrar's office and several academic departments.

Eventually, the case against the school was settled out of court. The players are now regrouping to sue the *Globe*.

I was talking to the editor of the *Springfield Union News* before I took the Nets job and he told me he hoped I wouldn't hold a grudge against them because of what had happened. But it was out of my hands. These kids were damaged and I hope a jury sees that. I hope the jurors take a long look at the stories that were written, at the slant of the articles, and then say, "How could you do this to these kids?"

The real reason I hadn't lost my mind over this is that I felt our record spoke for itself. I have no control over how anyone in the media wants to perceive the program, but the bottom line is that numbers don't lie. During my time at UMass, our players' GPA was 2.5.

We stand by our record. Have some of our kids had bad semesters over the last six years? Yeah. It's usually happened after an NCAA tournament run.

In fact, we made academics a top priority during my tenure.

When I was putting together my staff, I needed to fill certain positions. When I brought Dave Glover in as a graduate assistant to run our academic program and coach our post players, it was probably my biggest hire. I first met Dave when he was a camper at Five-Star and I was a counselor. Then we worked together in the summers for seven or eight years. Dave went on to become a high school teacher and coach in Texas and Connecticut. He had a master's degree in education, so it seemed like a good fit. He stayed in our program three years; then he went to Michigan and worked with the football team.

He returned to UMass as assistant to the athletic director/academic advisor—just as the *Globe* stories hit.

"Did it hurt me personally?" Glover asks. "No. But it pissed me off. It really did. What hurt me was how badly it hurt the kids.

"I can remember one kid sitting here and talking about the situation as if it really didn't matter. And then a big tear rolled out of his eye, and he said, 'People think I'm stupid now. They don't understand the pressure I'm under.'

"I said, 'Look, the best way to put this whole thing behind you is to finish school. Get mad. You don't have to take that. You don't.'

"The other part that was hard for me was there were so many misrepresentations. The newspaper people covering the story and a number of people involved in it lied. I understand that people get caught up in digging out a story. I understand that there was some sensationalism there. It wasn't only that they didn't tell the whole story—which they didn't—but they also used a lot of information that was not factual. They used a lot of hearsay stuff, and there were some things they put in there they knew were not true.

"What bothered me most about it was that the story itself could have been told differently. It could have been brought to light by saying, 'Hey, that team's not doing as well academically as they should be.' And the point could have been made without hurting the kids. It wasn't necessary to name names. In retrospect, it was probably pretty stupid because what it did was it rallied everyone around those individuals. If you want to hurt the program or hurt the university, the way to do it would have been to imply that there's some kind of institutional control problem, not by picking on individuals.

"So, in a way, as unfortunate and as ugly an incident as it was, it made my job easier because I had kids who were definitely challenged, who were motivated, and who were still stinging from a slap in the face. They came to me and said, 'Whatever I have to do, I'll do.'

"We heard the question, 'What kind of classes were they really taking?' The media had this notion that there was something wrong with the courses. Well, the kids were taking the same classes that everyone else at the university was taking. Every single credit taken counted toward their major. There is no basketweaving.

"The course 'Sports and Society' was one of the classes the papers chose to pick at. 'What the heck kind of class can that be?' they asked. That's a very difficult class here. A lot of kids struggle in it. The professor is very tough. The program is one of the top in the country in sports management. God bless the media. They took a twist on it, and it's very easy to present something like that in a negative light.

"Then came the implications that the kids were being given grades. The media said the university was sympathetic and gave them grades, or professors felt bad, so they gave them grades. Not so. The kids did the work. They were here night and day. They did what they had to do.

"It was an interesting year. I couldn't even sleep at night, I was so worried. My worry was for the kids. And they all came through with aces."

Dave has always low-keyed his role there. But his philosophy is solid. "The credit should be given to the kids. Oftentimes, there's this philosophy people take when it comes to academic support and student athletes. When the kids screw up, it's because they're bad kids and it's up to them. When the kids do well, an adult stands up and says, 'We do a great job with our kids.'

"I think it should be the reverse. When the kids are doing poorly, I think the adults should stand up and say, 'We have a flaw in our system. Our support system is failing the kids somewhere.'

"If a kid's a bad kid, he doesn't belong in the program. If there's a problem, there's a problem in the system. Who knows what it is? Maybe the coaches don't support academics. Maybe the university doesn't support their efforts. But to blame the kids is too simplistic. If that's what it is, then you'd better throw all the kids out and get new ones.

"It doesn't work that way.

"We had nine out of thirteen kids make the honor roll last year. Pretty good percentage. A lot of people want to say, 'Gee, Dave, you did a helluva job.' My response to that is, 'No. The kids did a helluva job.'

"I didn't go to school for them.

"There are a lot of people who judge the kids based on the stereotypes that the media has developed for them. For every one illiterate football player or basketball player who makes headlines in the NFL or NBA, there are 10,000 student athletes who graduate on time.

"People don't understand. Student athletes graduate at a higher rate than the regular student population. They graduate in less time and with higher honors. The stereotype is that there's something wrong with athletics because one kid cuts class every day, or is a bum, is a pain in the neck, etc., and doesn't take education seriously.

"Keeping student athletes on course to graduate is the model everyone else should follow. We really support the kids. It's too bad that all student athletes on every campus don't have a learning center like this one.

"The first thing I did when I returned to UMass was to tear apart all this structure and replace it with support. Simply to say we have study table is a useless statement within itself. That's structure. It's boot camp—you get in there, you open your book, you read. It's scheduled for the coaches' convenience. It's easy to have a study table for two hours a day. I could do that blindfolded.

"I had study table for fourteen hours a day, and kids came and went as they chose. When they chose. In between classes. We had one simple rule—you worked until your work was done. There was a certain measure of performance that is acceptable.

"People talked about what's acceptable and what's not acceptable. If a C was acceptable, then we had to raise a student's expectations. Just passing was not acceptable. And a D sucked. If one of our students got a D, he had to improve his grades on his own time—and tasks at study table increased. If a player was a 3.3 sophomore, confident in his skills, was he at study table? No. Absolutely not.

"The support mechanisms exist. A student can get access to them as he chooses. But to force somebody into an environment is wrong.

"Here's the dilemma: people have this idea that student athletes don't do any real work, and sometimes they say, 'How in the hell did that kid get a 3.0 average?'

" 'Why couldn't he?'

" 'Well, you know, he's from the ghetto. He's a poor kid. He's seven feet tall.'

"Then they imply that something is wrong with these kids, or that they couldn't get these grades because they're traveling. They really couldn't be doing that well.

"Of course, they can.

"What people didn't see was how hard the kids worked. My response to that was, 'If you wanted to see how they did so well, go there at ten at night when this place was jammed and kids were all working on their papers, studying for their exams, or meeting with their tutors. Inus Norville put in twenty hours a week studying. It's just that nobody saw it, didn't know where it was happening.'

"The one thing people said was, 'Well, the teacher must have been cutting them some slack,' i.e., giving them a grade. I don't know of a faculty member who would say, 'Here, this is free. Free grade. Don't do anything. Don't work.'

"That doesn't happen.

"Life would be a lot easier if it did.

"The second thing I heard was, 'Did they really do their own work?'

"My response is, 'Boy, that's a real insult to the faculty. Don't you think the professor would know whether that's the kid's work?'

"If you can't work in this system, then you're a bum. If you're a bum, then you deserve to flunk out.

"I had one simple rule of advising: you took whatever class you wanted, but it had to count toward your degree. And it was written in stone: you could not take something that didn't count toward your degree. I wouldn't approve it. Other than that, they did whatever they pleased.

"What we did—and I think it was successful—was a three-part program.

"Number 1: You respected the kids as individuals first. Not everyone is the same. Academic support should be tailored to how people learn.

"Number 2: We gave all the students choices. We allowed the individuals to choose what to study, when to study, and how to approach their learning—so long as they were productive.

"Number 3: We hired good people to work with our kids. I'm a big believer in having a staff of well-trained people who serve as a good resource for the kids and assist them—with the kids doing the work for themselves.

"When you say we graduated 75 percent, I think Coach Cal would say we failed 25 percent somewhere. The graduation rate for the student body is significantly less. The average graduation rate for schools around the country, according to a report put out by American College Testing, is only 53.3 percent.

"I told our players, 'As long as you view it as graduate or not graduate, are you doing something productive right now? For example, did you leave school to play basketball or make a lot of money, knowing you can come back and finish up your degree? Did you have a terrific job opportunity, and when you have a chance, you'll come back and grab that one class you didn't get?'

"That's one thing. Did a kid go four years and still end up forty credits short and took crap classes the entire time he was here? That's a different issue. It didn't happen at UMass on my watch."

I guess the media scrutiny was the price we paid for success. According to an NCAA study, before we got to UMass, the school hadn't graduated a basketball player from 1982 through 1985. But it didn't matter because the school wasn't winning any games. When they weren't winning and weren't graduating anybody, nothing was written about the program. Nobody in the media cared then.

Suddenly, they were all concerned. Why?

"When people from the outside looked at this program, the only way they could envision it happening was by cheating," Tony Barbee, one of the earliest UMass recruits, said. "That's the farthest thing from the truth. You can build a program like this with integrity, from the ground floor up, if you have people who want to be successful. When I was recruited, I was told, 'If you want to come here, you're going to class, you're getting good grades or you're not going to play.' At UMass, they recruit kids who want to get a degree.

"It's not just basketball.

"They're not going to recruit criminals. They recruit nice kids from nice family backgrounds who want to achieve. You have to take a chance on people because if you don't gamble, you never win."

The graduation rate at UMass for students who have completed four years is 44.7 percent. It is 62.1 percent for those students who have completed five years.

I had a winning hand with the 1995–96 players.

Both Edgar Padilla and Carmelo Travieso come from very proud families. Their parents did not want to take anything from anyone. They wanted to earn their way. They knew their sons needed an education to make it. For them, this is really special. It's the American Dream. I heard somebody say, "Well, they're from another country." Guess what? We all are, except for the Native Americans.

I go back to Philadelphia and see Tyrone Weeks's mom. She has a smile from ear to ear because her son is in college. Her son is going to get a degree. And her son is the first family member to break the cycle and get out. Nothing makes me prouder.

Marcus Camby has an opportunity to be the first college graduate in his family. He can come back anytime and get his degree. Donta Bright could become the first college graduate in his.

A good majority of our kids—though not every one of them—were the first college graduates in their families.

In spite of all the things that were written in that *Globe* story, we never had a kid ineligible while I was the coach at Massachusetts. We never had a kid flunk out of school. Sure, we had kids on probation. Each year, we might have had one, but I don't think there were any this past year. And that's a normal student. If you're dealing with thirteen to fifteen kids, and you don't think one of those kids might have some academic problems, then you're kidding yourself.

On our basketball team, we had kids with 1,400 on the College Boards; we had kids with under 700 on the College Boards. And we had kids in between. We had 3.8 students, and we had 2.2 students. We had a wide range of kids—from Puerto Rico, from the Dominican Republic, black kids, white kids. Our team mirrors the campus. The players fit in, they feel good about who they are, and they've done well.

Most of our kids didn't come from money. A lot came from tough economic backgrounds. For them, earning a 2.0 GPA in their core subjects might be like a suburban kid coming here with a 4.0 cume.

That's one of the things I've always loved about UMass. The school is dedicated to educating the citizens of the Commonwealth, not shutting them out. This school is about giving everyone a chance—especially me. The administration knew I wouldn't really have my own program until I went through a full cycle: a four-year recruiting class, top to bottom.

Since my second year here, I was able to sit down with our admissions people and go over our recruits on a case-by-case basis. In my eight years at UMass we took only four players who didn't meet minimal academic standards. That's one every other year. Some people would have you believe we admitted twenty.

When the first student came in who didn't have the test score, the admissions people asked me what I thought.

I said, "Judge me by him. If he does fine, then maybe we would think about other kids."

Kennard Robinson helped us open the door. Kennard was a 6'8" kid from New York whom we had seen in summer camps.

He played for Bobby McKillop—who is now the coach at Davidson. Kennard was the first Prop. 48 recruited by UMass in any sport. Whatever he lacked academically, he made up for as a person. He'd attended Long Island Lutheran, a strong academic high school, and we felt he would do well.

He did.

Kennard graduated in four years. He worked his tail off; he made the dean's list. I had professors writing me notes, saying, "If this kid is a Prop. 48, I do not believe in Prop. 48." Bill Cosby sent him a great letter after he read a story about how Kennard was doing academically. I told Kennard that he had done as much as anybody for the program by becoming an academic success story.

When the other guys saw Kennard's success in the classroom, they started to feed off it, and the program became a little bit competitive academically. They would tease one another, "How could you get a C on that test?"

That's when we turned the corner. I'd seen it before. When the kids actually take a little bit of pride in what they're accomplishing, then the message has been sent, and the program should start to be successful on its own.

If I had been coaching at a school where the median Board score was 1,300, I probably couldn't have done it. But the average UMass applicant scores slightly under 1,000, so a kid with 750 can cut it if he comes from a high school background. I have a proposal for college presidents: whatever the median Board score for a specific school is, admit athletes who've gotten 250 points below that number.

If a coach is at a school where the average SAT is 1,300, prospective student athletes have to score at least 1,050. The main reason is that you care about the kids and know they can't get by if they score too far beneath your median. If your average

SAT score is 1,000, you can bring them in at 750. That way, kids don't go somewhere where they can't survive.

But I know the presidents will never go for that. The main reason? These rules are trying to create parity at academic institutions whose mission is to educate the highly motivated and the financially secure—this country's elite. And there are many fine private institutions for them.

Many students believe that being with people similar to themselves prepares them for life. But I don't believe that.

If a student wants to be with people from all different races, economic backgrounds, religions, then he or she should go to UMass. It is about society there. It is not a campus where everybody is one race, one religion, and where the parents are all doctors and lawyers.

And I believe diversity is important for the Commonwealth. The private schools drive the state too much. Higher education in Massachusetts is for everybody. It's not about exclusion. It's about inclusion. We've got to support it because this gives every person in Massachusetts a chance to get an education. A large portion of the students on the UMass campus are probably the first college-educated people in their families. This is their opportunity to go to college, to get a great education at a reasonable price on a campus that has real diversity, and to make a success of themselves.

I believe in public education so much, I want to tell everybody. I guess that's why I was the first UMass employee to address both houses of the state legislature. The first time was in 1992. Since then, I've done it three times. And the bottom line is this: as public education goes, so goes the Commonwealth. Public institutions can touch the lives of students who may not have the financial means to attend some other schools.

And the financial support the legislature gives these schools is returned to the Commonwealth in the form of educated citizens.

I also told them that there's only one academic institution in which the state has instant name-recognition.

UMass.

And it's not just for basketball.

It's for whatever the school does.

Because it's not Northeastern. It's not Boston College. It's not Boston University. It's the University of Massachusetts.

The school has become better known in the business world as well. The increased success we had in the classroom has made our players much more attractive to employers. We've been able to get on the phone and get kids jobs. I called people and said, "This is what the kid wants to do. This is what he's doing. What can we do for him? Where can we place him?"

Jeff Meyer, who graduated in 1994, isn't playing basketball. But that's okay. He's working for Spalding. The CEO is a UMass graduate. Derek Kellogg isn't playing, either; he's working at the state house.

In 1996, four of the five seniors—Dana, Giddel, Rigo Nuñez, and Teddy Cottrell—graduated. Eighty percent is about right. Donta is a semester short. Donta and Dana still want to play. Ted Cottrell? We'll figure out what he wants to do. Rigo Nuñez will have an opportunity to work at Bertucci's, the local Italian restaurant, or in the banking industry in Boston. The point is, they'll all be set up. It was important the kids knew if they came with us, that when they were done, they'd have opportunities.

Julius Erving understands that. So does Bill Cosby. We're lucky. They've both helped us with summer jobs for our kids.

Julius is part-owner of the Coca-Cola bottling plant in Philly. He's always been into helping kids and preparing them for life after basketball. He is an unbelievable role model. Forget about what he was as a player. He comes to games. Instead of asking Julius for money, we asked him to rub shoulders with the players so they can see how a successful person acts. He just oozes class.

You'd better understand; he's one of the two best players ever to play the game. He and Michael. I was starstruck when I first met Julius. I was stumbling over my words at his Hall of Fame induction.

But he's a regular guy.

So is the Cos.

I have an autographed picture of Bill Cosby that I proudly displayed in my office. He went to Temple as an undergraduate, but he received his master's degree in education from UMass and has a house in South Deerfield, near Amherst.

He called me when we went to the Sweet 16 in 1992 and we've kept in touch. He came in and talked to our team during halftime of the St. Bonaventure game at the Atlantic 10 tournament in 1996 and told them they belonged in the Final Four.

He's one of the most exceptional individuals I've ever met in my life. He is as funny in private as he is in public. When he came in and talked to my team, he cracked everybody up with his routines. But it's just Bill Cosby being Bill Cosby. If you want to strike a chord with my man, talk to him about education. If he'd ever thought I was using these kids and not teaching them life skills, he wouldn't speak to me. His feeling is, you don't exploit kids, especially black kids. You teach them; you help them grow. You put them in situations where they're going to have success. His question to me was, 'How are they doing in school?' Why? He's concerned about building human beings.

I learned early you don't ask somebody for a dollar when they can give you a million. You don't even ask them for $10,000. I told Bill people had asked me to talk to him about donating money to the school.

"I would never do that," I told him, "but I have a player, Anton Brown, who is graduating. Is there any way you can help Anton? My asking you this is like my asking you for a $1 million because you'd be doing something for the future of one of my players."

When Anton graduated, Cosby hired him as his personal secretary. And Anton, who is now working in the NBA league office in New York City, worked toward his advanced degree because Bill Cosby helped him.

"After I graduated, I tried out for the CBA team in Hartford, and I was one of the final cuts," Anton says. "I went to New York—I had some relatives there. I wanted to get into the workforce. I went through the classifieds, and then I decided to use my networking contacts.

"So I gave Bill Cosby a call.

"I knew him from when he had talked to our team at the A-10 tournament. I left a message for him with his assistant.

"A couple of days later, I got a call back. My uncle said, 'Bill Cosby's calling for you.'

" 'Get out of here.'

"But it was, and he asked me to come down. I spent the next two years as one of his assistants before I went with the NBA. I'll never forget him for that."

There are other UMass success stories.

The class of 1992 was the first while I was there to complete four years. Since that time, ten of thirteen players accountable to NCAA standards have graduated, a rate of 75 percent. Will

Herndon, who transferred from Richmond, is not included in the NCAA numbers. If you want to paint the picture in the worst possible light and include all the seniors who have ever played for us, including Herndon and the three players who were on academic probation when we arrived in 1988, sixteen of twenty-five players have graduated and three others have to complete just two or three classes to earn their degrees.* This includes John Tate, who is expected to finish in December 1996. Since 1990, the first year our program had seniors on the roster who had played a full season, sixteen of twenty-one—excluding Herndon—have graduated.

To prove my point, *USA Today* recently ran a list of teams that finished in the Top 25 and where they would have finished if they were ranked by graduation rate. UMass finished third, behind North Carolina and Villanova.

	Degree	Year	Present Position
1990			
Mike Byrnes	Sports Management	1990	Graduate student
Carey Herer	Sports Management	1990	Sales manager, Starter Co.
Sean Nelen	English	1990	Liaison for South Korean government in New York City
Chris Bailey	Graphic Arts (3 courses short)	—	Buyer, Nordstrom
1991			
Matt Anderson	Economics	1991	Graduate student, UMass
Rafer Giles	Sports Management	1991	Facility Manager, Richmond Coliseum
Ben Grodski	Exercise Science	1991	Teacher, Long Island, N.Y.
John Tate	History (2 courses short)	—	Sales rep, Pitney Bowes

1992

Anton Brown	Criminal Justice	1992	Public relations intern —NBA League Office
Francois Firmin	Economics	1992	State Street Bank, Boston
Will Herndon	Criminal Justice	(transferred)	Counselor, Shuman Center
Jim McCoy	Criminal Justice	—	Pro basketball, Sweden

1993

Tony Barbee	Sports Management	1993	Asstant. coach, UMass
Tommy Pace	Sports Management	1993	Sales, Foot Action USA
Kennard Robinson	Business/Real Estate	1993	Pro basketball, Indonesia
Harper Williams	Education	(1996)	Pro basketball, Spain

1994

Jeff Meyer	Management	1994	Sales, Spalding International

1995

Derek Kellogg	Real Estate	1995	Massachusetts State Treasurer's Office
Lou Roe	Sports Broadcasting	—	Pro basketball, NBA
Michael Williams	Sports Management	—	Pro basketball, CBA

1996

Donta Bright	Education	—	
Dana Dingle	Sports Management	1996	
Rigoberto Nuñez	Spanish	1996	
Ted Cottrell	Exercise Science	1996	
Giddel Padilla	Hotel/Restaurant/Travel Administration	1996	

*1989: Seniors David Brown, Duane Chase, and John Milum were on academic probation when we arrived. Brown and Chase were dismissed from the team for breaking the law, and withdrew from the university. None of the three graduated.

CHAPTER 11

GEOGRAPHY LESSONS

When I accepted the job at UMass, they held my press conference at the Basketball Hall of Fame in Springfield, Massachusetts. They figured it was the closest I'd ever get to being inducted.

But six years later, I had another reason to make the seventeen-mile trip from campus: I wanted our kids to play there.

Over the years, this traditional early-season tournament had hosted many teams with marquee value: Duke, Georgia Tech, Kentucky, and North Carolina.

I fought like hell for over a year with the people who organize the game. I wanted us to open our 1995 season there, but they didn't look at us as a worthy opponent for Arkansas, the team that had won the NCAA championship the previous spring. They felt this was a big game and we didn't have enough national recognition.

"What are you talking about?" I said. "The year before, you had UConn. How could you put UConn in there and not us?"

They claimed it was because UConn was a Top 10 team.

"UConn finished 15–13 in 1993," I told them. "They went to the NIT. We went to the NCAA Tournament."

Some people on the committee looked down their noses at us. John Cawley and Bert Weinbaum were two people who pushed for us. But others would say, "Who is UMass?" They wanted Kentucky. We had to twist their arms, so I called Rick Pitino and asked if he had a problem postponing his appearance for a year.

He said he had no problem.

When I got on the phone with the organizers again, they tried to tell me Rick couldn't move.

"I've already talked to him," I said.

"Why don't you wait until next year?"

I'll tell you the reason I fought so hard for this. Derek Kellogg, our point guard, was from Springfield. He was a senior and had been a three-year starter for us. He deserved to play in that game. I told them if they didn't allow Derek to play in that game, they could forget about taking us the following season.

They tried to tell me this game was bigger than any one person.

"Hey," I said, "it wasn't bigger than Travis Best, Vinny Del Negro, a couple of local kids who played in the game with Georgia Tech and North Carolina State."

We had them, so they put us in.

It was another game where we were double-digit underdogs. Everybody told us why we were going to lose. Everyone said we'd have to move mountains to beat Arkansas.

Maybe. But we had Lou Roe.

I don't think Arkansas had a lot of respect for us. They thought it would be an easy game. We got a lot of mileage over a statement that Arkansas's All-American forward Corliss Williamson made at the SEC media day. Somebody asked him if Arkansas's second team was better than our first team.

"Yeah, yeah, whatever," Williamson said.

There seems to be some controversy now over whether he was kidding at the time. But our guys took it personally. It made for great bulletin board material. "That angered me," Roe recalls. "It was like he was saying they were the national champs and they were playing Prairie View, a small Division I school in Texas with a losing tradition. He might not have remembered us, but I was on the All-American team my junior season.

"We hung the statement up in the locker room. Every time I looked at that statement, I went into the weight room and got with the weights. When I came to practice, I really worked my butt off. So did the rest of the team. We were really focused on what we needed to do to compete with that club.

"We were arguing, fighting with each other in practice. We were tired of practicing. We wanted to compete."

In a game like that, it's not about coaching emotion. In other games, you have coaching intensity because you know you're going to win. But in that Arkansas game, it was about coaching basketball.

We have always played well in cause games—and this was no exception. We had plenty of ammunition. For one thing, Arkansas was the defending national champion and had all of its starters back.

Nobody had given us much of a chance, especially since we had suspended our starting guard, Mike Williams, because of an academic situation. But our players had gathered emotional energy from the *Globe* story about our grades. We closed practices to the press all week, but the players were confident.

Lou took out his frustrations on Williamson that night, scoring 34 points and grabbing thirteen rebounds. We opened the game with a slam dunk to set the tone. That was only the beginning. Late in the half, we had built a 50–31 lead. At one point early in the second half, we increased our lead to 68–40. The final score was 104–80. We never let up. "When we went out, they were like some new meat and we just tore them apart," Roe says.

"It was like getting caught in a dream that you don't want to end," says Kellogg, who played thirty-five minutes and ran our offense flawlessly. "It was a perfect setup for me and UMass."

Nolan Richardson said later his team hadn't approached the game with the seriousness it should have, that they were still caught up with being national champs. "They had a Corliss Williamson day, a Scott Thurman Day. Everybody had a day," he said. "You went to UMass and said, 'Hell, they ain't had no day.' But they took their day out of us."

People tell me Richardson was sitting on the bench and telling his players, "I told you." I think he used that game to propel them to the Final Four.

We gave the Tipoff Classic the best game it's ever had. There was electricity in the building. The people didn't want to leave. They just stood and cheered and chanted, "We're No. 1. We're No. 1."

It was incredible because there had been a lot of media people who came to that game just to write nasty stories about us in the wake of the *Globe* articles on academics. One writer from the *Providence Journal* was so sure we were going to lose that he had already written a story ripping our program—'Who do they think they are now?'—before the game was even played.

I know because a friend of mine, Ken "Jersey Red" Ford, who is a teacher in Fall River, Massachusetts, saw him, read the story, and told him, "I can't believe this is what you're going to write."

After the game, Jersey walked up to him and asked, "What are you going to write now?"

I got to enjoy the win for about thirty seconds because we had a blowup behind the scenes. Mike Williams went kind of crazy and ran out of the locker room. He had been fine until there were about four minutes to go; then he figured out we were going to win the game without him. And he couldn't deal with it.

After we beat Arkansas, we were the first team in the history of New England to go No. 1 in the polls. When the rankings came out the next week, we all acted like it was no big deal. But it was huge. Are you kidding me? We were going around saying, "Can you imagine? UMass, a New England team, being No. 1 in the country?"

People asked me, "How did you do that? You got to play a great schedule *and* you got to play the No. 1 team *and* you beat them?"

It's simple. When teams play a weak schedule, they're not going to be No. 1. They can be good programs, but they're not going to be No. 1.

Our ranking was not long-lived. We played Kansas in the Wooden Classic the next week, and they beat us. But I felt we had earned some respect in-state. And it had been a long time coming.

I'm glad Derek Kellogg was there to enjoy it. Derek had grown up just three miles from the Civic Center and had come from a big family. He had played for Cathedral High and was a late recruit for us. He wasn't even the top-rated guard in the city. Travis Best was. Derek was considering Holy Cross, Siena, and Fairfield because he didn't know how hard we were recruiting him.

When we offered, he jumped at it.

And the radio talk shows jumped all over me. People said I should be fired for wasting state money. But if we were taking a chance on Derek, he was taking a chance on us. He was our first in-state recruit. And he ended up being a three-year starter.

"When I was growing up," Kellogg said recently, "the Big East was it. Even in the Springfield area, people had just started recognizing the fact that UMass had a basketball program and they were becoming good for two or three years before I got here. When we were freshman, we constantly had to explain to people where we went to school. We'd tell them we played in the same league as Temple. Now when we say, 'UMass,' we get instant respect.

"I remember being at UMass, watching CNN and seeing us crack the Top 25 for the first time. Everybody was hooting and hollering. Finally to see us in the Top 10 on a regular basis was gratifying."

I kept referring to us as the state school, but when I first got to UMass, I felt like an outsider because we couldn't recruit the area. I told our administration we might not have a Massachusetts recruit for the first two or three years because we had no credibility in the area. After that, I said, we'd start getting Massachusetts players.

In 1994, after we played North Carolina at Madison Square Garden, someone criticized me for the lack of local players on our roster. I answered, "That's okay because, at the time, the Tar Heels didn't have a player from the state of North Carolina on their team, either. So what's the problem?"

We'd had some success in Springfield in the past with Derek Kellogg and the Padilla brothers. But our biggest success story in-state was probably Carmelo Travieso.

Carmelo Travieso, our starting guard, grew up in Boston and was recruited by both UMass and BC. Carmelo used to attend BC games as a kid. He never knew much about our program back then—we were too far away. But when BC suggested he go to prep school for a year, he signed with us. What we've done with Carmelo has done wonders for the program in Boston.

People cannot believe this. That includes Leo Papile, who coached him on the Boston Amateur Basketball Club.

Leo's very close to Jim O'Brien at Boston College. He was in his wedding party. I know that and I accept that. That's not a problem. If you talk to Leo, he is stunned by what's happened to Carmelo. He was the fifth- or sixth-best player on Leo's team. That's the guy we took, and Leo said he'd be good for us. "What about this guy, that guy? They're better." But Carmelo was a good fit. Carmelo was the guy we liked. We turned down Tommy Pipkins from Pittsburgh, who ended up going to Duquesne and becoming Freshman of the Year in the Atlantic 10.

In the end, we took the right guy. We had some arguments on the staff because both Tommy and Carmelo were good players. At this point, it's in Leo's mind that if we could make a pitch for Carmelo, hide his weaknesses, then work on those weaknesses and really explore his strengths, what can we do with these other kids? So, if a kid goes to Leo and says, "I really want to go to UMass," Leo's going to be fine with that. Why? Because Leo cares about his players, and he knows there are certain kids who shouldn't go to BC.

It's helped us with Monte Mack, a 6'2" guard from South Boston who's played for Leo the past four years. We also signed Mike Babul, a 6'6" swing man from North Attleboro, Massachusetts, who reminded me of Tony Barbee.

North Carolina was recruiting both Mike and Willie Dersch of Holy Cross High in Flushing, New York. They were honest with the kid. They told him they were waiting on Dersch to make his decision. In that case, Mike said, he didn't want to be their second choice, so he came with us.

Most Minutemen on the UMass roster these days are from New England. UMass's next goal should be to close down Boston and New England. If a kid can really play, his first thought should be, 'I'm going to UMass.' I'll be honest. If UMass signs three kids next year, they could all be from New England.

We'd always been a blue-collar team, and that, to me, symbolized New England. We were a New England team. Even the fans in Boston had to recognize that when we played BC in December 1995 in the Commonwealth Classic at the Fleet Center.

There had always been a strong rivalry between UMass and Boston College. Legend has it that back in the '80s, during the state budget crisis, one state official made the offhand comment: "If a student wants to win a national championship, he should go to BC."

BC had the money.

BC had the political clout.

BC had Doug Flutie, who led the football team to the Cotton Bowl and won a Heisman Trophy.

Before 1970, BC used to be a regional school. These days, it views itself as a worthy first cousin to Notre Dame, attracting students from all over the country. In fact, the BC media guide says only 20 percent of its undergrads come from in-state. At UMass, 60 percent of the students come from inside Route 495, the big loop that surrounds Boston. But their parents went to BC.

Boy, times have changed. In more ways than one.

"People in Boston don't give the western part of the state enough credit, nor do they know too much about it," Kellogg says. "So for a school from Amherst to come from obscurity is an amazing thing. Just now are you seeing the national press and the Boston papers giving UMass what it deserves."

During the mid-70s, UMass played games in its league and then against teams like Boston College, Providence, and other schools in New England. That's where the rivalries were.

"When Julius and I were in school," Al Skinner recalls, "we had a winning record against BC, so I never thought they had a leg up on UMass. As a matter of fact, I thought we had the better program, even if we didn't have the recognition.

"The Boston papers didn't really show any interest in our program. The only time they covered us was when we played Harvard, Northeastern, or Boston College. But I don't think we were particularly well received. Even the Boston Celtics didn't feel like making the trip to Amherst. They waited until we came to Boston before they scouted me."

Aside from a game in a 1990 Abdow's Classic tournament in Springfield—sponsored by Abdow's, a local restaurant in Springfield—BC and UMass had not met since 1979. I got the feeling BC coach Jim O'Brien never wanted to play us. He probably wished we'd go away. We were recruiting competition for him.

Ted Sarandis, a talk show host for Sports Radio WEEI in Boston, began beating the drum for this game back in 1993. He turned it into a crusade because he felt this would be a great way to promote college basketball in that town. He spoke at our banquet in Boston in '94 and pushed for it. He spoke to Charlie Flaherty, the speaker of the state house of representatives at the time, about making a subtle push for it. He urged UMass and BC alums to write to our then-president Michael Hooker, and the BC president, the Reverend J. Donald Monan, about playing it. He spoke about it so often, he actually received complaints from the Celtics' front office, because WEEI was carrying their games at the time.

I was all for it. We wanted a presence in Boston. We wanted to recruit there. But, at the time, BC coach Jim O'Brien apparently had some reservations. He wanted to keep us out. Boston had always been a Big East town. The Commonwealth was beginning to produce more and more Top 50 prospects, and

BC was self-conscious about us coming in and recruiting in their backyard.

I couldn't blame him.

Just take a look at Leo's roster on his Boston Amateur Basketball Club. Two years ago, it included Wayne Turner of Beaver Country Day School, who went to Kentucky; Randell Jackson of Winchendon School, who went to Florida State; and Scoonie Penn of Salem, who went to BC.

Leo's team was so deep and so talented, almost everyone missed on Pat Bradley, a 3-point shooter from Everett. He was a late-bloomer who had a big AAU tournament in Winston-Salem and ended up starting for Arkansas as a freshmen last year.

But the push for this game was bigger than any one individual. The BC alums begged for the game. Ours did, too. Personalities held it up. It had to go above the coaches. And when our AD, Bob Marcum, and their AD, Chet Gladchuk, met at the Football Foundation Dinner in New York, the wheels were set in motion.

Bob knows the other ADs, so he could sit down with Chet and say, "Hey, we've got to throw the egos out of this. If the coaches don't like each other, so what? This game needs to be played, and it's financially in our best interests to do it."

Bob and Chet had the vision to understand how big this game could be. It didn't take long before they cut a deal to play this rivalry in the new 18,974-seat Fleet Center when it opened in December of 1995.

That is not to say everything went smoothly.

But every time there was a disagreement, Bob and Chet settled it by flipping a coin. BC won the flips to determine which team would wear home white, which team would sit on the Celtics bench, which team would use the home locker room, and who would be the official scorer. We won the flips to determine practice time and selection of game ball.

Tickets were scaled at $50 for lower-level seats and $35 for upper-level seats. Student tickets went for $25. But when we had first proposed those prices to the people at the Fleet Center, Bob Marcum told me they'd balked at the idea.

They said, "Oh, no. You guys can't charge that. You're college."

We said, "Well, what do you charge? We've looked at your prices for the Bruins and the Celtics."

"Yeah, but you're college."

"What does that mean—we're going to play half-court?"

BC got 9,000 tickets; UMass got 9,000 tickets. It was like a good old-fashioned high school playoff game. It was like an NCAA tournament game.

We sold out our allotment of tickets within an hour and a half, at the prices we wanted—$50, $35, and $25. That's an NBA ticket.

And the papers covered the matchup like it was an NBA playoff game. The fans were so revved up, it developed a life of its own. Instead of the usual Celtics or the Bruins, the focus of the entire state's sports fans was on a college basketball game. It may have seemed like a Hatfield-McCoy feud on the surface, but it was all in good fun. It's amazing how many people have ties to one school or the other.

Bill Bulger, the new UMass president, is a Boston College grad. Paul Cellucci, the lieutenant governor of Massachusetts, is a BC grad. Charlie Flaherty is a BC grad and a big UMass fan. State treasurer, Joe Malone, a Harvard graduate, and I have developed a tremendous friendship, so I consider him a UMass fan, too.

I've always had great respect for Joe, not just because of his political office and Ivy League education, but because he worked his way through school by being a chauffeur and a bartender. He's a regular guy. Joe started a program called "Savings Makes Cents" in which he would go to grade schools around the state and speak to the students about opening bank accounts and saving a little bit of money at a time. He asked me to get involved in kicking it off. From there, he and his brother Chuck began coming to our games at Amherst.

He, along with corporate leaders like Ben Camarate of T.J. Maxx, Bob Morse of Sheraton ITT, Dave Collela of the Colonnade Hotel, and Joe Crognali of Bertucci's were always people I could confide in when I needed advice.

Now, back to BC.

The hype started early that week and carried over to game time.

"The build-up was incredible," Sarandis said. "We were just hoping it wasn't going to be like the Super Bowl, when you have a week of hype and the game doesn't live up to it. But the game lived up to the hype."

It snowed that day, but that didn't stop anybody. The restaurants in the North End had all kinds of special functions. On the morning of the game, there was a huge pep rally for both schools down at Quincy Market.

George "Trigger" Burke, a Quincy lawyer who had played for UMass in the '50s and is the only UMass player other than Julius to have his number retired, took a maroon-and-white limo to the game in honor of his alma mater.

There were players from the state on both rosters. We started Carmelo, and BC started Scoonie Penn, whom we had recruited out of high school.

It's hard to tell how our players felt about this game. They had just played Kentucky and Maryland, two nationally ranked teams. Marcus said he would have rather played UConn.

Over 18,000 squeezed into the building, the largest crowd ever to watch a college basketball game in New England.

But once the game started, it was obvious how much was at stake. We eventually won, 65–57, but not before we had to rally from a deficit in the first half. And not before Edgar knocked down a three-pointer with 1:23 to play to break a 57–57 tie; and Marcus made a monster block on Danya Abrams's baseline layup with 49.6 seconds to play.

Bob Kraft, the owner of the New England Patriots whose wife Mira is on the UMass Board of Trustees, came into the locker room afterwards, all smiles. He talked to our team. He looked at Tyrone and said, "Wow, you're a big human being."

"Why don't you sign me as a tight end," Tyrone told him.

The atmosphere was great. When it was over, I think people walked away saying, "Man, did we waste a lot of time. We should have gotten this thing together a lot sooner."

The governor of Massachusetts, William H. Weld, must have enjoyed it. He told me he was rooting for both sides, and he said this game should be played every year. Afterwards, when the media asked me if we would play again, I said, "I hope so."

Jim O'Brien was noncommittal. When he said he didn't know if the game would be played again, everybody went off on him, saying, "What are you doing? Don't you understand how much you benefitted?"

He went on to suggest the game would be played if his administration wanted to play it and that he had no control over the matter. "Hey, I didn't want to play the first one," he said, "but if they make me play the second one, I'll do it."

I guess the BC administrators enjoyed themselves. The

Minutemen are going to play the Eagles for the next five years.

Because of that game's success, there's been talk about playing other big games at the Fleet Center, maybe with the arena's hosting a doubleheader similar to the John Wooden Classic in Anaheim.

But the biggest news to hit New England basketball actually occurred the day I left UMass. UMass and UConn held a joint press conference at the Hall of Fame to announce the resumption of a rivalry that had been dormant since 1990. I'm sorry I had to miss it.

The game was put together by Dave Gavitt, the former Big East commissioner and the president of the NCAA Foundation. Gavitt had worked quietly behind the scenes for the past eight months after UConn AD, Lew Perkins, and Bob Marcum asked for his help.

It's a five-year deal. The first game will be held December 27, 1996, at the Hartford Civic Center. It will be televised on ESPN. Then the game will move to the Fleet Center. Revenues will be split on an equal basis between the two schools. I would have liked to get the Mullins floor put down in Hartford and let them put theirs down in Boston. This is a marketing dream. Tickets should go for $75 on the floor and $35 upstairs—with each school getting approximately 8,000 seats. I guarantee there won't be a problem with selling out the place.

UMass and UConn are located just fifty miles apart. The schools used to play on a regular basis, even after UConn joined the Big East in 1979 and UMass became part of the Eastern Eight at about the same time. UConn dominated the series, winning thirteen of the last fourteen games.

The last time the two teams played, the Huskies beat us, 94–75, at the Cage. Our team was still young at the time. Jimmy,

Anton, and Will were only sophomores; Tony and Harper were freshmen. That was the year UConn had Nadov Henefeld, Tate George, and Scott Burrell. They won the Big East and got to the Final Eight.

But we gave them a game. We were down 7 points with five minutes to go. They made a couple of threes at the end and wound up winning by 19. Afterwards, Jim Calhoun knew we were getting dangerous and refused to continue the series.

I don't blame him. He was playing a tough schedule; the last thing he wanted was another rivalry. But I think what happened was that our program was reaching a point where he may have thought, "Hey, UMass could beat us."

Actually, *not* playing each other has only increased the hype for this game and helped UMass's program.

Over the years, New England basketball had been centered around Providence, Holy Cross, and Boston College. Now you really have two huge state universities, UMass and UConn—located in primarily rural areas—that are the powers. But try telling that to the rest of the teams from this region who play in the Big East. Particularly Connecticut.

Diehard UConn fans must feel they have a divine right to rule New England. I heard it all the time on the weekly radio show with Mark Vandermeer. They loved to pick up the phone and dial our number in Amherst, looking to take cheap shots at our program, our league, and our players.

They couldn't handle the fact we were ranked No. 1 five times in 1995 and ten this past season.

"UMass would have at least five losses in the Big East."

Click.

"Ray Allen and Doron Sheffer are a much better backcourt than Edgar Padilla and Carmelo Travieso."

Click.

"When was the last time an Atlantic 10 team went to the Final Four?"

"This year."

And I didn't own a crystal ball.

How about this? One guy came up to me and said, "Geez, could you imagine Connecticut with Marcus Camby?"

"Could you imagine us with Ray Allen?" I countered.

We were a thorn in UConn's side and we were located right in their backyard. We made their job a little harder. They couldn't share the mantle. I said, "Okay, then I got to take it."

When we beat UConn to the punch and made it to the Meadowlands in 1996, I'm sure it hurt Calhoun. The same week his team lost to Mississippi State in the Sweet 16, we beat Georgetown in the East Regional Finals.

Calhoun did a great job getting it going at UConn—I'll be the first to admit it. He rejuvenated the program. His teams play hard. He's got them in the Top 10 almost every year. He's been to three Sweet 16s and two Elite Eights. But he's not the only good coach on his campus. Last year, Curry Kirkpatrick was doing a story on our program for *College Sports Magazine* and showed me a quote from *Sports Illustrated* in which Jim Calhoun said, "It was written somewhere that the best coaching job in the country over the past fifteen years was done here."

"Yeah," I said. "By Geno Auriemma."

Geno coaches UConn's women's team. He coached them to a perfect 35–0 season and a national championship in 1995. We're friends. Other coaches' successes don't bother him.

I called him a couple of times during this past season when we were in the midst of our winning streak just to get his ideas on how to keep our players going. Coaching is coaching. I've talked with Joanie O'Brien and Theresa Grentz at Illinois in the past. I don't think we should look at women's coaches and say they don't know as much as men's coaches do. It's the same sport, and we can get good ideas from everybody.

When UConn and UMass were battling for No. 1 in the polls in 1995, I chastised Calhoun for not playing what seemed to be a natural rivalry. So did the *Boston Herald,* which called Calhoun a wimp in one of its editorials and claimed that the state of Connecticut was nothing more than a speed trap on the way to New York.

The potential for a UConn-UMass matchup incited passions throughout New England. It would have been fun to see it played last year, when Marcus and Ray Allen were still in school and both teams were ranked in the Top 10.

When Marcus was at UMass, he told me there were two games he had always wanted to play—Duke at Cameron Indoor Stadium and UConn anywhere.

Even though UConn fans gave Marcus flak about his academics, he felt it was a chance to play against a team that had wanted him badly. Marcus has never been one to hold a grudge. In fact, he is close friends with Ray Allen and even accepted an invitation from Ray to attend one of UConn's home games. He sat right behind their bench.

The closest Marcus came to playing UConn during his career was on Sega Genesis. He used to play "Coach K's College Basketball" all the time. The game was programmed for UConn vs. UMass. According to Marcus, UMass won every time. And he scored all the points.

I wish UMass had a chance to play everybody in New England. What about a round-robin concept like the Philadelphia Big 5 used to have in its heyday, with UConn, UMass, Boston College, Rhode Island, and Providence? If UMass could schedule

Connecticut, Providence, and BC, the school wouldn't have to go out and play all these national games. The Big East teams would have to pencil in only two games on their schedules and designate which league games they wanted to count in the New England standings. The same with Rhodey and UMass.

We're talking ten games total, five of them nonleague.

UMass-UConn, UMass-BC and UConn-Rhode Island could all be separate attractions played at alternating sites because those would be sellouts. Then why not schedule a doubleheader—UMass-Providence and BC-Rhodey—one year in the Providence Civic Center, one year in Boston?

My point is, I think those schools should go after one another to generate more excitement for college basketball in New England. I think there should be rivalries within the state, within the region.

I want the New England teams to do well so the area can be the focal point for basketball in this country.

For whatever reason, college basketball in New England has always had an inferiority complex. Holy Cross—with George Kaftan and Bob Cousy—did win a national championship in 1947; but basically, outside of Providence, the games were always regional deals played in tiny gymnasiums.

Providence was different, first under Joe Mullaney and then when Dave Gavitt coached there. They got to the Final Four in 1973. They had players like Marvin Barnes and Ernie DiGregorio. They played in the 13,000-seat Providence Civic Center. The rest of the schools in New England—particularly those in the Yankee Conference—used to scramble for an NIT bid.

Hopefully, those days are gone.

I was always telling our fans, "Never cheer against another team in the region because it only comes back to bite you. If you have to cheer against someone else, turn off the TV. If you want to enjoy a college basketball game, fine, but you have to cheer for all the New England teams—UConn, BC, Providence, Holy Cross, Northeastern, BU—and the Atlantic 10 teams."

I got away with that because the fans I knew were a little different from most. They got caught up in it, but they didn't get angry with it. It wasn't like it was life or death to them. They never thought about an opposing player, "I'd like to choke that kid." No. And in most cases, our people were very happy with our team. It was, "Boy, this is great. I wish this could last forever."

But nothing lasts forever—as we were about to learn.

CHAPTER 12

THE STREAK

It was a near-perfect season, but it didn't start out that way. We had scheduled an exhibition game against the Converse All Stars—a team of ex-college players—at our place to open the season.

We lost.

We were down 10 at one point. We showed no emotion, had no intensity on defense. We turned the ball over. We had no chemistry. Each player was trying to get his own shot. It was scary because we were going to play nationally ranked teams like Kentucky, Maryland, Wake Forest, and Georgia Tech. We had a game against Boston College in Boston, and we were going to the Rainbow Classic in Honolulu—all in the first month of the 1995–96 season.

I'm not afraid to lose games, but I was concerned we might start out the season 1–9 before we even got into Atlantic 10 play.

Afterwards, we had kids crying. Donta Bright came into the locker room and said he wanted to quit. We talked for an hour. He felt that his pro aspirations seemed to be going down the drain. "Donta," I said, "if you're worried that you have to make it into the NBA, it's like having to win the lottery. You may make it. But what you have to do is play. Show them you deserve the opportunity."

I had him call his mom. Patricia's a special lady. She just wants him to do well. She wants him to get a college degree. She doesn't want to live through her son, but she does want her son to be a success. And that's what she told him.

He stayed. But Marcus Camby came to me later and said, "These fellows don't think we can win." And this was only about a month after Tyrone Weeks had said, "Let's go undefeated."

Unacceptable.

At that point, I thought we were an NIT team. I felt our players didn't understand how hard we play. They didn't play together; we didn't play any defense. And those were the foundations that program was built on.

Our opening game against Kentucky, in the Great Eight at Auburn Hills, was only ten days away; and we still had a lot of question marks.

Could Donta Bright and Dana Dingle play on the floor together?

Did Marcus have the stamina to play more than twenty-two or twenty-three minutes a game? He hadn't before.

Were our guards good enough? We had lost Derek Kellogg and Mike Williams. Edgar Padilla had never played thirty-five minutes a game, which is what he was going to have to do.

Was freshman Charlton Clarke good enough to contribute? Could we get some bench play out of Tyrone? Was his foot healthy enough that he could help us?

We had leadership questions, too.

Who was going to be the team leader? Could Marcus do it? Would Donta play well enough to do it? Was Edgar good enough, and did he have enough respect from his teammates to do it?

I told the staff that I thought we were going to have to be the leaders. Then our players grew up. In a hurry.

Maybe the best thing that happened to us was that we didn't win the exhibition game. I didn't mind losing a game if it didn't count. It gave me a chance to get the players' attention.

I went back to coaching the way I had done four years earlier. I told them my job was to make practices harder than the games. And I did it. You can ask them. I kept talking to them about breaking through because we kept hitting a wall, and then we'd stop playing. I told them I wasn't going to accept that anymore. I got tougher and more agressive. I told the players I was not going to settle for their efforts. They were going to raise their efforts to mine.

We conducted football-style practice the next eight days. Some of our players required stitches. If a player screened someone and his feet didn't come off the floor, I went nuts. If a kid was on defense and got screened, I went nuts. I told them, "You'd better try to go right through them. If someone comes to screen you, punch him in the mouth." No one won. I had somebody send me an article from the *Lexington Herald Leader* that said UMass was Marcus Camby and a bunch of schmoes. I spent all week calling our guys schmoes.

One day, the Air Force Academy hockey team, which was in town for a game, slipped in to watch practice. I was absolutely losing my mind.

Afterwards, one of their coaches came up to me and told me he had watched us in practice and absolutely loved what we were doing. Teaching. Yeah. Going nuts. "I can see why your teams win," he said. "You knew what had to be done."

So did our team. That's what made us special. I've never coached any team that wanted to win as badly for themselves as this team.

And I tried to give them every advantage going into that game against Kentucky. I even resorted to some mind games. I went to the papers in Boston and told the writers we wanted to try new things—that I was thinking of trying a box and one in which one player plays man-to-man defense against the opposing star while the other four players remain in a box zone defense. I said the same thing on my TV show. We had no intention of playing a box and one. But I knew Ken "Jersey Red" Ford would tune in.

Jersey is one of my closest friends. We talk all the time on the phone. His son, Greg, used to sit on our bench before he went to college. But Jersey's even closer to Rick Pitino. He had been the cook at Rick's fraternity when Rick attended UMass and has become somewhat of a local celebrity in Lexington since Rick took the Kentucky job.

I knew as soon as Jersey heard what we were supposedly doing, he'd be on the phone with Rick that night. And that's exactly what happened. I can imagine what he said: "John said it on his show. You wouldn't know it. He's giving out secrets because he thinks you don't watch his show." I know Rick had his staff breaking down tape, looking for box and one and triangle and two defense because we had never played it. We got their staff wasting time, worrying about things that were never going to happen.

You know how I know?

We were at the shoot-around the day of the game, and Dick Vitale—Dickie V.—came up to me and said, "How's everything going? I hear you're working on a box and one, triangle and two." I didn't want to say I knew Rick had picked that up from my TV show, so I said, "Are you kidding me? I just put it out there. I was just messing around."

When we went into the game, I was laughing inside.

I can do that with Rick.

What most people can't do is beat Kentucky. We jumped on them early, racing to a 29–10 lead, then held on for a 92–82 victory. Marcus went off for 32 points, nine rebounds, and five blocked shots. He carried us down the stretch. After Kentucky rallied from a 60–50 deficit to pull within 76–74, Marcus made a classic spinning turnaround jump shot into a double team, then came back to make a pair of free throws as UMass increased its lead to 6. Kentucky never recovered. For our players, the practices had been so grueling, this game seemed easy. Dana added 19 points, 15 in the second half. Edgar and Carmelo played the entire forty minutes. And I started thinking, "You know what? We're pretty darn good."

Right after the game, Rick came over to me and said pretty much the same thing.

"You guys played great," he said. He's a generous guy. He knew he would catch some grief. But he was happy for me. He should take pride in what we've done at his school. After all, he was the guy who helped me put this thing together. I never was a member of his staff, but it feels like I'm one of his guys. He's got Billy Donovan. He's got Tubby Smith. He's got Herb Sendek, Ralph Willard, and Obie O'Brien. He's got those guys. And he's got me.

Marcus's performance solidified him as the player to watch. In that game, he needed to take over. If you're a good player, you get out there and get it done. But special players make everyone on the court better. Kentucky played behind him in post. They didn't think he was as good as he was. They hadn't seen him play. They hadn't seen how we used him.

And they had no idea how our guards would play. If Marcus Camby was the National Player of the Year, then you could make a case for juniors Edgar Padilla and Carmelo Travieso—a couple of skinny, 170-pound kids—as the best backcourt in the country.

They are almost inseparable, like identical twins, both on and off the court. Edgar and Carmelo were even born on the same day— May 9, 1975—just a mile apart in Puerto Rico. They are very good friends. They eat together, room together on the road, and sometimes exchange clothes. Occasionally, they even speak Spanish to each other during games, just to confuse the opposing team.

"People confuse us a lot. Sometimes, they think I'm Edgar and he's me because we're together a lot," Carmelo says. "The bond is there. I'd rather play with him than with anybody in the country because he understands the way I play and I understand the way he plays. We have similar styles and personalities. We both have the same goals and beliefs."

"Even if the backcourt we face is supposed to be better, we're not going to give in. We're going to go at them. We're going to drive and push and take a kneecap out or something. It's not going to be easy playing against us."

Edgar ran our offense and led the Atlantic 10 in assists and steals. Carmelo, who emerged as our best perimeter defender, picked up the nickname, "Trey-ieso" after he burned Temple for eight three-pointers during an 84–55 rout at Mullins. Both played over thirty-seven minutes a game.

And that's just the way they had planned it when they met for the first time at the ABCD camp in Irvine, California, after their junior year in high school. "We came from the same backyard and we hit it off right away," Edgar says. "We were getting recruited at the same time and made a pact at the time that we wanted to become the first Hispanic backcourt to play major college basketball," he added.

Edgar signed with us the following fall. Carmelo followed. They are classic examples of what coming to America is all about.

When Edgar was growing up in Puerto Rico, he used to shoot a rag ball into an empty paint can that was hanging on a fence. Carmelo learned how to play by shooting at a couple of bicycle rims. "It always seemed like we had to do a little more to catch up," he said. "We had to try harder to get even."

Edgar was persuaded to come to the United States when he was fourteen by his older brother, Giddel, who got him to move to Springfield, Massachusetts, and live with his uncle and sister. Edgar didn't know any English when he arrived. He used sign language or had Giddel translate when he first played organized basketball over here. Edgar was a quick study, emerging as the Western Massachusetts Player of the Year when he played for Springfield Central during his junior year in high school. But he became homesick and returned to the island to complete his secondary education.

Carmelo came to this country at age four after a hurricane destroyed the house where he had lived with his family in the Dominican Republic. "The rain was hitting me in the chest so hard, it felt like rocks," he said. "As we were running, we could see buildings collapsing and trees falling, shanty houses flying around.

"When we went back the next day, everything was destroyed. We moved back to Puerto Rico and, about six months after that, to Boston."

Carmelo learned the game from his older brother, Raul, and polished it playing at the Boys and Girls Club in Dorchester. He spoke only Spanish when he arrived. He attended Spanish-speaking classes in elementary school and never felt comfortable speaking English until he requested English-only classes in junior high school. Carmelo was recruited to Thayer Academy, where he led his team to the New England Class C Prep School Championship.

The two had always kept in touch. But it was up to us to break down some language barriers when we were recruiting them. Edgar's mother and father are deaf. When we recruited him, his sister, Millie, used sign language to communicate to them. So for me, all communication was delayed. I could never get into a flow of what I wanted to say. I would say something. Then stop. I'd say a few more words. And stop. If I told a joke, there was delayed laughter.

Carmelo's mother still does not speak English, so when I recruited him, I had to use Raul as an interpreter with the family. I would speak. Then wait for a response. It was the same idea in both homes.

During Carmelo's first year, he couldn't defend anybody. I called him into the office at the end of his freshman year and said, "Carmelo, I love you. But if you don't get stronger and tougher on defense, you can't play here. You've got to be a tough hombre." As for Edgar, his major problem was passing. He was wild. It was one assist—and three turnovers. Guys on press row would put their hands up to protect themselves when he had the ball. There was no definition to his game.

They grew up with the program and answered the challenge.

We catapulted to the No. 1 ranking the week after we defeated Kentucky and stayed there for the next nine weeks. We put together a twenty-six-game winning streak before we finally lost to George Washington on February 24 at Mullins. Then we came back to win a fifth Atlantic 10 tournament.

When the season started, I said the players were going to have to fill a vacuum. We had different people lead us. And it was fun because they all accepted their roles.

This team epitomized what UMass basketball is all about. They overcame a brutal schedule, winning eighteen regular season games against teams that qualified for the NCAA tournament. In addition to SEC power Kentucky, we defeated Maryland, North Carolina State, and Georgia Tech from the ACC; Memphis and Louisville from Conference USA; Syracuse, Pitt, and Boston College from the Big East. We defeated Temple three times, and Virginia Tech and George Washington in league play.

"If you had told me this was going to happen at the beginning of the season, I'd have never dreamt it," Marcus said. "Especially after we lost an exhibition game to a bunch of guys who looked like they worked at a 7-Eleven. That kind of woke us up."

We didn't just break barriers.

We tore them down.

In the previous two seasons, we'd had a history of playing poorly immediately after we had beaten a No. 1 team. When we defeated North Carolina, we lost our next game to Kansas. After we beat Arkansas, Kansas got us again.

The same thing could have happened this time. But instead of folding, we rallied from 16 points down to defeat Maryland, 50–47, in the Franklin Bank Classic. It wasn't easy. We had far too many turnovers, and I had to yank Donta Bright, Dana Dingle, and Inus Norville—all in the first few minutes—because I wasn't pleased with their efforts. Even Marcus struggled in the first half, shooting two for seven. We shot only 19 percent. But

Marcus cranked it up in the second half, and his turnaround jumper gave us the lead for good with 1:59 to play. And our defense shut Maryland down when we made our critical run.

I had expected a similar kind of war when we played at Temple. Every time we'd gone to Philadelphia, I'd said to myself, "Here we go again. It's a hostile environment. It's on national TV. I'm going to have to wear a flak jacket." We had never played well in McGonigle Hall. We were ranked No. 16 one year and lost. And the only time we had won there prior to the 1995–96 season, Mike Williams had had to stick in a twenty-eight-foot bank shot at the buzzer.

We still think that was a fluke.

But this year's victory wasn't. We wanted to spank Temple. Boom. We did it—59–35, in a 9:30 P.M. ESPN game that seemed to stun both their players and their fans. We didn't want to come back to Amherst with anything hanging over us. I think we took care of that. We really defended. We were all over them. Temple shot just 20.6 percent and did not make a three-pointer.

"Coach told us after looking at the film that Temple takes only two kinds of shots—three-pointers and bad ones," Edgar said. "So we denied the threes."

Later in the season, we played Virginia Tech, which ranked 10th in the country at the time, in a big Atlantic 10 game at Blacksburg. The game was scheduled for Saturday, February 17. We had decided to charter down on Thursday night, immediately after our game with La Salle at the Mullins Center. We had to leave pretty quickly because there was a threat of a driving snowstorm that was sweeping through the South. But we had a meal for the kids in a restaurant; and we all messed around, including me.

We finally boarded the plane, but it was too late. They had

shut down the airport in Roanoke, so we had to fly into Greensboro, North Carolina. By the time we landed, it was two o'clock in the morning and we didn't have a hotel.

Guess what? They were all booked. We ended up finding a motor lodge—I'm not sure the rooms had windows—and that's where we stayed. The kids got to bed at 3 A.M.

I told the pilot, "We're not paying you if you don't fly us to Blacksburg tomorrow."

"Take a bus," he said. "It's about two hours."

I got into an argument with the guy. The next day, we ended up busing down. It snowed. It was freezing.

We finally checked into our hotel at 4:30 P.M. Friday and went over to practice. We didn't do much because we had been traveling all day. It was an unbelievable trip.

Our performance against Virginia Tech the next day made it even more incredible. We had never played well in a noon game since I came to UMass. I told the guys that when we got into the NCAA tournament, we might have to play at that time in a subregional. It was unrealistic to think we could go down there and beat them convincingly. This campus had been waiting for us for close to a month. Tickets to this game had sold out within an hour, and scalpers were asking between $75 and $100. Their students had been living in tents for two weeks, waiting for an opportunity to pick up the few remaining tickets to Cassell Coliseum. They were going crazy, just like the Dukies.

I knew we had a good team when the players said, "Let's shoot around on game day."

I told them, "That means going to the gym at seven o'clock in the morning."

"So what?" they said. And they did it.

We came back four hours later and played one of our best

games of the year. We executed as well as we had all year—at noon, rolling to a 74–58 victory. Marcus scored 31 points—15 in a ten-and-a-half minute stretch at the start of the game when Tech insisted on single-covering him. Marcus hadn't been single-covered since our opener with Kentucky. He wasn't complaining.

"It was an average game for me," he said. "I can play a whole lot better."

Average?

I was speechless.

Marcus seemed unaffected by the atmosphere at the Coliseum. "Once you play at McGonigle, you're not fazed by anything," he said.

My first three years at UMass, I used to tell our players, "Hey, we've got no shot to win this game. Just go play." Then I could go to the media and say the same thing. It became a running joke.

During the last four years, we were the biggest game on everybody's schedule. I can go right down the line—from Memphis to Louisville. They had record crowds when we played Louisville and Pitt.

Look at our league games. Temple sold out only one game—our game. And McGonigle Hall doesn't seat 15,000; it seats closer to 4,000. When we played GW, that game sold out.

We thrived on it.

I think it's important to challenge your team. It's important to play neutral-site games. I don't know how important it is to play road games. We have enough of those in our league. If you want to play a road game, okay. We played at Louisville, and there's a game scheduled at Wake for 1996–97.

I wanted to have a lot of neutral-site games because they simulate NCAA tournament games. We have fans. They have fans.

The Louisville game was a great college game and it toughened us up. We played in front of a record crowd of 20,000 on Cardinals coach Denny Crum's birthday. It was a hotter ticket than their game with Kentucky. Scalpers were selling tickets out front for $300 to $400. Their fans stood the whole game. They screamed their guts out.

Our team was more prepared to play close games because of the schedule we played, which was as tough as anyone's in the country. They responded in close games. They expected to win. That's how they were. We won four overtime games, including victories over Pitt, Xavier, and St. Joseph's, when we needed to make big plays in the final minute.

We had fallen behind, 68–66, in overtime at Pitt when Carmelo hit two three-pointers in a row to ignite a 10–0 run that wrapped up a 79–71 victory. We were down 68–65 at Xavier when Edgar stepped up and made a three-pointer with fifteen seconds left to force overtime. And we needed a fadeaway jumper from Donta with 3.8 seconds left in regulation to force overtime with St. Joseph's at our place.

We relied on balance—on more than one player. If you have a star system, where one guy carries you, an opposing coach can come in and say, "Hey, guess what? We've got to stop that one guy, and we can beat them." If you have a team where five or six guys can beat another team, it's a little harder.

It's hard to know whom to zero in on defensively, so you'd better hope you're right.

During the 1995–96 season, most coaches were wrong.

Whoever they let free on our team scored. It was like there were six holes in the dike, and you had only five fingers.

Our kids learned how to cope with adversity, too, especially after Marcus collapsed before our game at St. Bonaventure, January 14. Marcus missed four games. But we had other guys step up. When the best player goes down, everybody's role changes. Guys who were not playing many minutes had to play more. Guys who were not scoring much had to shoot and score more. If players truly put out in practice on a daily basis, then they are able to move from one role to a bigger role with a great deal of success.

Tyrone came off the bench to score 15 points and grab twelve rebounds as we defeated St. Bonaventure, 65–52, in Olean. Three days later, Donta went for 32 points as we defeated Rhode Island, 77–71, with a late surge at Mullins. Afterwards, Marcus phoned to congratulate his teammates in the locker room, and Edgar told him we were keeping the streak intact for him.

Marcus accompanied us to Pittsburgh for the games with Duquesne and Pitt. But he didn't show up for the Duquesne game because he didn't want to steal the publicity from the guys who played the game. Carmelo played like a star, making seven threes and scoring 33 points as we held off Duquesne, 93–89. And Dana poured in 24 points.

Dana Dingle had originally thought he might become a major league baseball prospect. His first cousin, Willie Randolph, was the starting second baseman for the New York Yankees from the mid-70s to the mid-80s. And baseball was his first love. "I went to see him play a couple of times at the stadium," Dana recalled. "But my own schedule was real busy."

Dana grew up in the Parkchester section of the Bronx, where he was a first baseman and outfielder for all the age-group teams in his neighborhood from the time he was five years old. "I did a little of everything," he recalled. "I was a power hitter, a place hitter, and I stole a lot of bases."

But once Dana discovered basketball in eighth grade and

made the Riverside Church traveling team, he brushed baseball aside for good. "It was hard to give it up," he said. "But then I realized basketball was more exciting. If you're by yourself and you want to go play baseball, what are you going to do? Throw a baseball against a wall? You can't really practice by yourself. That gets kind of boring."

Dana took up basketball full-time at St. Raymond's High School. He averaged 20 points and ten rebounds as a senior and signed with UMass over Texas A & M and Western Kentucky. The Big East never gave him a sniff. "It surprised me a little bit," he admits. "I saw the players they took over me and the players they recruited at my position. I always felt I was better than them. But I guess the coaches didn't think so because I was a late-bloomer."

We liked the fact he could rebound. "That was the first thing I learned to do in high school," he said. "I was quick, and I used to find a way to get to the ball, even though I was skinny."

When Dana signed, a lot of the guys in his neighborhood made fun of him. "A lot of people I know never even heard of UMass. People didn't even know Dr. J went to UMass. They didn't even know they were Division I." They stopped laughing a long time ago.

Three days later, we played Pitt at Fitzgerald Field House. I thought we had the game under control, but we blew an 11-point lead in the second half. I had the answer to our problems sitting on the bench with me. But I had decided to keep Marcus out until I was completely sure he was ready to go, so I stuck with the players on the floor. Carmelo had another big game, making seven more threes and scoring 27 points as we defeated Pitt, 79–71, in overtime.

Marcus's absence actually made us a better team in the long run. It got us to understand that if we weren't sharp, we were in trouble.

Before the season, I had told Bob Marcum that we had a fragile team. We had three guys worrying about next year, a couple of guys worrying about whether they were good enough, a couple of guys wondering whether they were being accepted. What I felt we had to do was get a sports psychologist in there and try to crystallize our thinking.

Bob told me about Bob Ratella, a sports psychologist from the University of Virginia. The main thing I wanted him to do was put our players at ease, convince them that the future is pretty good, and that they were fine. He was wonderful with Dana Dingle, getting him to talk, getting him to feel more comfortable with who he is and where he's going. The same thing with Donta Bright.

I kept talking to the guys about doing a little more than they thought they could do. And I wanted to practice what I preached.

I would get on the treadmill before practice and I'd run three miles.

I pushed it to three and a half.

I kept saying to myself, "I'll never get to four."

But I got to three point eight.

Then, one day, I got to four miles.

I called one of the players over and made him verify it.

After that, I used to have the trainer do that every day.

I'd go to four point one, four point two. I'd come out. I'd be sweating. I'd say "Verification. What'd I do today?"

What I was trying to tell the players was it's a long season but I'm challenging myself, too.

The players knew they had a chance to make history, but they rarely brought the subject up publicly. "After I get away from you guys, I get to go back to the hotel and I don't have to think about it," Dana said to the media, playfully. "Then, the next day, I see you guys again. But we try to block it out. We don't have you guys on the court to ask us how we're playing the game."

Occasionally, I used my own brand of psychology to keep the streak going. The night of our game with Memphis in Worcester, I came into the locker room and just shook my head.

"I think I'm crazy, guys," I said. "There are people who are saying Lorenzen Wright is better than Marcus Camby. Am I nuts? I can't believe that.

"There are people saying their point guard is better than Edgar Padilla.

"There are guys saying their four man, Michael Wilson, is better than Donta Bright. Wait a minute, I understand the guy can jump, but better than Donta Bright? What are they talking about?

"I must be nuts when I say we're the better team here."

Ed Schilling, our new part-time assistant, told me he really liked that one. Our players bought into it, too. They defeated Memphis, 64–61.

It might not have mattered what I said the day our streak finally ended. George Washington defeated us, 86–76, February 24 at the Mullins Center.

GW had played us well in the past. Our team knew that. They knew they were going to have to make an extra effort and do a little bit more than they were used to doing. I didn't think they were ready for that. UMass basketball is about playing as if you're going to the electric chair, and you didn't see that from us that game—there wasn't that fire and passion.

I wasn't around to watch the bitter end.

With 10:31 left in the half, I got tossed out of the game by official Larry Lembo, who claimed I was out of line with some of my comments to him. Subconsciously, that gave the kids an out for why they didn't play as well. It gave them a reason to stop playing. It gave them a reason not to finish the game the way they could have because there were chances to get back into the game and cut the lead to 5 or 6 points. Every time they did get it that close, they kind of backed off defensively—someone broke down. I think my not being there had a bearing on it.

The job Bruiser did in that game, and in the game against St. Bonaventure, proved that he was ready to be a head coach. But this team still relied on me in a game situation: to step up and make sure the game is coached in a manner so that we win.

I watched the game on TV in the locker room.

I was more embarrassed than anything else. I had never been thrown out of a game before. I just told the players, "Hey, we'll get ready and move on. Now we're 26–1. Now we'll move on."

I had maybe four or five technicals a year during my career at UMass. Most of my screaming and yelling is at my team. A good official doesn't need to call technicals. He knows how to disarm a coach. He knows we're only looking for consistency, even if it's consistently bad. But if you're going to make a call at my end, just make sure you call the same thing at the other end.

People love to watch teams like UMass, Kentucky, North Carolina, Indiana, and UCLA because of how we play. It's about finesse. It's about speed. It's about chemistry. It's about playing together. It's about hard, tenacious defense, not being dirty. I don't believe in thuggery basketball. Basketball that is a cross between football and mud wrestling is something that has no place in the sport that I coach.

The game is getting too rough. The people who know basketball—the John Woodens of the world—look at this and say, "It's getting ugly."

No one wants to see a return to what happened in the Big East. It got so rough, people turned their TVs off. They didn't want to watch a possession that ended up at the foul line.

The officials all talk: "This is the way we're going to call this game. We're not going to allow hand-checking." Then they allow body-checking. If the game is going to be physical, fine. I'll go recruit some football players.

In the NBA, they got away from hand-checking because it hurt the game. People don't want to see players out there just pushing and shoving.

In the end, it was good to get the streak off our backs. I'm not sure we would have advanced to the Final Four if we had remained unbeaten during the regular season. Other teams would have had that much more incentive to beat us.

It was that much more of a weight on our own shoulders. As much as we said it was no big deal, it was. There aren't that many coaches who can ever say they were No. 1 in the country. Well, we were. That's special. But it can also put a little heat on you.

What I tried to do during that period was take the heat off the players rather than motivate them. I just told them, "We don't need to win every game. We're trying to win a national title. And our job is to make the game hard for the other team. That's all. Push the ball on offense and put pressure on them by constantly trying to score and attacking the glass. Then, defensively, make it hard for them to score by putting pressure on the ball, by contesting shots, by being a great rebounding team.

"If you make the game hard on them, they want to beat you so bad it creates problems for them.

"If that's not good enough, we lose the game. And that's it."

In the end, losing that GW game helped our basketball team.

We didn't play real well as we finished out the season. But we went to Louisville and played great basketball in the final game of the year and it carried over. We went to the Atlantic 10 tournament and played great. We even found a way to defeat George Washington in the semifinals.

GW had beaten us four times in a row. No one had done that. And their coach, Mike Jarvis, punctuated one of their recent victories by doing his thing at half-court. He pumped his fist in the air and didn't come down to shake my hand.

I shook his after we beat them, 74–65, in the semifinals of the Atlantic 10 tournament at the Philadelphia Civic Center. Donta scored 14 of his 19 points in the second half, and Inus came off the bench to stifle GW's big center Alexander Koul defensively. Then, in the finals, Carmelo hit seven threes and was named Atlantic 10 tournament MVP as we dusted off Temple, 75–61, to win a fifth straight title.

Like I said, we were ordinary guys trying to do extraordinary things. Just like Fran Tarkenton.

CHAPTER 13

CAMBYLAND

Marcus Camby comes from the same neighborhood in Hartford as NBA guard Michael Adams and world championship boxer Marlon Starling.

Adams went to Marcus's high school. He was a 5′9″ guard who was a star at Boston College and later played for the Washington Bullets and Denver Nuggets. Marcus was best friends with his nephew.

"He was a really quiet guy during his whole career," Marcus says. "He was short. People said he had an ugly jumper. But they forget he averaged 26 points one year in the league.

"Marlon Starling didn't get much credit, but he went out and became the welterweight champion of the world. All of us have been proving people wrong our whole lives."

Marcus has become as big as either of them. He converted an entire community into UMass fans. Before Marcus signed with us, UConn was the only basketball team in the state, aside from the Celtics, who played a couple of games a year in Hartford.

By the time he became a star, there were busloads making the trip to the Mullins Center. "My mother, two sisters, and Jackie

Bethea were at almost all my games," he said. "One time, during Midnight Madness, the people from my neighborhood almost filled up an entire section."

They were true believers.

But Marcus also had his doubters. "People were always telling me I couldn't make it," he said. "There's always somebody trying to hold you down. But you just have to fight through it and listen to the ones who love you."

Marcus still has posters of NBA stars like Grant Hill, Hakeem Olajuwon, and Michael Jordan hanging on his bedroom walls. For inspiration. There is also an autographed picture from David Robinson of the San Antonio Spurs, inscribed, "I've seen you play. You have most of what it takes. Do you have the drive?"

I know he has it. He's shown it all his life.

By now, most people have heard the stories about how Marcus learned to play by shooting at a milk crate hooked to a clothes-line pole behind his house. He would cut the bottom out of the milk crate, and he broke more than his share trying to dunk. He was seven at the time.

The rest of the country first saw him in 1992 at the U.S. Olympic Festival. He was just a tall, skinny kid playing in the same tournament as blue chip recruits Rasheed Wallace, Jerry Stackhouse, John Wallace, and Donta Bright. Rasheed Wallace, who signed with North Carolina, had the biggest reputation of anyone there. "Everyone was talking about him," Marcus recalled. "So I think when I went down to San Antonio, a lot of people were focused on him. I took it upon myself to make things happen and make a name for myself."

He did just that, by dominating Wallace and the rest of the high-profile centers in that nineteen-and-under competition, launching a brilliant career. With UMass.

Marcus showed he had determination during our drive to the Final Four this past season. Anytime he laced up his size 14-EEE sneakers and put his 7'0" frame on the floor, he gave us a chance to win because he was the best player in the country.

When one student held up a sign that read CAMBYLAND before our game with Wake Forest, he knew what he was talking about.

Marcus won every National Player of the Year award in 1996. I don't remember the last time that was done. He handled himself well at both the Wooden and Naismith awards dinners. He spoke a very short time at each. When I accepted the Naismith Coach of the Year award for myself, I went up and said, "I told Marcus Camby not only did he win *his* award, but he also won this award."

We had to wear tuxes to the Wooden dinner. It was funny because Marcus didn't fit into anything. His shirt was hanging out and the coat was halfway up his back. Finally, he came over to me and said, "Coach, I can't wear this coat."

We got him another coat and a new shirt. But once he put on the Wooden jacket, he looked a lot better.

It was a perfect fit, as I had predicted when I first walked into his house in 1992 and outlined his career. I told him, "You come in; you have no pressure on you. We have a great team, and you're going to fit in. Your goals your first year should be to become the Atlantic 10 and National Freshman of the Year. After that, your goal is to become Atlantic 10 Player of the Year, National Player of the Year, win the national title, and earn a degree. Your final goal is to be drafted and be a lottery pick."

We didn't want to throw him to the wolves, but to bring him along slowly, give him an opportunity to grow. When he was uncomfortable, we stopped him. He played only nineteen minutes a game his freshman year and only twenty-three minutes as a sophomore. The first time he played thirty minutes a game was this past year.

The results speak for themselves. Marcus was Atlantic 10 Freshman of the Year his first year and A-10 Player of the Year the next two seasons. He was a first team All-American. We did not win a national title, but he led us to the Final Four. He was the No. 2 pick in the draft, chosen by the Toronto Raptors. And he promised me he would get his college degree.

Marcus is gifted. What he didn't have when we first arrived was the consistency and the work habits to be great, the "positive psychology" that a player needs to be great.

"Positive psychology" is an attitude. When you're down, no one knows it; when you're sick, no one knows it. You always come across as being ready to go. And you always, like Michael Jordan does—and that's why he's great—figure out what gets you going. You don't ever come in down. If you're not feeling good, you figure out a way to get yourself going.

Marcus eventually picked that up. He played the entire season with the detached confidence that all of the great ones have.

We tried to create a forum for Marcus to become a candidate for Player of the Year. Look at what we did for him with scheduling. We opened with Kentucky, the pre-season favorite to win the national title. We played the most difficult nonleague schedule of any team in the country. Any team. Anywhere. Why? Because I wanted him shown against the best people. We were on national television twenty-five times. Why? So he would get national exposure.

He played against all of the best big men in the country— Danya Abrams of Boston College, Todd Fuller of North Carolina State, Lorenzen Wright of Memphis, Samaki Walker of Louisville, Marc Jackson of Temple, and Tim Duncan of Wake Forest.

We specifically scheduled an ESPN game with Wake the third game of the season to give him a chance to go head-to-head with the 6'11", 242-pound Duncan, who Lakers GM Jerry West was saying would have been the No. 1 pick in the 1995 NBA draft had he chosen to leave after his sophomore year.

Marcus felt very challenged by Duncan because everybody was saying Duncan was this and Duncan was that. He even had an index card tacked to the wall of his dorm room that read, "December 6. Tim Duncan. #1 Player in college."

You have to understand that the hype to build up that game was unbelievable. It was a heavyweight championship kind of hype. When I came into the shoot-around, I saw Tim Duncan and said, "Hey, Tim, why don't you and Marcus play one-on-one, and the rest of us will eat pizzas? Should the rest of us be involved in this game?" Tim looked at me as if I was crazy. My point was, isn't it getting a little bit out of hand with this Tim Duncan vs. Marcus Camby stuff?

The NBA didn't think so. We got requests for twenty-two scouting passes. Fifteen scouts showed up. I think they thought they were going to see history in the making. After a shaky start, Marcus got the better of Duncan.

Marcus scored 17 points, grabbed nine rebounds and blocked three shots as we cruised to our third victory this season over a Top 25 opponent. He shot six for nineteen in thirty-seven minutes. Duncan finished with 9 points, twelve rebounds, and four blocks in forty minutes, but he shot four for eighteen and scored only two field goals in the second half while going scoreless for a stretch of 18:01. "I didn't try to turn it into a personal battle," Marcus said. "But, early in the game, I tried to do some things on my own. I've had guys put their hands in my face all the time, but their arms were never that long."

Marcus, who missed his first five shots before finally nailing a baseline jumper over Duncan with 11:24 to go in the first half, may have been anxious on offense, but he smothered Duncan with his man-to-man defense in the post. "I thought he played a great game," Duncan conceded. "He definitely altered my shot."

Wake actually did a good job getting the ball to Duncan, but UMass never allowed him to dominate inside. "That was the first time he's had someone of equal size in back of him," Wake coach Dave Odom said.

Okay, so there weren't many fireworks on display. Marcus and Duncan are two different players. Duncan is more of a pure low post player, with good size, great hands, and great athletic ability. But it didn't surprise me when Marcus outplayed Duncan. Marcus has more versatility to his game and it proved to be one of our greatest strengths as the Minutemen attacked Wake's zone. No matter what Marcus says, I think he was nervous about this game. Both players spent the first part of the game feeling each other out. We made Duncan out to be Olajuwon—and they were making Marcus out to be Olajuwon.

We shot just 39.6 percent in this defensive tug-of-war; but we had the superior supporting cast, particularly at small forward where Donta shot eight for fourteen, and exploded for 22 points. Donta got 14 in the second half as we cracked open a 34–34 tie with a 10–3 run. He got us started when he scored on a layup off a pass from Marcus. Then Marcus made a spinning baseline jumper over Duncan, and Carmelo stuck a jumper as we put Wake to sleep for good, 60–46, with a suffocating defense that forced the Deacs into a brutal seven for twenty-eight in the second half.

The Wake game solidified Marcus as the guy to beat in the National Player of the Year sweepstakes. And he didn't do anything to change the voters' minds. Marcus could hurt you in so many ways. Single-cover him and he'd get 35 to 40 points. Double up on him and he's more than happy to kill you with passing.

Marcus is an enigma to the NBA guys. They look at him, and some people don't like him. They just say, "Where are you going to play him?" As a coach, even in the NBA, I will go after the best players. I don't care about position. I need a point guard and a couple of big guys. As to the rest of the guys, I would say, "We're going to get the best players I like." I've done it at UMass, and we had success with it. Some years, I got a lot of guards; other years, I got a lot of forwards. Still other years, I got a lot of centers. I'll tell you one team that I had. Jeff Meyer was a center. Lou Roe, in high school, had been a center. Marcus Camby was a center. Donta Bright was a center. Dana Dingle was a center. Ted Cottrell was a center. I'm naming seven, eight guys. Tyrone Weeks was a center.

So we said, "Well, they're the best players for us. Let's just figure out who would play forward, power forward. Let's just play forwards." And that's what we did.

I think it will be the same way for me with the Nets. We need three big guys with size, two guards who can handle the ball, but the rest . . . we want players who play hard, who rebound. Obviously, shooting is more important in the pros, but I think playing hard is also a desireable skill. And I think in Marcus's case, Toronto will sign him and say, "We'll figure out how we're going to play him."

Marcus flirted with immortality all season. He also had to deal with his own mortality. He threw a major scare into our coaching staff midway through the season when he collapsed just ten minutes prior to our game at St. Bonaventure. His blackout occurred within five days of a fatal tragedy on the UMass campus when a

member of the swim team, Greg Menton, died from an unde-
tected heart defect during a meet with Dartmouth.

Marcus was unresponsive for ten minutes before being taken
to Olean General Hospital by ambulance. I was so concerned
that I felt compelled to skip the game and accompany him to the
emergency ward.

Things had gone well at the shoot-around. Everybody had
been good. At the pre-game meal in the morning, everybody
had been good. There was no indication that anything was
wrong. We went into the locker room. I wrote the scouting report on the chalkboard, as I do before every game, and Donta
came flying into the locker room as I'm finishing the board and
said, "Coach, Marcus fell out. Marcus fell out. You need to come
out here."

I said, "What are you talking about?"

He said, "Hurry up, hurry up."

I jogged out. Marcus was right there in the hallway, lying
down, with a doctor standing over him. I knelt down next to
him. My first reaction was, "Come on Marcus, get up. Get up." I
thought, "He's okay." When they rolled him over, his head was
back and mouth was open. And I thought, "He died."

He was unconscious. The doctor was monitoring his heart.
For that short period of time, it was like one of my children was
dying right in front of me. It was a shock—a physical reaction.

Then his leg kicked, and you could see that he had become
semiconscious. But at that point, I had no idea of what had happened to him.

When they got him on the stretcher, I went in and saw the
team. Jimmy Baron, the Bonnies' coach, came up to me and said,
"Coach, we'll do whatever you need, whatever you want to do. If
you want to cancel the game, we'll do it."

"No," I said, "we'll play the game. I'm not going to do that.

You've got these people here. But I'm not going to coach. I'm going to go to the hospital."

At this point, Marcus still had not come around. He was semi-conscious. His eyes were open, but he was almost comatose.

When I met with the team, I told them, "I want you to understand. If this was any of you who was unconscious, I would be going to the hospital with you. It does not matter that this is Marcus. Okay?"

If one of my daughters got light-headed and fainted on the way to a game, I wouldn't go to the game. I would go to the hospital to be with my daughter.

As Marcus came back past us on the stretcher, the team and staff said a prayer in the hallway. We held hands. As he came through, everybody touched him. Then he was wheeled out. I just looked at Bru and said, "Do a good job. I know you will."

I hugged him and left.

In the ambulance, I held Marcus's hand and rubbed his head. I was praying. I told him, "I love you, Marcus. Are you doing okay?" He started to respond to talking. He nodded. He was conscious, but he wasn't speaking. He was squeezing my hand, and I was squeezing his—all the way to the hospital.

I asked about his heart rate. I was told, "His heart is fine." In fact, his heart rate had been very good from the time the doctor got to him, which was thirty seconds after he hit the floor.

After we arrived at Olean General Hospital, Marcus started answering a few questions he was asked. The doctors did some tests on him right away. But he wasn't fully alert until twenty-five to thirty minutes later, when he went in to have a CAT scan.

Then he asked me, "What's the score of the game?"

Someone gave him the score.

He knew there was a game going on, but he didn't know what

had happened to him. He remembered getting on the bus. He remembered waking up in the hospital. He didn't remember going through a pre-game talk, about warm ups.

I was sitting in the waiting room, and the game was on outside. I asked to have it turned off because I didn't want to be hearing or thinking about the game. I didn't care about the game. I just wanted to focus on him. A priest from St. Bonaventure came in. We prayed.

His mother had seen what happened on TV. Her phone began ringing with calls from friends wanting to know if Marcus was all right. I called her as soon as he regained consciousness. Eventually, I went into his room. I started talking to him. I could see he was better. I said, "They're going to have to do some tests."

That evening, when the doctors finally told me they felt comfortable that there was no danger to his life, I felt like we had just won the NCAA tournament.

Marcus wanted to go home with the team. I said, "Look, you're going to stay here overnight." They felt there was nothing wrong with his heart, but they wanted to conduct some other tests. I stayed. After the game was over, I had Bruiser and our trainer stay. The rest of the team left and drove back to Buffalo for the night and then flew back to Amherst on a commercial flight. I wanted us to go back with them, but the doctors had a few more tests they wanted to do before they would let Marcus travel.

The doctors at Olean wanted us to go by Medivac. I said, "You said nothing was wrong. Do you understand that if we travel by Medivac, the country is going to say, 'If nothing's wrong, why are you traveling by Medivac?' "

They said, "It's a precaution. What if, while he's traveling, something happens. We want to get a read on it. John, you need to do this because we want to keep everything hooked up so that if he has another fainting spell, we'll have a good idea of what is causing it."

Obviously, it didn't happen.

We went up in the Medivac plane and when we landed in Worcester, they took him out on the gurney, put him right into the helicopter, and flew him to the Medical Center. That's how he got there.

I was driven by car.

While we had been sitting in the Medivac, I saw the chopper and said to him, "Look, I love you, but I am not riding in this helicopter. You go in the helicopter, and I'll meet you over at the hospital."

Marcus laughed.

We went to the UMass Medical Center in Worcester, and more tests were done. They had done a spinal tap in Olean the day before, but Marcus's head was still absolutely throbbing. From this experience, I learned that spinal fluid is the same fluid that bathes your brain. When they tap your spine, they're also tapping fluid from your brain. Your brain moves a little bit, which causes a massive headache. His head was just pounding.

Marcus spent four days in the hospital in Worcester.

During that time, people were constantly trying to compare his situation to that of Hank Gathers and Reggie Lewis. Gathers had died of a heart attack during a West Coast Athletic Conference game. People said Lewis's death was drug-related and immediately started asking questions about substance abuse. It made me mad because people didn't know the particulars of what we knew. It wasn't Marcus's heart. It wasn't an aneurism. It wasn't drug-related. It wasn't a stroke. It wasn't any of those, and the tests proved it.

The other thing people didn't know then, including me, was

that 50 percent of all blackouts go undiagnosed. When that was told to me, it was pretty simple. "Hey, this kid is not taking care of his body if you're telling me it's not his heart and it's not his head. I know he doesn't eat right. I know he doesn't take good care of himself. I know he weighs only 215 pounds. I know he's seven feet tall and he runs like a deer. I know we challenge him and he's expending energy. I know we've traveled all over the world, playing basketball."

I said to him, "You've got to take better care of yourself."

He had been taking some cough medicine at the time of the blackout. He'd been run down. He'd had a cold. His blood sugar was a little low; it fluctuates. His grandmother died from diabetes; it's in his family. He's also a little anemic. What I think it adds up to is the kid needed to take better care of himself.

Maybe something will prove me wrong. I'm not a doctor. But I'm telling you that I went through every one of his tests with him. I was there. I saw the results. I know what it's not.

Marcus was a perfect patient most of the time, but he did balk at one of the tests, pulling the covers over his head and refusing to get out of bed, according to Dr. Joel Gore, a cardiologist at UMass Medical Center.

Marcus gave autographs to the nurses, posed for pictures with the doctors, and visited the pediatric ward.

Marcus has a human side to him.

All Marcus did while he was in the hospital was beg me to get him out. The main reason is that all the tests they did—the spinal tap and everything else—made him sick. It wasn't fainting that made him sick, it was the tests afterwards. Every time they did a test, he got sick. He was looking at me, saying, "I need to get out of here. I'm telling you I'm all right. If I stay in here, something may happen to me. Coach, you've got to get me out."

Dr. Gore, who was overseeing the whole thing, was really

good. He was bringing him junk food. He knew Marcus needed salt, so he brought him potato chips. I think Marcus really appreciated that.

I wanted Marcus to come to Pittsburgh that weekend, just to be with us. How about this one? He was at the Duquesne game, but he did not want to sit on the bench and be the focal point. So he stayed at the hotel. He felt that if we won and someone played well, the media weren't going to interview that player, they would interview him.

He decided to shoot around the next day. The trainers called the doctors the morning of the game and said, "Everything seems to be going well, but it doesn't look like Coach is going to play him tonight."

Dr. Gore said, "Why? Why is he holding him out? We had cleared him to play. When is he going to start playing?"

That's what Marcus wanted to know, too. He came to me and said, "You know I want to play tonight."

I called his mom and said, "Janice, the doctors have cleared your son to play. The doctors *want* your son to play. How do you feel about that?"

She hesitated, then said, "You're not going to play him a long time, are you?"

I said, "No. If I play him, it will be for a short time. But he wants to play. Just how comfortable would you be with my putting him in?"

She said, "Well, if he really wants to play and feels comfortable, I would say okay."

I thought about it all day: "Well, maybe I'll play him." Then I just said, "Hell, there's no way. I'm not going to play him."

So I didn't, even though Marcus was dressed for our overtime victory at Pitt. I wasn't afraid he would pass out. But he had missed four games, and he hadn't been in live practice. He'd run up and down the court, done conditioning and shooting. But that's all he'd done. I just didn't feel comfortable. It was more for him. I didn't feel like having him go out there, have a shaky game, and have everybody say, "Wow, you know, he's not the same player."

During that game, he came up to me twice—with about three minutes left in regulation, and then in overtime—and said, "Put me in. I want to play."

I said, "No. Just sit down. We're all right. We'll figure this out."

So we didn't play him.

The day Marcus came back, we played St. Bonaventure at our place. You've got to understand: the tickets around here are hard to get anyway. But that game was the hardest ticket we've ever had. Joe Malone was there. Senator John F. Kerry was there. The UMass president and chancellor were there. They were all there. It was a Who's Who of the state. Everybody wanted tickets.

And a lot of people got them. We had a sellout crowd, even though most of the fans had to venture out in a downpour. The reason wasn't St. Bonaventure. It was Marcus Camby.

Before the game I'd told him, "You play a little bit. And if you feel anything, you come out. I don't care what it is. You stop. You quit." He felt okay, and everything went well. I think part of his being scared was my being scared.

His mom was nervous. She was there, along with Jackie Bethea—and all his friends and family. Everybody was there for him, and everybody wanted him to play.

Marcus wanted to play, too, even though he admitted to being a little nervous when the P.A. man at the Mullins Center announced the starting lineup. "I felt like it was my freshman year all over again," he said. "My palms were getting sweaty. I was just anxious to get out on the floor."

He sure didn't play like a freshman. Marcus reacted to the thunderous applause and adoration he received by scoring 19 points, grabbing seven rebounds, and blocking a school-record nine shots as we beat the Bonnies, 72–47.

He looked rusty at first, missing his first two shots. Then he made his next six, reestablishing the fact that we played at another level when he was in the game.

"I think I was forcing it a little bit at first," he says. "Then Coach Cal took me out briefly and told me to play defense, rebound, and block shots. After a while, the offense just came around."

Marcus shot six for eight and made seven of eight free throws. He played twenty-six minutes and punctuated his performance by scoring his 1,000th career point when he nailed a baseline jumper to give us a 60–39 lead with 7:32 to play.

"They ran a play for me—a pull-up jump shot off the dribble," he said. "I hit it and after that I said, 'Yeah, I'm back. I'm back.' I had that shot going, my inside game going, my outside game going, and I was hitting my free throws. And I felt fine. It was a great day for me."

It was a great day for all of us. How did we know he was ready? We pushed him. I'd be leaving practice and what's he on? The StairMaster. The same thing in shoot-around. He was alive, ready.

So I had no problems starting Marcus. In the NBA or the NFL, if a guy is a starting center and he gets hurt, he starts when he comes back. That's how it is with us. If Hakeem Olajuwon went down and was out two weeks, he starts. I don't think that's any reason to mess around.

Marcus did have the benefit of coming back against a team he could dominate. Our entire team dominated the Bonnies. We got 15 points apiece from Donta and Edgar, shooting 53.2 percent and making nine three-pointers. Forward Robert Blackwell led the Bonnies with 10.

"I feel relieved," Marcus said to the media. "After today, you guys will finally leave me alone."

Wishful thinking.

I have to give Marcus credit. He focused on each game during the rest of the season. We told him, "Forget about the NBA. Worry about now. Worry about the NBA when this season ends." He did that for us this year. And it was hard. I'm not so sure some of the other guys we had last year did that.

Two weeks after Marcus returned, we heard that Chris Daniels of Dayton had died suddenly. That wasn't a good day for Marcus. He had a respiratory infection, and he was coughing a little bit. While he was running in practice that afternoon, he got chest pains—and it scared us. We found out later that the pains were mostly from the cough, but at that point, I was just thinking, "Is something wrong with him? Is he okay?" We told the doctors about it, and they said, "Nah, nah, nah, nah. That was his chest. There's a difference."

But Marcus was shaken up. I was, too. I sat him down and said, "Hey, man, at any point in time, if you feel anything, you step off this court."

He looked at me and said, "Don't worry about that."

I later learned that Daniels' problem was arrhythmia, a condition Marcus doesn't have. But in the back of his mind, he had to have been thinking, "Maybe something is wrong with me, too."

As a team, that day, we took time out to say a prayer for Chris and his family. We wanted to let our players know they're not invincible, they're all human beings. That life is fleeting—we're here today, gone tomorrow—and let's just be thankful. In Marcus's case, I think that put things in a different perspective.

Marcus is a very reserved, almost introverted person, but he's

246 JOHN CALIPARI WITH DICK WEISS

learning to give up some of himself. He's learned to come out of that shell to help other people, especially young people. He's much more comfortable around young people because he knows he has a better impact on them. He knows they really look up to him. He's not into trying to impress adults. He doesn't feel comfortable in those situations.

While Marcus was in the hospital in Worcester, undergoing tests, he met a young man dying of kidney disease. Marcus went down to the boy's room twice and spent an hour, two hours with him. The young man's uncle said it was the first time in a while he had seen his nephew smile. Some of the most special moments of this boy's life were spent with Marcus Camby.

The boy died two weeks later.

It touched all of us.

The uncle wrote about his nephew in the Worcester paper, and we got a copy of the article. The story was incredible. The uncle said our team would have a sixth man, and it would be this youngster.

I read it to the team before our game with Georgetown.

Marcus was an education major. He tutored fifth- and sixth-grade special education students at the South Hadley Middle School as part of a course he was taking.

"I used to help with geography and spelling," he says. "Usually, I'd be nervous and upset before a game, but the kids make you so happy when you walk through the door. The whole class would run up to me, ask me to help them."

Marcus has plans to become a principal when his professional basketball career is over.

In about twelve years.

Marcus has never forgotten where he came from. After the season, he returned to his roots and spent a couple of hours a day at the Kelvin Anderson Recreation Center, just kicking back with Jackie Bethea and the kids. "I'm not going to change because of a different lifestyle," he said. "I'm from the projects. I don't want anybody to think I'm any different."

When people ask me what Marcus did for the program, I usually say, "He was the kind of guy who gave us a player that no one else in the country had. He was different. He wasn't a dominating player all the time, but because he was seven feet tall and could block shots, he could be unstoppable. He didn't always dominate. But when you threw him in with the other guys on our team, he would just change the complexion of any game."

And he's had an impact on UMass's recruiting, too. Now, if there's a player who wants to be Player of the Year, he can come to UMass and the program can help him get there. It's been proven. There aren't many programs in the country that can say they've had a Player of the Year. We're talking North Carolina, Kansas, and Virginia. And now, UMass.

But how many programs out there are going to highlight a guy, put him on national TV a lot, and schedule games so he's thought of as the Player of the Year?

Just a few—and UMass is one of them.

CHAPTER 14

MARCH TO THE MEADOWLANDS

If you think about it, the best UMass basketball has always been played in March. Particularly over the past five years, when our record in the final month of the season was 30–5.

We won five straight Atlantic 10 tournaments. We went to five consecutive NCAA tournaments. We went to a Sweet 16 in 1992. We played in a regional final in 1995.

And, in 1996, we finally made it to the Final Four.

Everything we did was built on getting our team ready for a tournament run. We talked about it at the beginning. Obviously, we started the season by playing a great schedule. But we were also playing to have fresh legs and fresh minds—and to have a hunger—in March.

I didn't want to bury our players and wear them out. I didn't want them just playing the string out. I wanted them inspired. I wanted them on a high in March.

And they were when it counted.

We played our two best games of the year when we defeated Arkansas and Georgetown to win the NCAA East Regionals in Atlanta.

Maybe that's why it hurt so much when we finally lost to Kentucky in the NCAA semifinals at the Meadowlands.

I admit it: I cried. We all did.

It took us almost ten minutes to compose ourselves in the locker room afterwards. If we had to lose to someone, I'm glad it was to Kentucky and Rick Pitino. But that didn't make it any easier for our team. It still hurt. We had set a goal of winning the national championship when the season began. And we came so close.

I just wish the NCAA hadn't paired us against Kentucky in the semifinals because we could have let it all out in the championship game. It would have been an unbelievable finish: No. 1 vs. No. 2. But it didn't happen that way.

At least, we gained some respect in the eyes of people who thought we could never get this far.

We had been on a roll throughout the season, beginning the year with a stunning 92–82 victory over the same Cats. The Wildcats waited four months for their revenge. But that should not detract from what we accomplished on the road to the Final Four.

Each year, I've taken one or two subjects and said, "This is what they're going to hear the most." And I'll just say it in every interview. The main reason I do this is that the more you say something, the more it's believed, and the more the media zero in on what you're saying.

In 1995, it was "positive psychology." I talked about how you have to give off positive vibes; that you can't be negative because everybody else feeds on it. We had a couple of guys who thought it was all right to be negative in their psychology: the way they walked, the way they came to a meeting, the way they acted when they didn't feel like being at practice. Negative psychology affects everybody, so we talked about positive psychology: being with one another, challenging one another to do the right things.

This time, I followed that up by talking about breaking barriers.

With about two or three weeks left in the regular season, we tried to zero in on the teams we might be playing if we advanced to the Elite Eight or the Final Four. John Robic and Ed Schilling started breaking down how those teams would try to play and what they'd try to do.

We came up with a couple of things. One, we felt there would be a lot of pressing, so we spent five minutes a day on the press. We also thought we'd need to play some zone and would need to press a little bit ourselves if we got down. So we worked on all of those things.

We didn't necessarily try to prepare for the first couple of rounds because it was a smorgasbord out there.

I thought we'd be a one- or a two-seed and would be sent either to the East or the West Regionals. I didn't know what would happen with Connecticut after they had defeated Georgetown to win the Big East tournament. I thought originally the committee might put us in the same region, with one of us first and the other one second.

As it turned out, we were the first seed in the East, and UConn was the top seed in the Southeast. The committee made Georgetown the second seed in the East. We ended up in the same side of the bracket as Arkansas, Georgetown, and Kentucky, three high-pressure teams. So we'd guessed right.

We hardly looked like a Final Four team at the start of our opening-round game with 16th-seeded Central Florida. We struggled to a 45–39 lead at half.

What is needed in these situations is for guys to step up. Certain guys have to dominate at times. It isn't Xs and Os. Edgar

Padilla and Carmelo Travieso took care of business, clamping down on the Knights defensively with full-court pressure that destroyed any attempts UCF made to get the ball over half-court in the opening moments of the second half. Edgar personally popped UCF's bubble, bunching 6 points and five steals into less than two minutes to fuel a 12–0 run as we turned a close game into a 92–70 rout.

"When you start making steals in the open court and picking off passes to the post, it makes the other team think instead of just react to what we were doing," Carmelo says. "Their guys were thinking out of bounds, 'Who should I throw it to?' and we were just waiting for them to throw it."

Edgar finished with 15 points, eight assists, and seven steals. Carmelo made six three-pointers and finished with 21 points.

And Marcus Camby wound up with four stitches in his forehead after he was whacked by Central Florida forward Reid Ketteler with 9:44 to play. Marcus returned to the game with 5:26 remaining and finished up with 14 points and seventeen rebounds. But he shot just seven for twenty-two. That had me concerned.

I knew that Marcus was going to have to dominate for us to get to the Final Four. He couldn't keep playing like he had been playing. He wasn't shooting the ball well. He wasn't being aggressive.

I thought the pressure was getting to him. He was a candidate for Player of the Year. He had all these things going for him. He was up against it, and he was a little panicked.

I told him, "You don't have to be great. You just have to do what you do best. If you have a great game, we're going to win by 30. Just be you, and we'll win by 15. But you've got to go out and play and be you, at least."

But it was hard.

He'd never been in that situation before. And everybody was expecting him to do X, Y, and Z. Marcus always thought of himself as just an ordinary guy. I kept telling him, "Don't be afraid to be special. Don't be afraid to step out, to do the best you can. If you flop occasionally, that happens."

The rest of the team were all doing the best they could. But they were all feeling it. We all felt the pressure to win.

Especially in our second-round matchup with Stanford.

That game scared us.

We knew they had guards who could beat us—and they almost did. Brevin Knight had 27 points and nine assists. If you had asked Stanford coach Mike Montgomery before the game, he'd probably have told you, "If Brevin gets those kinds of numbers, we'll win going away."

As it turned out, we won 79–74—but not until Donta Bright had made a clutch jump shot from just inside the foul line with thirty seconds to play to give us a 3-point lead, and Pete Sauer missed a three-pointer on Stanford's next possession.

And not until I shook up Marcus.

I told him to take a seat at the beginning of the second half of our game against Stanford because his concentration had been drifting.

I walked out and told him I was going to start Tyrone Weeks.

I said, "You have three fouls."

"Tyrone has three, too," he said.

"I know that."

And I walked away. That wasn't for public consumption, but he knew what I was doing. When I finally put Marcus in, he blocked three of Knight's shots in the first nine minutes of the half and went on to score 22 points, grab eight rebounds, and block seven shots.

I had been hoping to spend a rare day off with my family after that win. But my plans changed when I received an invitation to a long-standing St. Patrick's Day breakfast in South Boston from William Bulger, the new president of the University of Massachusetts.

When I said I didn't know if I could make it, there was a long pause on the other end of the line, so I figured it must be important.

It was.

Until his recent appointment to UMass, Bill Bulger had been the powerful president of the Massachusetts state senate since 1979. When I walked into the Bayside Club Sunday morning, the place was packed with important political figures, who were there for the pre-parade festivities. Local television carried it live.

I had no idea, though, that I would wind up talking to the president of the United States. Bill Bulger called me up to the podium and, all of a sudden, I was on the phone with President Clinton, a huge Arkansas fan whose Razorbacks were scheduled to play us that Thursday in the NCAA Sweet 16 at the Georgia Dome in Atlanta.

Tony Lake, a former UMass professor, is the president's national security advisor. He's a big basketball fan, so I said to President Clinton, "Have you and Tony made a bet on the game yet?"

He started laughing.

"Yes, we have," the president said. "But sometimes I have to root for you guys because when you lose, he goes into a deep depression and it affects the rest of the world."

Then I asked if he planned to attend the game. "They never lose when you come to the game," I said.

"You know . . ." Clinton said, "I can't be there."

"Very good," I said. "Glad you can't be there."

With that, the entire place cracked up.

When I got back to Amherst that afternoon, I didn't even watch much of the Sunday afternoon games. First, it was off to the Mullins Center to visit with my staff, who were busy video-taping games from the East Regionals from the two satellite dishes outside the building. Then it was off to an hour-long meeting at three with Bob Marcum about travel plans. This was spring break, and the team planned to fly south after practice Monday night. We wanted to make sure the coaches' families were included on the charter flight home.

I also wanted to make sure no one served the team oatmeal with raisins before the game the way they did in Providence before the close call with Stanford. That had been bad luck for us earlier this year. I'm less superstitious now than I was five years ago. But you get into a routine about what you do—how you travel, how you eat, the meals you order, the hotels you stay in. If you won when you had stayed in a certain hotel, why would you change?

I didn't watch any tapes. I hurried home and hung out with the girls. I even found time to practice with Megan on my new indoor putting machine. Ellen is pregnant with our third child, so I drew baby-sitting duty and took Erin and Megan with me that night to Rafters, a local restaurant, to eat hamburgers and ribs at a team get-together. Quality time.

Erin knows how to get on her father's good side. "Dad," she said, "you should be able to beat Arkansas because they're not as good as they used to be."

"But," I told her, "they're still good."

And we almost had to play them at less than full strength.

Carmelo had built up a reputation as the team's practical joker, so when he fell off the stage while making his way to an NCAA tournament press conference the day before the regional semifinals, his teammates started chuckling.

Only this time, it was no laughing matter.

Carmelo bruised his lower back following a five-foot fall into a metal frame that was being used to support the platform. He spent an hour in the locker room where trainer Ron Laham applied ice to the injury. He missed the team's 3:30 P.M. shootaround in the massive Georgia Dome. "I don't remember exactly how I fell," Carmelo said. "I went to step around Marcus's chair to get to my seat. I thought there was a wall behind the platform, but there was nothing but air. I ended up grabbing onto a ladder behind the stage to break my fall.

"It was scary. I'm not in training to be a stunt man. I didn't know how far the drop was. I couldn't believe it. I just kept saying, 'Oh my God, not this.' I just laid there, waiting for the doctor to come and check me out. Then I got up and told him it was fine.

"Right now, it hurts like crazy."

Our trainer did not seem that concerned about the injury. "He's obviously going to be sore, but it's nothing else. He didn't hit his head or his shoulder. We'll just keep icing him."

Carmelo was supposed to draw the defensive assignment on Arkansas freshman guard Pat Bradley, who was, ironically, from Everett, Massachusetts, a suburb of Boston. Bradley had been one of the major surprises of Arkansas's wild ride to the Sweet 16, surfacing as his team's best 3-point shooter. He was averaging 11.5 points his last eleven games and hit twenty-three treys in his last five performances. Bradley grew up as an enormous Celtics fan. "L.B. [Larry Bird] No. 1," he said. He never saw too much of UMass in high school. And we never saw much of him.

Arkansas coach Nolan Richardson had discovered Bradley

when he played for a Boston AAU team in the seventeen-and-under nationals at Winston-Salem. He became enamored with Bradley's long-range shooting stroke and offered him a scholarship that fall.

Aside from Arkansas, Bradley was recruited by Boston University, Hartford, and St. Bonaventure. Given the fact that he never got a sniff from a Big East school and UMass never got a chance to evaluate him the fall of his senior year because he'd been injured, Arkansas seemed like his best bet to play big-time basketball.

All week long, Richardson had suggested his team—which had won a national title in 1994 and been to the championship game in 1995—was a team with nothing to lose. "We're not expected to win this game," he said. "We want to win this game. UMass has to win to keep its No. 1 ranking."

He obviously didn't know me. I wasn't going to let his comments affect me. I was more affected on the day of the game when Marcus got caught in traffic on the way back from a local mall.

I was the one who had told Marcus and the guys, "Don't stay in your rooms all day because it's going to be a late game. Don't be lethargic. Go out. Go to the mall. Go do what you want to do. Come back, and we'll go to shoot-around at four."

Marcus got caught in traffic and was late for the bus. He hadn't been late for anything all year. But that day he was late. He walked in. He didn't apologize or say anything to the team. He just went to the back and sat down. I got a little mad. If he had said "I apologize," it would have been all right, but he didn't really know how to react.

I just made a decision that I wasn't going to start him. I told the team and I told him. He apologized to the team, and I said,

"Well, I'm not going to start you tonight, but you'll handle it like you've handled everything else." And he did.

When you think about it, I had no choice but to sit him at the start of the game. I had to make a point. I have to be consistent in how I deal with all my kids, even my star.

Marcus had no problems with it. It was no big deal. But he was little more than a spectator as we defeated Arkansas, 79–63, to advance to the Regional Finals against Georgetown. I put him in with 1:13 gone. We already were ahead, 7–0. He immediately hit a jumper, but he was not much of a factor as we cruised to a 40–24 lead at the half. Marcus did finish with 15 points, but he spent close to eight minutes on the bench after picking up his third personal foul early in the game.

Tyrone, who started in place of Marcus, powered his way to 16 points, and Dana added 12. The two combined for 19 points in the first half. Carmelo recovered from his sore back long enough to make a pair of three-pointers early in the second half and finish with 14 points.

I wish I could tell you our bandwagon was getting full.

But no one had us advancing. And I mean that literally.

Everyone thought Georgetown was unstoppable, especially Dick Vitale. He picked us to lose.

"That's okay," I said. "He's very rarely accurate in his picks. As a matter of fact, he picked the Germans in World War II."

They kept running that film clip all week on ESPN.

I had to laugh. I said, "I'd like to see the pools on our campus to find out how many of our own students picked us. We haven't been to the Final Four. We haven't won the national title. Until we do, people will say, 'Aah, they can't do this.' "

It was just another barrier to break.

I wasn't mad about it. We do not teach an "Us against the

world" mentality. That's not what this country was built on. It's about "How many people can I help who will eventually help me?"

Actually, the fact so many people thought we couldn't win helped us. It let our guys know they didn't have the respect they felt they deserved. People bought into the theory that the Atlantic 10 was a bad league and Georgetown had been there before. They had won a national title. It's that old Big East mentality. They're a media machine. They crank out so much hype from the machine that, after a while, people believe it.

The day before we played Georgetown, I took the team over to visit John Gilpatrick and Travis Roy, two paralyzed hockey players, at the Atlanta Spinal Hospital. We could just as easily have been going over there to see Carmelo. He had fallen far enough that he could have broken his neck and been paralyzed. Our kids looked at these kids who could barely move and yet who still had a great outlook on life. I said, "Look at these two kids—upbeat and positive. And sometimes you guys get down. How could you ever be down after seeing that?"

I think Georgetown felt they were playing a team people told them was "not as good as everybody thinks." They didn't understand Marcus was a pretty good player. I don't think they had enough respect for our guards.

Other teams said, "They're not that good."

There was no "Win One for the Gipper" speech. I said, "You know what you have to do. Nobody thinks you can win the game. This is a great game for us to go out and just play ball." We went out on the floor together and the guys really performed. The chemistry that day was great. Maybe now, no one will view UMass as second-class citizens in their own backyard.

Marcus scored 22 points, grabbed seven rebounds, and

blocked three shots in twenty-eight minutes that night as we defeated Georgetown, 86–62, to win the NCAA East Regional before a crowd of 32,328 at the Georgia Dome. Marcus, who was selected the Most Outstanding Player in the regional by a media panel, totally took over the game at the beginning of the second half, scoring 8 of his team's first 11 points as we went on an 11–1 run, surging to a 49–35 lead with 17:02 remaining.

It was good to see us come out with all kinds of emotion and passion. We simply squeezed the air out of the Hoyas after that, cruising to a spot opposite Midwest Regional winner Kentucky in the NCAA semifinals and making a dramatic statement for the quality of our program.

I told my teams, "I want you to be the predators, not the prey. We want to hunt, not to be hunted. We want to be on our toes and have our opponents on their heels. We don't ever want to be on the defensive, even when we don't have the ball."

And that's what we did to Georgetown.

We'd had a chance to go to the Final Four in 1995, but the team let their dream slip away in the second half of an East Regional final against Oklahoma State. This year, Marcus wanted to make sure it didn't happen again.

I thought he was terrific, but that's Marcus. It didn't stun me because I'd been seeing it all year. The only thing I asked him to do at halftime was to play with more emotion and passion. "Block out everything on the outside. Just be with us and get done what you have to get done." He was the Player of the Year. We fed off him. We fed off his emotion. And he did his job.

Carmelo, who joined Marcus and Donta on the All Regional team, finished with 20 points and splashed home six threes, but he will be best remembered for the job he did on Georgetown's brilliant sophomore guard Allen Iverson. Iverson scored 22 points, but Carmelo tied and gagged him when it counted, holding him to just 6 points in the second half. He did a fabulous job of making the game hard for Iverson—continually making him drive into our defense instead of shooting shots. But everyone else helped Carmelo. It was a team effort.

At one point, Iverson missed eight straight field goal attempts. He did not score his first field goal of the second half until there was only 8:46 left—and we were comfortably ahead, 63–49. "He was a little frustrated," Carmelo said. "I tried to keep harrassing him, to be physical. I just kept playing him the way he didn't want to be played. I got a lot of help from Edgar and the rest of the guys when he drove in. I saw him just kind of give up a little bit and I picked up my level."

With eight minutes left, I was saying to myself, "They can't come back." Then I said, "I'd better not think that way." So I blocked it out.

With about four minutes left in the game, I knew we were going to the Final Four. What was nice was that it wasn't coming down to a last-second shot, so I could enjoy the last part of the game.

I did not want to look ahead to Kentucky just yet. When UMass students began chanting, "We want the Wildcats," with 2:18 to play, I waved them off.

People wondered why we didn't cut down the nets after we beat the Hoyas to advance to the Final Four. Part of the reason I wasn't going to go running out at half-court, pumping my arms and going nuts, was because I didn't want to show up John Thompson. John Thompson is a Hall of Fame coach. He's won 10,000 games. He's coached All Pros. He's been a benchmark for me and other coaches.

And my team had enough class that they weren't going to sit

on rims. Hey, they enjoyed this. They were excited. But part of our team is the sportsmanship we show. Later, the managers cut down the nets and brought them to us.

Iverson, who shot just one for ten in the second half, appeared dazed that his season was over.

So did Spike Lee.

Our players had first met Spike when we'd gone to the Garden to watch the Pistons, with Lou Roe, play the Knicks the night before our game with Fordham. At the time, he had tweaked our guys, saying we couldn't beat Georgetown, that we had no answer for Allen Iverson.

After our win over Georgetown, Donta spotted Spike, a huge Hoya fan who had done a profile of John Thompson for HBO, in the stands. Spike was wearing a Georgetown jersey with Iverson's number on it.

Donta took off his own jersey and casually flipped it to him.

"He had the wrong shirt on," Donta recalled.

Spike handed the jersey back to Donta and wished him luck.

When we went into the locker room afterwards, each of our players picked up the stat sheets to see how many points the player he was guarding had scored. "Check out No. 44," Edgar said to me. No. 44—Victor Page, Edgar's man: zero points.

Then we all kicked back. There was almost a sense of relief. We wanted to step away and cool down before we did anything else. Everybody was laughing, joking, putting the nets around one another.

We tried to low-key our matchup with Kentucky. "We beat them once before this year and we're looking forward to beating them again," Edgar said.

"Actually, I was hoping another team—no name—would be there, but they won't be," Marcus said, referring to UConn.

The week leading up to the Kentucky game was so hectic we couldn't get anything done, so we decided to leave Tuesday night for New York.

Bruiser had asked me, "Do you mind if I leave early for New York because St. Joe's is playing in the NIT?" I asked when they were playing. He said, "They play the late game." I said, "Why don't we practice and take the whole team down? Why don't you call them, to see if they'd mind. We'll show support for them."

I did it, too, for Jack Powers, the executive director of the tournament, who has been really good to us. I said, "I hope you understand we're here to support St. Joe's. We're also here to support the NIT."

It was a long bus ride down to New York. The driver went about thirty miles an hour. They had given him a brand-new bus and told him, "If you get a scratch on it, you're fired." He was a young guy, a good guy. Anytime a car passed him, he slowed down. A truck passed him; he almost pulled off to the side of the road.

We finally got there midway through St. Joseph's overtime win over Alabama. ESPN wanted me to go on television. But I told them, "This is not about me—or us. This is about St. Joe's and I'd rather not go on because this is their night. Our night's coming up."

Afterwards, Phil Martelli, the St. Joseph's coach, invited me into the locker room. "They've already met a poor Italian," he said. "I want them to see what a rich Italian looks like."

I just said, "Win the whole thing, man. We're going to try to do the same. You guys have been great all year."

I told them our kids had really enjoyed the game. Phil had a great line: "We gave you twenty tickets to our tournament. I was hoping you'd give us twenty tickets to yours."

Tickets?

Forget it.

The team got 250 tickets and I got ninety-two. I gave them out to my father, my mother, my sisters and their families, my high school coach and his wife, some of my high school team-mates, my college coach and his wife, my college roommates. I told my AD this was an opportunity to reward some people who had helped me along the way.

I was questioned in the newspaper about giving a couple of tickets to people who had shady backgrounds. But the reality is, a lot of people had touched my life over the years. I was not involved in business dealings with them.

All of our former players were invited and given tickets if they wanted to come. I wanted to make sure our staff could bring their families.

I thought we might catch some flak for arriving for the Final Four early, but since we were graduating four of our five seniors on time, this was never an academic issue. I'm a person who likes his team to be together all of the time, and I like to be with them all of the time.

Our team stayed in New Jersey. We practiced; then we told the guys to go to the movies, go to the mall, just enjoy themselves. I said, "You live this only once. Enjoy yourselves. We expect to win the game."

Our Wednesday practice was one of the best we'd had all year. And on Thursday, I felt we were going to be in good shape.

There were some distractions. I guess we should talk about the rumors about me and the St. John's job that surfaced in the midst of Final Four week.

People who were big St. John's boosters were trying to talk to me about doing it, and the stories hit the New York papers. The *Post* was throwing around numbers like $1 million a year.

I'd be walking down the street, or having dinner, and people would be coming up to me: "Please come to St. John's. Please come to St. John's."

I never talked to their AD, Ed Manetta. I never talked to him. I wouldn't know Ed Manetta if he walked in here right now. People say I met with him, we were negotiating. That was not true.

Bob Marcum came into my office when I returned from the Final Four. Manetta had called and asked permission to speak with me.

Bob asked if I had any interest in meeting with them.

I said, "No."

I didn't want to be pulled into a situation where they needed to say, "They interviewed John Calipari and, in the end, they couldn't make it work."

That's why I said to Bob, "Just tell them I have no interest."

As it turned out, they eventually hired Fran Fraschilla of Manhattan, who had been my roommate when we were both eighteen and worked as counselors at the Dean Smith Basketball School at North Carolina.

Fran and his wife, Meg, are great friends of mine. Let me tell you about Fran. He's one of the brightest coaches, hardest workers, and best recruiters out there. He has an understanding of how to work with alums and the media. In my mind, there was not a better choice for the St. John's job. I think he'll have that program back on top within a short period of time.

At the press conference before the Kentucky game, most of the questions were directed toward Marcus, who seemed to be the biggest obstacle standing in the way of Kentucky winning a sixth national championship and the school's first since 1978. "They're playing for revenge," Marcus said. "We're playing for respect."

Rick Pitino and I didn't talk during the week of the Final Four. We communicated through Jersey Red, who was staying at Kentucky's hotel. The morning of our game, I called and said, "Kenneth James Aloysius, well, it's a beautiful morning. I don't know what Rick's doing. He's probably in strategy meetings.

"Why don't you tell him I'm going roller-skating with my daughters. Then I'm going out to have a great lunch with my family, and later I'm going to have a nice, nice nap. I realize he probably won't be able to sleep because of all the pressure."

Jersey immediately called Rick and told him, "Oh, we've got to get him."

Jersey called me back at two-thirty in the afternoon. He told me he had just run into a guy in the hotel who stopped him and told him that on the Monday of the Final Four, a Boston newspaper would do an exposé on all the class time our players had missed. They made it up, but I fell for it.

Jersey was probably howling with laughter.

Normally, Jersey would come to a couple of games. When we beat Kentucky in the season opener, he told me, "The next game I come to, you guys are going to lose."

He'd said that early in the season. What he meant was, "You guys are good enough that you're going to be playing Kentucky in the final game. I'm going to be there and you're going to lose."

His brother, "The Faa," is a sportswriter down in Jersey City. He and Jersey haven't spoken in twenty years. We had Father Jay Maddock of Fall River rooting for us. And Rick had Jersey. Jersey once told Rick, "As long as my brother is anywhere close to your bench, you have no shot of winning. He is the Prince of Darkness."

When you're playing Kentucky, which has so many players, it's like playing blackjack. And Rick is the dealer. He deals himself blackjack and you lose. He wins all pushes. I think you have to look at it in those terms. They played a great game against us during a 81–74 Cats victory. It's not that we played bad. We didn't play as well as we could play. But they had a lot to do with that. They had so many guys, so much room for error.

I knew we were nervous and a little scared. And that surprised me. But we were all up against it. This was the first time we had been to a Final Four.

Tony Delk led Kentucky with 20 points. Antoine Walker added 14. Kentucky shot 50.9 percent and attacked the basket well enough in their half-court sets as they effectively coped with our man-to-man defense in late game situations.

The Wildcats came after us defensively with an army of players, smothering Edgar and Carmelo with trap pressure that limited them to a combined five field goals, and forcing us into nineteen turnovers. They made Marcus work hard for his 25 points, eight rebounds, and six blocks by constantly double-teaming him. Kentucky was willing to concede Marcus his numbers. "We knew he was going to get his points," Walker said. "Our job was to stop the other guys."

We never quit, even after Kentucky scored the first 7 points of the second half to take a 43–28 lead. Each time Kentucky looked like it was about to pull away, we closed the gap. Kentucky went up, 59–49, when Ron Mercer made a three-pointer. But we cut the lead to 63–60 with an 11–4 run of our own. Donta came up big during the rally, making a jump shot from the left baseline with 5:28 to play and then scored on a tip-in with 4:57 left to get us within 3 points.

We were right there.

Then Tony Delk, Kentucky's best perimeter shooter, limped to the bench after suffering leg cramps with 4:04 remaining. He did not return until 1:49 remaining.

We could never take advantage of our opportunity. We had

played so well in close games all year, but this time, we got away from how we normally play. Donta took a bad fade-away jumper, and Edgar shot an air-ball from 3-point range.

Kentucky never panicked. Their center, Mark Pope, made a pair of free throws, and Antoine Walker made another free throw to send Kentucky up 66–60 with 3:04 left. Then Walker made a big defensive stop on Marcus and hit Jeff Sheppard with a length-of-the-floor outlet pass for a driving layup to send Kentucky up by 8.

We still had one last desperation run left in us. We got within 73–67 and then cut the lead to 3 when Edgar hit a three-pointer from twenty-two feet with 1:02 left. But then Mark Pope made a pair of free throws on Kentucky's next possession, and Antoine Walker scored on a breakaway dunk; and time finally ran out on us.

We gave ourselves a chance to win against a great basketball club. We refused to lose. We never stopped playing.

I started subbing with twenty-five seconds to play. Kentucky people couldn't believe it. You know, maybe you keep fouling. Maybe they miss. Sure, if we were down 1 or 2 points. But we were down by 7 and I knew it was a one-in-a-million shot.

I thought it was more important to let our players know how I felt about them. I thought it was more important that I take Marcus out and tell him, "You had an unbelievable season." I wanted to hug Carmelo, Edgar, Donta, and Dana and tell them the same thing.

So I did.

CHAPTER 15

PROS AND CONS

Marcus Camby couldn't resist playing a practical joke on the media who showed up for his April 29 press conference at the Mullins Center.

"I'd like to announce . . . ," he said, "that I'm going to transfer to UConn for my senior year."

Then he proceeded to say what everyone had suspected all along—that he had made a decision to make himself available for the NBA draft.

With that, he hugged his mother and his fellow players.

He handled the announcement well. He kept it light with that UConn joke. Everyone cracked up. Then, as he was talking about his college experience, he said, "I've really enjoyed my three years at UConn—er, UMass."

The positive things he said about UMass were very special to me. All of his National Player of the Year trophies were on display on a table behind him.

Marcus leaves a legacy of excellence. He led our team to a 92–14 record in three years, including a perfect 9–0 record in Atlantic 10 tournament play and an 8–3 record in the NCAAs.

If he had stayed, the school might have won a national championship.

But this had to be a selfish decision. People say that college basketball is becoming a two-year sport, three years tops—at least for the top five or six players in the country. I think what's happening is that everyone's thinking the same way: "These kids are making decisions based on money."

In his own mind, Marcus made the right decision. He wanted to provide for his mother, and the money the NBA was offering was too tempting to pass up. Even though there is a rookie salary cap, Marcus could make up to $9.1 million over three years if he is the top pick in the draft.

We had a couple of short discussions early on, and one long meeting. During one of our talks, he broached the subject of living off-campus if he returned for his senior year.

We've always had a policy of making the kids live in the dorms, but I told him that would be all right, considering his situation. After he left, our other three juniors came in and asked the same thing. "You got no shot," I told them. "You have plenty of time to live on your own."

Marcus can afford his own place now with the money he's making. I just wanted to make sure he knew what he was doing.

"Here's the best picture I can paint for you," I said. "You go into the league. You're a star. You play well. You have an impact on your club. You're the Rookie of the Year. You end up playing in the All-Star game and life is grand. You have the money. You're dealing with success. You're still being a positive role model. You come back in the summer and earn your degree.

"Now, let me paint the worst picture. You go into the league as a lottery pick. You're on a bad club. They expect you to carry the team and you can't do it. You end up getting beat up physically and you start to get down. Your team starts 2–18 and they ridicule you as being a bust. You can't go to the mall or anywhere else, because you get shit on.

"Can you deal with that? If you can deal with that, you should go. Because that's the absolute worst that can happen.

"Hey, look, you can play in the NBA," I added. "The question is, can you carry a bad team? Can you go in and make an impact? That's an answer only you know because you're the guy who has to look in the mirror."

His eyes flickered a little bit.

Then I told him, "I'm with you one way or the other."

When Marcus told me he wanted to announce his decision, I said to him, "Okay. But I want to tell you this. There's no crying. This is a happy day. We're going to go in and laugh and hug. The players are going to be there. You've done so much for me and my family. You've done so much for our program. I'm happy for you. I'm happy for your family. This is a celebration, not a funeral."

He agreed.

His mother was great about the whole thing. She told me afterwards she wanted Marcus to do what was best for him, but she also wanted him to get his degree. She tossed and turned over that issue, the same way she had tossed and turned when Marcus thought about turning pro at the end of his sophomore year. Marcus could have been a high lottery pick then, but then he got pushed around by Big Country Reeves in our loss to Oklahoma State in the NCAA East Regional Finals and he started to have second thoughts, especially after he spoke with Julius Erving a couple of weeks later.

"Julius was like, 'It's a tough league out there. You got to be mentally and physically strong,'" Marcus recalled. "I said, 'Oh man, I don't know if I'm ready for that yet.'"

I told him, "Hey, you've got to do what's best for you. If you want to leave, fine; if you want to come back, fine. We won before you got here. We won while you were here. And we'll win when you leave.

"If you work hard this summer, you're going to be the Player of the Year, and we'll have a chance to win a national title. If you're not going to work hard this year, go steal the money because you're not going to move up much in the draft next year. Go take it now."

He stayed because he knew he wasn't ready. For people who say he's dumb, that was pretty smart. He knew.

When Marcus returned to school, he had added a tattoo on his left shoulder. He has a green-and-magenta etching of a basketball with the name "Mr. Camby" emblazoned underneath.

It was a sign he was growing up.

"When we played against Kentucky at the Final Four," Marcus says, "I had a great showing. Plus, all the individual awards and my team's success really pushed me over the edge. I'm mentally ready now. I think I can come in right away and get the job done."

Marcus was one of forty-two underclassmen and high school players to declare for the pros last spring. When he announced his intentions, he hadn't selected an agent yet. He eventually went with ProServ, a Washington, D.C.–based sports management firm.

There are good agents out there. There are guys I have a lot of faith in, who care about the kids and who are very ethical. There are other guys who are trying to get started or are not as credible, who will do anything to get a kid. I discovered that the hard way three weeks later when the story broke linking Marcus Camby with prospective agents.

I'm not into fighting agents. I'm into finding solutions to

problems. Here's the problem: players are leaving early. How do we get players to stay the four years or at least to consider staying?

Some players should not stay. Here's why. One, they don't want to go to school, then don't stay. Two, they're physically, mentally, and emotionally ready to leave. It's like they're twenty-five, twenty-six years old.

But what about those kids who shouldn't leave, who need the money, who have families bugging them to leave? Inus Norville came to our banquet in jeans and an open shirt because he didn't have a suit. He came in tennis shoes; he didn't have dress shoes. I asked myself, "What would Inus do if he were in that situation?" I think Al McGuire said it best: "You open a refrigerator; if there's a can of corn in there—boom—you go."

A monthly stipend might be one answer, but I don't like talking about something that has absolutely no shot of passing at the coaches' annual convention. Schools are trying to save money, not spend it.

While I was at UMass, I was a member of the NCAA's agent and amateurism committee along with David Berst and Cedric Dempsey of the NCAA, President William E. Kirwan of Maryland, Chet Gladchuk of BC, Mike Tranghese of the Big East, Nolan Richardson of Arkansas, and Texas football coach John Mackovic. There were also student athlete representatives.

Here's my solution to the problem.

First of all, understand that the NCAA has an insurance policy program. If a player applies for this insurance through the NCAA and he is a potential first-round draft pick—judged by the NCAA, the NBA, and the American Underwriters' Insurance Company—he is eligible for insurance, and that group decides how much he's eligible for. There's a death benefit in the policy.

My point is that if an athlete is eligible for insurance, why shouldn't he be able to take out a loan against that insurance policy? For example, after his freshman year, he takes a loan against that policy for $10,000 to $15,000. A lot of kids aren't eligible for a loan until they're sophomores or juniors. A player doesn't need a loan after his senior year because he's going to pick an agent and go.

A kid like Marcus has a lot of financial obligations. He has a family. Marcus's mom still lives in the same house he grew up in. She has no car; she's baby-sitting for money. If this loan program had been in effect, it would have given Marcus and players like him another option. Marcus could take out a loan for $30,000 going into his senior year. He could give his mom $20,000. They could get her an apartment to live in, and he would hold off going pro for a year. Or he could get himself a cheap car; he could buy some clothes, so he's like a student whose family is doing well.

Otherwise, he's looking to go. Why should he stay? What would make him stay when other students have cars and money because their parents are lawyers and doctors? He's sitting there with nothing, and he's the guy who has the future. He could leave now and be a millionaire. But he knows he's not physically or emotionally ready. He needs another year.

We could take care of this through the loan program. The reason I like this concept is because it's not taking anything out of anybody's pocket. It's working on the player's future earnings.

It's not going to affect everybody. We're talking about the twenty to thirty kids who are the potential first-round draft picks. Those are the kids the agents zero in on anyway. They're not dealing with second-rounders.

Can you imagine how exciting the NCAA tournament would

have been last spring if Jerry Stackhouse and Rasheed Wallace had stayed for another year at North Carolina instead of leaving after their sophomore seasons? The same with Joe Smith of Maryland. The TV ratings would have gone through the roof.

Maybe Stackhouse and Smith were ready to leave. It looks like Rasheed Wallace was not. But let's give them an option.

Let the NCAA fly these players to its headquarters in Kansas City, hold a seminar for them, explain the loan option. We need to take money out of the equation. Some kids are flunking out. Some kids are leaving because they want to go. But other kids are leaving based on the money. Marcus was one of forty-two players who applied for early admission to the NBA.

It was like a broken record this past spring.

Marcus Camby.

Allen Iverson.

Ray Allen.

Stephon Marbury.

How many of these kids are all saying the same thing: "I had to do this to help my mom"?

If we had the loan program, their coaches could say to them, "Well, take a loan. We've made it possible for you to take care of your families." Those are the kids we should try to save.

Some people have suggested if the NCAA allows student athletes to take out a $20,000 loan on their insurance policies, the kids will blow the money. Good. I say it's better to learn from a $20,000 mistake instead of a $20 million mistake.

NCAA executive director Cedric Dempsey actually broached the subject at a meeting of the National Association of Collegiate Directors of Athletics at Marco Island, Florida, last spring. He stopped short of embracing the loan program, but he did say it needed to be fully explored because the world of the student athlete is changing and the NCAA needed to reevaluate its rules.

I'm sure the decision by more and more kids to turn pro early will dilute the level of play in the college game. But this is America. If the kids want to leave, they have the right to do so. If they want to test the waters and go pro, they should have that opportunity. They're free to do that.

I tell kids, "If you fail, you fail. If you make it, you make it." I just want them to try.

Marcus is too skinny to play center in the NBA and is more likely suited for power forward.

"Length is strength," he said. "I'm not going to try and gain forty pounds and play center. That's not my natural position."

At least Marcus will get playing time.

Lou Roe did not get much time with the Detroit Pistons during his rookie season.

I went out to see him play against the Knicks the night before we played Fordham in the Garden and was very disappointed he didn't get into the game. But I did have a chance to meet with his coach, Doug Collins, and discuss what was going on. Then I met with Lou for about twenty minutes.

It's the first time in his career that Lou isn't playing, and it's hard for him.

I told him, "Here's what happens in the NBA: they pay you to play, and they expect you to do it. Nobody calls to wake you up in the morning. If you don't come, you're fined. They don't say, 'Hey, let's work on shooting.' You work on shooting if you want to play. You have to get the coach. The coach isn't getting you in the NBA."

For all those young guys coming in, it's hard.

Lou had a special relationship with all of us at UMass. He had a special relationship with me. I loved him. I used to hug him and tell him that. But he also knew I could get on him.

In the NBA, it's a job.

"I need a hug."

"You ain't getting one from me. You can get married and get one."

It's totally different in the NBA than it is in college. I was dealing with seventeen-, eighteen-year-old kids. For the coaches, it is about molding them, teaching them life skills, and getting them on their way so they can make it in society.

In the NBA, it's about winning, about performing. If a player doesn't perform, he gets traded, he gets cut. If he does perform, they love him.

I'm going to tell you about what happened in New York City that drove me crazy. Obviously, I like Charles Smith. I was at Pitt for two years when he played. He is a beautiful person. I don't care about Charles Smith the basketball player. I know him as Charles Smith the person. Charles and I had dinner after the Fordham game and he spoke to my team.

But during his own game, Charles pulled up to shoot a jump shot and the Knicks fans booed him. And when it went in, what did they do? They cheered. That's how the NBA is.

I think Lou is finding that out. As a rookie, he can't approach things like a veteran does. Pro teams play eighty-two regular-season games; and a veteran is playing thirty-five minutes a game. So what's he doing on an off-day? Not a whole lot. But if a rookie is playing only seven minutes a game, he'd better be spending that off-day on a treadmill, running sprints, busting his butt. Joe Dumars is making $7 million dollars. Lou isn't. This is a tough time for him. He's never been there before. We always played him.

Our goal at UMass was to win a national title. That's what we planned on. That was the premise of our program, not just winning games, not just getting to the Final Four. But winning it all.

The people there thought that was out of the question. They were shocked we went to a Final Four.

They're not shocked anymore.

It will be up to Bruiser Flint to keep UMass basketball at that level, but he is dedicated to recruiting the same kinds of players. It may take a little longer for the team to grow up because Bruiser has to replace the entire starting frontcourt. And they have another killer schedule. But he does have Inus Norville and Tyrone Weeks back to go along with Edgar Padilla, Carmelo Travieso, and Charlton Clarke. Edgar and Carmelo both participated in the summer games in Atlanta for the Puerto Rican national team. If they continue to improve, the potential to win another Atlantic 10 title is there.

One of the reasons for our success when I was at UMass was the fact we were able to keep our staff together for a long period of time. John Robic had been with me since the beginning. Bruiser came my second year. Dave Glover was there six of my eight years. In addition, Brian Gorman has been there for eight years, and Mike Connors, our administrative assistant who was the interim coach at Army, has been there the past three years.

I brought Ed Schilling on board this past year. He's a Five-Star guy from Logansport High in Indiana who compiled notes and tapes for a motivational book of lectures from Howard Garfinkel's camp and has made a tape of ball handling and dribbling drills.

We created a tradition at UMass for who we are as well as a tradition for how we play, how we act, what kind of sportsmanship we have.

Dick Vitale called me earlier this spring and asked why I wasn't at the Magic Johnson High School All-American game in

Detroit. "All the big-timers are here. You should get involved with Shaheen Holloway and Jamaal Magloire."

I told him we'd signed our guys.

I do like this recruiting class. The class of 2000 at UMass includes 6'9" forward Ajmal Basit from St. Anthony's High of Jersey City; 6'5" forward Winston Smith from St. Patrick's High of Elizabeth, New Jersey; 6'5" Chris Kirkland from McKeesport High in Pennsylvania; 6'6" swing guard Mike Babul from North Attleboro High in Massachusetts; and 6'2" guard Monte Mack from South Boston High in Massachusetts. Then there's Lari Ketner, who is 6'10", 270 pounds. He sat out this past year and had his foot operated on. He'll be coming back this summer. In time, he's going to be exactly what UMass needs in the post.

In the past, the recruiting experts always said our kids weren't good enough. Tony and Harper weren't good enough. Edgar and Carmelo weren't good enough. They've been good enough for us.

Lou Roe's jersey was retired last fall. I think they should retire Jimmy McCoy's jersey, maybe Tony Barbee's, and Harper Williams's. UMass needs to do that. People want to judge everybody against Julius Erving. But they can't. If that had happened when the Celtics had Bill Russell, no one else would have had his number retired until Larry Bird because those two would have stood apart.

That's not what retiring numbers is all about. It's about accomplishment. And Tony and Jimmy and Harper accomplished a lot.

That's why I used to get emotional on Senior Night because I knew I was looking at guys for the last time and I remembered what they'd done for our program. I always started the seniors, even if they were walk-ons. There have been games where our conference championship was on the line and I started them anyway. If there were five seniors, we started all five.

The pieces are in place.

It's helped that Bob Marcum had been there to oversee the development of the program. Bob came to UMass in 1994 from the Atlanta Motor Speedway. I was on the committee when Bob was hired. We screened a lot of candidates and there were a lot of people we liked. But when Bob interviewed, you could tell he knew the profession. He had the background we needed. He had been an AD at Kansas and South Carolina. And he was a former college football coach who understood what we were going through.

In the spring of '96, after I took the Nets job and the Marcus Camby story was hot, the media began asking Bob if I had left a sinking ship. "I'll tell you," he said, "if this ship is sinking, there's an awful lot of people calling to see if they can get on it. And, believe me, I'm not the captain of the *Titanic*."

Bob understands what building a program is all about. He was close friends with Woody Hayes, the legendary Ohio State coach, in the '60s, when he was coaching football at McKinley High School in Canton, Ohio.

"Woody once told me there are more good coaches than there are good programs," he said. "Good programs take longer to build and you'll have to go through some crises. And don't think you're always going to do it in three, four years. If you have good people in charge of those programs, invest in them and try to hold on to them as long as possible. And you will go from developing a few good teams to developing a good program.

"Woody assured me the next coach at Ohio State would win 'because we have a good program.' The next coach was Earle Bruce and he went 11–1 his first year."

I'd like to think we've built the same type of program here.

One of the biggest beneficiaries of our success has been fund-raising efforts. Donations to UMass athletics were about

$100,000 in 1991. Four years later, they had jumped to over $1 million. UMass had two corporate sponsors—USAir and Spalding—in 1993. In 1996 there were seventeen who paid a combined total of $323,639 to be associated with the sports program.

Basketball drives the engine.

Times have changed for the better. UMass was on national television twenty-five times and was on the Atlantic 10 package ten more times. That's visibility you can't beat.

The A-10 had four teams invited to the NCAA this year. I don't think it's important how many teams get into post-season play. What's important is how they do once they get in there. A-10 teams were 6–4 in the NCAA tournament and had a team reach the Final Four. A-10 teams were 6–2 in the NIT, and St. Joseph's reached the championship game in New York. The A-10's record in the post season shows we deserved to be there. And our trip to the Final Four has done wonders for the league.

Just ask the commissioner, Linda Bruno, who, by the way, has done a great job moving the A-10 to another level.

"That final week, with only four teams left, everybody knew Massachusetts was a member of the Atlantic 10," she says. "You can't print enough media guides for that kind of exposure.

"If I had to pick a year for us to achieve this success, this was a good year because it kind of brought everyone together. I think it's a sense of pride. Hey, we had a team in the Final Four. There are very few other conferences that can use that as a recruiting tool this entire year.

"We're still feeling the fallout. Suddenly, we have teams in pre-season tournaments. TV wants the league on more. Right now, we have noon games on ESPN five consecutive Saturdays in February 1997. We have ESPN2 games on Mondays or Tuesdays.

We're a regular on tournament week. Our championship game on ESPN had the third-highest rating. We also had one semifinal on ESPN and three more tournament games on ESPN2."

I just hope the league remembers to stand together through the good times and bad. You know what the major problem is in the A-10? The coaches don't stick up for one another. In the Big East, they protect one another. In the ACC, they protect one another. Do you know who gets the Coach of the Year in the Big East? Usually, it's the coach who needs it the most. P. J. Carlesimo got it when he was on the bubble of getting fired at Seton Hall. Jimmy O'Brien got it when they were ready to fire him at BC. Leonard Hamilton of Miami got it in 1995 when his job was on the line.

In the A-10, that would never happen.

Even though the Big East coaches may not like a particular coach in their league, they won't say that publicly outside the inner circle. It hasn't always been that way, though. I give former Big East commissioner Dave Gavitt full credit for this solidarity. He held a meeting of all the coaches to discuss the constant backbiting among them.

He said, "Hey, enough is enough."

I told Linda Bruno that she needed to send the same kind of message, because in the A-10, the coaches won't stand up for one another. When they go on TV, do they promote the league and other teams? No. The coaches talk about their own programs. They don't take the time to say, "How about the job John is doing up there at Temple?" They won't do that.

I brought it up again at the league meetings. And you know who chimed in? Bill Foster of Virginia Tech.

He used to coach at Clemson and he said, "When I first went to the ACC, there were hatchets out there. When Mike Krzyzewski, Jimmy Valvano, and Bobby Cremins came in here, we came together and the league took off. We protected one another. We promoted one another."

I think, eventually, things will change for the better in the A-10. Last year, several new coaches came in—Skip Prosser of Xavier, Bill Foster, Oliver Purnell of Dayton, Scott Edgar of Duquesne, and Phil Martelli of St. Joseph's—who should push things in the right direction. They're good coaches, and they have an idea of where they want to go.

I'll be honest with you, the backbiting hasn't hurt UMass. We became a national program. Last season, if you had asked any fan in the country to name our starting five, I bet they could. But if you had asked what league we play in, I bet they wouldn't know. Eighty percent would have said we were in the Big East. They just equate Eastern basketball with the Big East. UMass supersedes that.

But it has hurt other teams in the league.

I'll use Virginia Tech as an example. They were ranked in the Top 10 all year. Why did they get seeded eighth in the NCAA Midwest Regional instead of third or fourth? The A-10 was thought of as a ragamuffin league instead of a Top 5 league because the coaches kill each other.

There was one downside to the season, as far as the league was concerned. Last April, Temple's longtime assistant Jimmy Maloney unexpectedly passed away at the age of sixty-two. He was driving home over the Ben Franklin Bridge in Philadelphia when he suffered a massive heart attack. There was nothing anyone could do.

It was very sad. I'd always admired him as a coach and as a person. I thought what he had done for Temple basketball— short of John Chaney—was unmatched. He was the guy who helped John develop great guards like Eddie Jones, Aaron McKie, and Rick Brunson. His death puts things in perspective. Hopefully, the league will name a sixth man award after him in the future.

Bob Marcum has always had an eye toward the future of UMass. He would love to see the school get involved in Division I-A football because he thinks the future of athletics is tied to that sport. He can foresee a day when there will be eight conferences made up of twelve teams, all playing conference championships. "Those conferences will control the television exposures," he warns.

"It's such a windfall. The SEC sends a check for $500,000 to their member schools for that one game. The Big 12 is scheduling a conference championship game, too, and they're saying it is going to produce $550,000 for each school. Once that happens, I think you have a natural format for a national championship playoff. If we're left out of that mix, I think it's going to be difficult to get the necessary exposure to sustain our programs."

Bob finds it interesting when people say that New England couldn't support Division I football, especially after seeing the crowds for high school games at Thanksgiving.

"I notice that as BC has gotten better in football; they've increased the size of their stadium and put in new suites and boxes," he says. "I don't think you do that with the idea they'll be empty. If we ever went Division I-A in football, it would put us in an entirely different world. Now, you're more attractive to prospective conferences."

He also thinks UMass needs to build suites and boxes at the Mullins Center to cultivate the corporate sponsors even more. Most people think corporate sponsors grab all the seats, but there are only 60 available in Mullins. And there are more than 2,000 people on the waiting list. "Now you wish you had 12,500 seats. But we don't," Bob says.

I didn't have time to think about what we accomplished until I took my family on vacation to Sanibel Island, Florida, in May. We'd been running so hard this year, I hadn't thought in those terms. I thought about "What's tomorrow? Where is the next recruit? How about scheduling? What about this new weight room? What about the mail?" Then I'd go home. When I'm there, I like being with my family, so I don't think about it then, either.

Megan is just starting to figure out whether we win or lose. I'll ask her, "Did we win?" She'll say, "Yeah, dad. You won."

Erin, my oldest, is into it a little more. She knows and she plays and she cries when we lose. She plays the players. She knows how they play. She goes out and tries to play like them. She tries to defend real hard. She dives for loose balls. She jumps for rebounds. Most girls who are nine years old just reach for the ball. She shoots it every time. She's very competitive, like her father.

We challenged our players to reach beyond what they thought they could reach. If you do that, you're going to win. It wasn't always fun and it made them uncomfortable and it made them mad. But when they looked back, they said, "Boy, I never thought I could reach that high—but I did."

That applied to just about every player on the team. They all achieved goals they hadn't thought they could reach. But that was our job, to get them to reach for the stars.

Who would have thought we'd be mentioned in the same breath as UCLA, Indiana, North Carolina, Duke, and Kentucky?

Who would have thought we'd be scheduled to play Maryland, and the students at an ACC school would be chanting "We want UMass! We want UMass!" the game before they played us?

When I look back at my career, my definition of success is, did I make a difference? Did I make a difference on this campus? Did I make a difference in people's lives? Are my players better off now than they were when they arrived? Have I prepared them for life? If I can answer yes to those questions, and if I've accomplished those goals, then I've had success.

ABOUT THE AUTHORS

JOHN CALIPARI is the head coach, executive vice president, and director of basketball operations for the New Jersey Nets. Among his numerous awards, he was named the 1996 Boost/Naismith Coach of the Year, *The Sporting News* National Coach of the Year, the 1996 Atlantic 10 Conference Coach of the Year, and the 1996 *Basketball Times* East Region Coach of the Year. He lives with his wife, Ellen, and their two daughters in Franklin Lakes, New Jersey.

DICK WEISS is the nationally syndicated basketball reporter for the New York *Daily News*. He is also the CNN college basketball Analyst on Saturday mornings and an assistant editor for *Basketball Times*. He was the coauthor of *Full Court Pressure* by Rick Pitino. Weiss lives in Havertown, Pennsylvania.